Migration, Minorities and Citizenship

General Editors: **Zig Layton-Henry**, Professor of Politics, University of Warwick; and **Danièle Joly**, Director, Centre for Research in Ethnic Relations, University of Warwick.

Titles include:

Muhammad Anwar, Patrick Roach and Ranjit Sondhi (*editors*)
FROM LEGISLATION TO INTEGRATION?
Race Relations in Britain

Naomi Carmon (*editor*)
IMMIGRATION AND INTEGRATION IN POST-INDUSTRIAL SOCIETIES
Theoretical Analysis and Policy-Related Research

Adrian Favell
PHILOSOPHIES OF INTEGRATION
Immigration and the Idea of Citizenship in France and Britain

Sophie Body-Gendrot and Marco Martiniello (*editors*)
MINORITIES IN EUROPEAN CITIES
The Dynamics of Social Integration and Social Exclusion at the Neighbourhood Level

Simon Holdaway and Anne-Marie Barron
RESIGNERS? THE EXPERIENCE OF BLACK AND ASIAN POLICE OFFICERS

Atsushi Kondo (*editor*)
CITIZENSHIP IN A GLOBAL WORLD
Comparing Citizenship Rights for Aliens

Danièle Joly
HAVEN OR HELL?
Asylum Policies and Refugees in Europe
SCAPEGOATS AND SOCIAL ACTORS
The Exclusion and Integration of Minorities in Western and Eastern Europe

Jørgen S. Nielsen
TOWARDS A EUROPEAN ISLAM

Jan Rath (*editor*)
IMMIGRANT BUSINESSES
The Economic, Political and Social Environment

Peter Ratcliffe (*editor*)
THE POLITICS OF SOCIAL SCIENCE RESEARCH
Race, Ethnicity and Social Change

John Rex
ETHNIC MINORITIES IN THE MODERN NATION STATE
Working Papers in the Theory of Multiculturalism and Political Integration

Carl-Ulrik Schierup (*editor*)
SCRAMBLE FOR THE BALKANS
Nationalism, Globalism and the Political Economy of Reconstruction

Steven Vertovec and Ceri Peach (*editors*)
ISLAM IN EUROPE
The Politics of Religion and Community

Östen Wahlbeck
KURDISH DIASPORAS
A Comparative Study of Kurdish Refugee Communities

John Wrench, Andrea Rea and Nouria Ouali (*editors*)
MIGRANTS, ETHNIC MINORITIES AND THE LABOUR MARKET
Integration and Exclusion in Europe

Migration, Minorities and Citizenship
Series Standing Order ISBN 0–333–71047–9
(*outside North America only*)

You can receive future titles in this series as they are published by placing a standing order. Please contact your bookseller or, in case of difficulty, write to us at the address below with your name and address, the title of the series and the ISBN quoted above.

Customer Services Department, Macmillan Distribution Ltd, Houndmills, Basingstoke, Hampshire RG21 6XS, England

Citizenship in a Global World

Comparing Citizenship Rights for Aliens

Edited by

Atsushi Kondo
Associate Professor
Faculty of Economics
Kyushu Sangyo University
Japan

palgrave

First published 2001 by
PALGRAVE
Houndmills, Basingstoke, Hampshire RG21 6XS and
175 Fifth Avenue, New York, N. Y. 10010
Companies and representatives throughout the world

PALGRAVE is the new global academic imprint of
St. Martin's Press LLC Scholarly and Reference Division and
Palgrave Publishers Ltd (formerly Macmillan Press Ltd).

ISBN 0–333–80265–9

This book is printed on paper suitable for recycling and made from fully managed and sustained forest sources.

A catalogue record for this book is available from the British Library.

Library of Congress Cataloging-in-Publication Data
Citizenship in a global world : comparing citizenship rights for aliens / edited by Atsushi Kondo.
p. cm. — (Migration, minorities and citizenship)
Includes bibliographical references and index.
ISBN 0–333–80265–9
1. Emigration and immigration—Case studies. I. Kondo, Atsushi, 1960– II. Series.

JV6035 .C55 2001
323.6'31—dc21

00–069469

10 9 8 7 6 5 4 3 2 1
10 09 08 07 06 05 04 03 02 01

Printed and bound in Great Britain by
Antony Rowe Ltd, Chippenham, Wiltshire

Contents

List of Tables

Notes on the Contributors

Atsushi Kondo is Associate Professor of Constitutional Law at the Economic Department of Kyushu Sangyo University. He is the project leader of 'Citizenship for Aliens' sponsored by the Toyota Foundation and is currently researching issues relating citizenship and aliens' rights.

Stephen Castles is Director of the Refugee Studies Centre at Oxford University and former Director of the Centre for Asia-Pacific Social Transformation Studies at the Universities of Wollongong and Newcastle, Australia. He also helps coordinate the UNESCO-MOST Asia-Pacific Migration Research Network. His recent publications include *The Age of Migration: International Population Movements in the Modern World* (with Mark Miller, 1998); *Citizenship and Migration: Globalization and the Politics of Belonging* (with Alastair Davidson, 2000); and *Ethnicity and Globalization: from Migrant Worker to Transnational Citizen* (2000).

Gerard-René de Groot is Professor of Comparative Law and Private International Law at Maastricht University in the Netherlands. He is a specialist in the field of comparative nationality law and is currently doing research on the relationship between European citizenship and the nationality legislation of the Member States of the European Union.

Elena Dingu-Kyrklund is a multi-disciplinary researcher at CEIFO (Centre for Research in International Migration and Ethnic Relations) at Stockholm University. Together with Charles Westin, she is the author of *Reducing Immigration, Reviewing Integration* (1997), and *Widening Gaps: Unemployment and Integration* (1998). She is currently researching issues regarding citizenship, immigrant youth, criminality and immigrant women.

Donald Galloway is a Professor of Law at the University of Victoria, British Columbia, teaching Immigration and Refugee Law and Jurisprudence. He has recently published a book on immigration law as well as a number of articles on related issues. He is currently a member of Canada's Immigration and Refugee Board. Any views he expresses are not intended to represent the views of the board.

Benoît Guiguet earned his PhD in law at the European University Institute (Florence, 1997). He taught EC law, constitutional law and international relations at the University of Saint-Etienne and presently works with the International Labour Organization as an external collaborator. His main fields of interest are citizenship, migration law and sexual orientation discriminations.

Kay Hailbronner holds the Chair of Public Law, Public International Law and European Law at the University of Konstanz and is Director of the Centre for International and European Law on Immigration and Asylum. He was legal adviser for the Council of Europe (Secretariat of Human Rights) in matters of Aliens Legislation of Eastern European Countries. He has published various studies and monographs concerning aspects of immigration and asylum law. Forthcoming is a monograph on immigration law and policy in the European Union which deals with the legal framework for European migration policy under the Amsterdam Treaty.

Thomas C. Heller is the Shelton Professor of International Legal Studies at Stanford Law School and a Senior Fellow in Stanford's Institute for International Studies. He was associated as Jean Monnet Professor with the Robert Schuman Centre of the European University Institute from 1993 to 1999. In addition to his ongoing work in the regulation of international labour markets and immigration, his current research interests focus on comparative economic law, international regimes in environment and energy, multinational investment, and legal theory. His most recent work in the area of law, identity and political economy is 'Modernity, Membership and Multiculturalism', published in the *Stanford Humanities Review*.

Zig Layton-Henry is Professor of Politics at the University of Warwick and a former Director of the ESRC Centre for Research in Ethnic Relations. He is the author of *The Politics of Immigration* (1992) and editor of *The Political Rights of Migrant Workers in Western Europe* (1990). He is currently researching issues relating to citizenship and discrimination.

Paul Spoonley is Professor of Sociology and is Academic Director for the College of Humanities and Social Sciences at Massey University's Auckland campus in New Zealand. He is co-author of *Recalling Aotearoa: Indigenous Politics and Ethnic Relations in New Zealand* (1999) and *Exploring Society: a Sociology for New Zealanders* (2000). He is researching migration and the development of transnational communities in the Pacific region, and citizenship in bicultural/multicultural societies.

Gianni Zappalà was Research Fellow in the Intercultural Relations, Identity and Citizenship Project at the University of Wollongong from 1996 to 1998. He is currently Senior Researcher, Australian Centre for Industrial Relations Research and Training, University of Sydney.

Introduction

Atsushi Kondo

This book presents a comparative analysis, by researchers from a variety of disciplines, of citizenship rights for aliens in ten advanced industrial countries that have experienced substantial immigration. These are: Japan (Atsushi Kondo, constitutional law); the Netherlands (Gerard-René de Groot, international private law); Sweden (Elena Dingu-Kyrklund, international law); France (Benoît Guiguet, EU public law); Germany (Kay Hailbronner, international public law); the United Kingdom (Zig Layton-Henry, political science); Australia (Stephen Castles, sociology); New Zealand (Paul Spoonley, sociology); Canada (Donald Galloway, administrative law); and the USA (Thomas C. Heller, international law).

The spread of international migration raises questions about citizenship rights for certain categories of aliens. It is a subject for urgent debate in industrialised countries where many resident aliens live. Through our international and interdisciplinary research, we hope to develop the theory of citizenship and find a way to explain the problems of each country. Traditional citizenship theories have explained rights and duties of citizens of a country in a closed system which distinguishes sharply between citizens and non-citizens. During the last ten years, many researchers have pointed out that resident aliens too have broad elements of substantial citizenship.

The editor of this book inherited the idea of 'denizenship', that is the idea of substantial citizenship rights for non-citizen permanent residents, from the Swedish political scientist Tomas Hammar,[1] who has published two books in Japan on this topic.[2] Professor Hammar and I discussed this idea many times when I was in Stockholm University for a year and, with other researchers, we developed a systematic questionnaire for comparative research on aliens' rights. Sociologists and political scientists of each country began to study transnational citizenship, but the legal comparative framework is out of date[3] and we need to reconstruct it from the viewpoint of citizenship rights. The first aim of this book is to understand aliens' citizenship rights – especially residential, social, economic and political rights – because these rights encounter significant constitutional problems in each country. A second aim is to analyse the issue from the various viewpoints of each discipline.

Each national report has been guided by the questionnaire set out at the end of this introduction. The exception is the German chapter (Chapter 5), which focuses on reform of the German Nationality Act, which is the significant problem in that country. As an introduction, we sketch out the development of aliens' rights, categorise aliens and confirm the constitutional bases of aliens' rights. Every legal system has a hierarchy and constitutional law is the supreme law in most states, although there are some exceptions. International treaties have much influence on constitutions; domestic, social and economic conditions have effects; and the law is also influenced by the ideas of the time. The situation of aliens is different from person to person and from country to country. Some kinds of aliens are guaranteed more rights than others. We try to compare these points in every country. Japan and Germany[4] have declared themselves to be non-immigration countries but recently the situation has been changing. France has relatively long experience as a European immigration country. The Netherlands,[5] Sweden and the UK are recent post-war immigration countries, while Australia, New Zealand, Canada and the USA are traditional or classic immigration countries in the sense that the whole basis of their present societies has been founded on immigration.

Firstly, we analyse the **concept of citizenship and nationality**. Most importantly of all, we need to discuss the distinction between nationality and citizenship at the legal, sociological and daily language levels. These English terms vary from country to country and among various disciplines. On one hand, the British Nationality Act is the official name of the citizenship legislation in Britain, while Germany, France, the Netherlands and Japan also officially translate their laws as 'Nationality Acts'. Jurists, among other international lawyers, also refer to 'nationality' in defining state membership because all international treaties have adopted this term. On the other hand, Sweden, Australia, New Zealand and Canada use the term 'Citizenship Act'. In the USA the American Immigration and Nationality Act is the official name, but citizenship and citizen are key concepts in the various clauses. Political scientists, sociologists and social anthropologists are also inclined to use the term 'citizenship' in defining state membership because 'nationality' denotes membership of a common public culture, nation or ethnicity. Additionally, the British Nationality Act defines sub-categories of citizenship and the Maastricht Treaty introduces another concept of European citizenship. Many Member States of the European Union have dual concepts such as French nationality (nationalité) and European citizenship (citoyenneté). However, Sweden uses the same term '*medborgarskap*' for 'nationality' in domestic nationality laws and Union 'citizenship' in the Maastricht Treaty.[6] Furthermore, the specific term of 'nationals' can include small groups of non-citizen nationals consisting mainly of those born in outlying possessions of the United States (American Samoa and Swains Island). We therefore need to confirm our definition of English terms and specific words for the native language of each national reporter (Table 1).

Secondly, we discuss the **residential rights** and alien registration procedures. T.H. Marshall categorised citizenship rights for citizens and divided them into three parts – civil, political and social rights. However with some limitations (usually political rights) many of these rights are granted to certain non-citizens.[7] For example, Marshall argued that civil rights were necessary for individual freedom, liberty of the person and right to justice. These civil rights are guaranteed, but freedom of speech, thought and faith, and the right to own property, are only partly guaranteed for resident aliens at the present time.[8] Additionally, the most fundamental civil rights are residential rights

Table 1 English terms and native words

Definition	*State membership*	*Personal status or a set of rights and duties in a polity*
Japanese English	nationality (kokuseki)	citizenship (shiminken)
German English	nationality (Staatsangehörigkeit)	citizenship (Bürgerschaft)
French English	nationality (nationalité)	citizenship (citoyenneté)
Dutch English	nationality (nationaliteit)	citizenship (burgerschap)
Swedish English	citizenship (medborgarskap)	citizenship (medborgarskap)
British English	nationality, citizenship	citizenship
Australian English	citizenship	citizenship
New Zealand English	citizenship	citizenship
Canadian English	citizenship	citizenship
American English	citizenship	citizenship

but these rights can vary from person to person. The examination of residential rights is the starting point for the categorisation of aliens. We need to reconsider the categorisation according to the question: what kinds of citizenship rights are guaranteed to what kinds of aliens? Indeed, aliens do not have the full freedom to enter a country, but permanent residents are guaranteed residential rights. The current expansion of globalisation and the rise of transnational organisations are limiting the extent of this exclusion.

Thirdly, we investigate **social rights** and multicultural education. Traditionally, social rights were categorised as citizenship rights for citizens, but recently legal resident aliens have been guaranteed them as well as citizens. Being a common-market citizen such as a citizen of the EU does not make much difference.[9] However, irregular resident aliens are not granted social rights. Public assistance for multicultural education varies from country to country.

Fourthly, we are concerned with **economic rights** and the rights to employment as civil servants. It must be noted that fundamental rights for aliens are residential rights and the freedom to choose an occupation. Nevertheless, there remain some hurdles for employment as public servants. The traditional justification for the exclusion of aliens from being public servants is similar to the justification for excluding them from electoral rights.[10]

Finally, we discuss **political rights**. Electoral rights and other political rights such as freedom of speech are also granted to certain resident aliens to some extent. The challenge of political rights compels us to reconsider the theory of citizenship.[11]

When it comes to citizens' duties, generally, resident aliens are not liable to military service but are liable to other citizens' duties such as tax liability or obedience to the host country's laws.[12] Thus, we can omit an analysis of the obligatory elements of citizenship and focus on issues relating to residential rights, social rights, economic rights and political rights. We need to have clear reasons why the practices are the same in all states or different in some countries to others.

This research project is sponsored by the Toyota Foundation in Japan and has involved considerable networking in order to invite, confirm, guide and finalise the contributions of each author. First, the editor (Atsushi Kondo) spent a sabbatical year (August 1997–August 1998) researching this theme with Tomas Hammar and colleagues at the Centre for International Migration and Ethnic Relations in Stockholm. We designed the questionnaire after much discussion and amended parts of it after consultation with other contributors. The first conference was held at Stockholm University in July 1998 and the second conference was held at Kyushu Sangyo University in Japan in March 1999. We hope that political scientists, sociologists, migration researchers, lawyers, administrators and students will welcome this international and interdisciplinary book which compares the practical issues while the various disciplines of the contributors encourage wide-ranging analysis from a variety of theoretical backgrounds.

Questionnaire

Introduction

a. How do we explain the chronological development of aliens' rights? Which factors are influential in explaining changes over time?
b. How do we categorise resident aliens (in a broad sense)?
c. Are there any bases of aliens' rights in constitutional law?

1. Nationality and citizenship

1.1 How is (citizenship) acquired and lost in legislation and in practice, and what are the underlying principles?
1.2 Is there a distinction between nationality and citizenship (in your language), at the legal, sociological and daily language level?
1.3 Is there any way in which the concept of citizenship (citizenship rights) has been altered in recent years?
1.4 Is there any debate in your country about stateless persons?
1.5 Is there any debate in your country about dual nationality?
1.6 Which factors are influential in explaining changes in the naturalisation rate?

2. Residential rights

2.1 Are there any restrictions concerning the freedom of entry for foreigners?
2.2 Which kinds of residential status are used for foreigners and how do we categorise them?
2.3 What are the requirements for permanent residence status?
2.4 Are there any restrictions for permanent residents about freedom of re-entry?
2.5 Is there any discrimination among aliens in terms of their origin by home countries?
2.6 Are there any special problems in the alien registration procedure?

3. Social rights

3.1 Are there any restrictions about social rights for permanently resident aliens?
3.2 Are there any limitations for temporary foreign visitors?
3.3 Are there any limitations for irregular (over-stay and illegal entry) residents?
3.4 Are foreign former soldiers guaranteed any war-related compensation?
3.5 What are the rules about multicultural education?

4. Economic rights

4.1 Are there any limitations to property rights for aliens?
4.2 Are there any limitations to the right of self-employment for aliens?
4.3 What kinds of national governmental jobs are closed to aliens and what kinds of arguments are used to justify this closure?
4.4 What kinds of local governmental jobs are closed to aliens and what kinds of arguments are used to justify this closure?
4.5 What percentage of aliens are working in each governmental post?
4.6 Is there a distinction between some non-nationals and other aliens in the public employment?

5. Political rights

5.1 Why are electoral rights of the (national) Parliament closed to aliens?
5.2 What are the requirements to grant aliens local electoral rights? How is the reciprocity element to be explained?
5.3 What is the ratio of the turnout of aliens and nationals (or all the electorate)?
5.4 What is the ratio of representation of aliens (or all the electorate)?
5.5 Is there a distinction between the right to vote and the right to stand? What are the reasons?
5.6 Are there any restrictions in the political freedoms of aliens?

Notes

1 Tomas Hammar, 'Legal Time of Residence and the Status of Immigrants, in Rainer Bauböck (ed.), *From Aliens to Citizens* (Aldershot: Avebury, 1994), p. 189. As for the concept of 'denizen', see Tomas Hammar, *Democracy and the Nation State* (Aldershot: Avebury, 1990), pp. 13–15.

2 Atsushi Kondo, *'Gaikokujin' no Sanseiken: Denizenship no hikaku kenkyu* [A Comparative Study on Denizenship] (Tokyo: Akashi Shoten, 1996); Atsushi Kondo, *Gaikokujin sanseiken to kokuseki* [The Aliens' Electoral rights and Citizenship] (Tokyo: Akashi Shoten, 1996).
3 Jochen Abr. Frowein and Torsten Stein (eds), *The Legal Position of Aliens in National and International Law* (Berlin: Springer, 1987); Jochen A. Frowein and Joachim Wolf (eds), *Auslanderrecht im internationalen Vergleich*, (Heidelberg: C.F. Müller, 1985). Now, there is a comparative research: Bruno Nascimbene (ed.), *Nationality Laws in the European Union* (Milano: Butterworths, 1996). It is useful for study about nationality in EU States.
4 'In spite of large immigration flows – second only to flows to the United States – and in spite of public organizing and financing of most of them, Germany officially still considers herself to be *kein Einwanderungsland* (not an immigration country)'. Dietrich Thränhardt, 'Germany's Immigration Policies and Politics' in Grete Brochmann and Tomas Hammar (eds), *Mechanisms of Immigration Control: A Comparative Analysis of European Regulation Policies* (Oxford: Berg, 1999), p. 34.
5 'Although it is only gradually and grudgingly being admitted by the Dutch government, the Netherlands has in fact been an immigration country for most of the years since the Second World War'. Rinus Penninx *et al.* (eds), *The Impact of International Migration on Receiving Countries: The Case of the Netherlands* (The Hague: Netherlands Interdisciplinary demographic Institute, 1994), p. 1.
6 Only four Member States of the EU (Italy: *cittadinanza*, Denmark: *borgarskap*, Sweden: *medborgarskap*, Finland: *kansalaisuus*) are using the same term. The other eleven states are using different terms. It should be noted that the double use of the word *borgarskap* was perhaps 'oil on the fire' of the Danish fear of creating European citizenship because it could be the first step on the way to the decline of their own Danish citizenship. See Gerard-René de Groot, 'The Nationality Legislation of the member of the European Union' in Massimo la Torre (ed.), *European Citizenship* (The Hague: Kluwer Law International, 1998), p. 121.
7 T.H. Marshall and Tom Bottomore, *Citizenship and Social Class* (London: Pluto Press, 1992), pp. 8, 84.
8 Andrea Rea, 'Social Citizenship and Ethno Minorities in the European Union' in Marco Martiniello (ed.), *Migration, Citizenship and Ethno-National Identities in the European Union* (Aldershot: Avebury, 1995), p. 182.
9 Yasemin Nuhoglu Soysal, *Limits of Citizenship* (Chicago: University of Chicago, 1994), p. 124.
10 William Rogers Brubaker (ed.), *Immigration and the Politics in Europe and North America* (Lamham: University Press of America, 1989), p. 152.
11 Zig Layton Henry (ed.), *The Political Rights of Migrant Workers in Western Europe* (London: Sage, 1990).
12 Jens Magleby Sorensen, *The Exclusive European Citizenship: The Case for Refugees and Immigrants in the European Union* (Aldershot: Avebury, 1996), p. 58.

1
Citizenship Rights for Aliens in Japan

Atsushi Kondo

Introduction

People are more globally mobile than ever before. It is not unusual for wealthy persons to go abroad for work and study, and many foreigners have also moved to Japan. There is now a substantial number of foreigners born in Japan who have received a Japanese education.

Development of aliens' rights in Japan

Japanese people live in an island country that experienced a major period of isolation from 1639–1853.[1] The Japanese government concluded treaties of commerce with other countries and regulated immigration. Apart from the migration between former Imperial Japan and its colonies,[2] the numbers of immigrants were small, but about 777 000 emigrants moved mainly to America and Latin American countries between 1853–1945. After the Second World War, the Supreme Commander of Allied Powers strictly controlled immigration and emigration between 1945 and 1951. Subsequently, during the period of sustained economic growth in the 1950s and 1960s, the Japanese worked long hours and invested in automation without permitting foreign labourers to enter the country, and Japan's traditional policy of not admitting foreign workers for unskilled jobs has remained basically unchanged. However, since the 1980s (about twenty years later than in European countries) Japan has experienced an influx of large numbers of foreign residents for the first time in its history. This is because high economic growth in Japan created the necessary conditions for the immigration of migrant workers. Some recruitment strategies were established, not only for ethnic Japanese foreign workers – a form of 'front door' immigration – but also trainees – 'side door' – and 'back door' illegal foreign workers.[3]

After Japan ratified the International Covenants on Human Rights in 1979 and the Refugees Convention in 1981, many social security laws were amended and social rights were guaranteed for refugees and aliens who settled in Japan. Both treaties aimed for the equality of social rights between nationals and non-nationals. Consequently, the nationality requirement clauses were eliminated from laws such as the National Pension Law and the National Health Insurance Law, although problems remain with regard to employment as public servants and voting rights.

How to categorise resident aliens

According to the recent predominant theory, the 'settled aliens' (*teijû gaikokujin*)[4] are guaranteed almost the same rights as nationals. The Japanese term for the *teijû gaikokujin* is similar to Tomas Hammar's 'denizen'.[5] Both terms are used for 'permanent domiciled aliens' who have some citizenship-like rights. The residents of states in Europe are categorised into three classifications: citizen, denizen and alien. In the same way, the population of Japan is categorised into three classifications: nationals, settled aliens (*teijû gaikokujin*) and other aliens.

Although there are different definitions of the term *teijû gaikokujin*, all include the descendants of Koreans and Taiwanese who were previously subjects of Japanese colonies. They are also called '*Zainichi*' (resident aliens in Japan) or 'old comers'. These foreigners are guaranteed permanent residence, but shoulder many disadvantages owing to their lack of Japanese nationality.

There are also many other foreigners who entered the country later, particularly since the 1980s. These 'newcomers' are from various countries, including China, Brazil and others. Foreigners staying in Japan for 90 days or more are required to have alien registration.

At the end of 1998, there were 1 512 116 registered foreigners in Japan (approximately 550 000 of these *Zainichi*). Registered foreigners comprised about 1.2 per cent of Japan's total population (126 486 430).[6] Additionally, at the beginning of 1999 there were estimated to be about 270 000 unregistered foreigners.[7] Thus a total of around 1 800 000 foreigners live in Japan.

Constitutional bases of aliens' rights

Many textbooks state that there are some constitutional fundamental rights, such as the right of entry into a country, social rights and electoral rights, which are accorded only to people as members of a state, and that such rights are not accorded to foreigners. This position is grounded in the position of human rights and citizens' rights in the French

Declaration of the Rights of Men and Citizens. Also, German traditional status theory presented the negative, positive and active positions of citizens without conceding the third active position to foreigners.[8] According to the classics, citizens' rights came to be explained under the concept of post-state rights, distinct from the pre-state character of most human rights.

Under the Meiji Constitution, subjects promised loyalty to the monarch. Aliens were not granted the rights of subjects since they owed loyalty to other monarchs. Additionally, the rights of subjects in the Japanese colonies differed from the rights of subjects in the homeland. After World War II, in order to change Japanese society, Article 16 of MacArther's Draft of the Constitution stipulated that 'aliens shall be entitled to the equal protection of the law'. According to Article 13, 'All natural persons are equal before the law' and no discrimination shall be authorised or tolerated on account of 'national origin'. In the final form, the Japanese Constitution did not include these clauses. The Constitution now does not have any special regulations regarding alien's rights. Therefore, the former 'Word Doctrine' accepted aliens' rights as long as the holder of human rights clauses was 'every person' instead of 'national'. Today's dominant theory in interpreting the Japanese Constitution is the 'Nature Doctrine', which accepts aliens' rights so long as the 'nature of rights' admits these special rights. This is based on the universality of human rights and the constitutional principle of international co-operation. Therefore, there is no express distinction between rights for nationals and rights for aliens in the Constitution. In my opinion, rights should be guaranteed to all aliens as long as the holder is 'every person', and other rights are guaranteed to specific aliens according to the nature of the right at issue.

Citizenship and nationality

Acquisition/loss of nationality

Article 10 of the Constitution provides that the necessary requirements for being a Japanese national shall be determined by law. The Nationality Law of 1950 set such requirements. The former *patrilinial jus sanguinis* was amended in 1984 before the ratification of the Convention on the Elimination of All Forms of Discrimination against Women. In accordance with the present *bilinial jus sanguinis*, Japanese nationality by birth is usually acquired from the nationality of either Japanese parent. Exceptionally, if both parents are unknown, a child born in

Japan can acquire Japanese nationality in application of *jus soli* (Article 2). Additionally, there is a principle of 'unique' nationality, which is considered desirable, while statelessness and dual nationality is not. Therefore, a naturalised Japanese national loses his or her former nationality (Article 5). Likewise, a Japanese national loses his or her Japanese nationality when he or she acquires or chooses a foreign nationality (Article 11).

Distinctions between nationality and citizenship

Let us consider the question of the definition of the term 'citizenship'. As a legal term, the Japanese usually use the word *kokuseki* to mean 'state membership'. Although the Japanese government usually translates it with the English word 'nationality', ethnic character is irrelevant in this context. If foreigners are naturalised, they will receive Japanese *kokuseki* and consequently equal rights as natives. Likewise, the Japanese legal term *kokumin* is usually translated into the English word 'national', with the meaning of 'official member of the state', rather than the word 'citizen'.

New concept of citizenship (citizenship rights)

On the other hand, in everyday language, the Japanese use the word *shiminken*, which has various meanings and is usually translated with the English word 'citizenship'. A first meaning refers to a set of rights and duties in a polity. A second meaning is that used in the context of international law and refers to the notion of state membership. A third meaning used in sociology connotes the 'status of being a full member of the community'. A fourth meaning refers to 'the status of participants in the political life of the state'. Recently, in Japan, there has developed a fifth usage of the word *shiminken*, as in the French *la nouvelle citoyenneté*,[9] which introduces particular citizenship rights including voting rights for settled aliens. The word denizenship (*eijû shiminken*) is appropriate for some citizenship-like rights of denizen (*eijû shimin*) in Japan.

Stateless persons

In a formal sense, aliens are persons who do not have Japanese nationality. Most of them have foreign nationalities. However, there are about 2,186 registered stateless persons in Japan.[10] In the *Andere* case, when the father was unknown and the mother was missing after the birth, a problem arose concerning the interpretation of Article 2(3) of the Nationality Law, which stipulates that if both parents are unknown a child born in Japan can acquire Japanese nationality. The District Court approved the decision to grant Japanese nationality to the child, but the Appellate Court refused it on the grounds that his mother probably had Filipino citizenship. However, the Filipino government denied it because of her lack of a passport. In the end, the Supreme Court approved the decision to grant the child Japanese nationality. The reason was that the clause 'if both parents are unknown' was interpreted as, 'if both parents are undetermined' (Supreme Court judgement, 27 January 1995). In order to eliminate the occurrence of stateless persons, this clause should be revised to 'if a child does not acquire nationality by the Nationality Law of his or her own parents' country'.[11]

Dual nationality

A further problem regarding the acquisition and loss of nationality is that, according to the Nationality Law, a naturalised Japanese national shall lose his or her former nationality (Article 5),[12] and a Japanese national shall lose his or her Japanese nationality when he or she acquires or chooses a foreign nationality (Article 11). This principle of state-membership is 'unique'. However, dual nationality persons are increasing in number owing to international marriages.[13] At present, around 4 per cent of marriages are international marriages in Japan. In recent years, about 80 per cent of non-citizen Korean residents have married Japanese nationals, and each year almost 8,000 children are born to Korean and Japanese parents.[14] A Japanese national who also possesses a foreign nationality must select either Japanese nationality or foreign nationality before reaching 22 years of age (Article 14). This selection system was introduced as the result of an amendment to the Nationality Law from *patrilinial jus sanguinis* to *bilinial jus sanguinis*.[15] In Japan, it has been stressed that dual nationality has many disadvantages: frictions from different diplomatic protection rights between countries, conflict of loyalties, inefficiency in immigration control, bigamy due to difficulties in establishing personal identity, and the confusion of civil international law relations.[16] Currently Japanese scholars are starting to consider the advantages of dual nationality not only to the individual but also to the state, for integration.

Under Articles 4, 5 and 6 of the Nationality Law, aliens may be naturalised by permission of the Minister of Justice who has discretion to grant permission and check the following conditions are fulfilled:

1 they have been domiciled in Japan for five years or more continuously (or have had residence in Japan for ten years), or are spouses or children of Japanese nationals, or are children of a parent born in Japan and resident for a period of three years;

2 they have reached the age of 20 and have legal capacity under the law of their home country (or they are children under 20 years old living together with their parents);
3 they demonstrate good behaviour and conduct;
4 they are financially supported by personal assets, skills or spouses or another relative in the same household;
5 they are stateless or lose their former nationality when acquiring Japanese nationality; and
6 they have not been involved in any activities to attempt or to advocate the overthrow of the Constitution or the government by violence.

Factors affecting the naturalisation rate

Many Koreans refuse naturalisation, despite more than 50 years' residence in Japan, because they do not want to lose their ethnic identity, which is connected to their nationality. It should be added that they have not forgotten the history of Japanese colonisation when they were forced to take Japanese nationality and a Japanese name. An acceptable solution to this problem is urgently needed. The amendment of the Nationality Law in 1984 eliminated the phrase 'Japanese name only' in the administrative guidance on naturalisation.

The naturalisation rate of Japan (0.6% in 1991; 0.8% in 1993; 1.0% in 1995) is increasing, but it is relatively low in comparison with other industrial countries.[17] The Japanese government is currently discussing the facilitation of naturalisation rules.

Residential rights

For aliens, limits are imposed on the freedom of residence and movement. However, Article 22 of the Constitution states that:

> Every person shall have the freedom to choose and change his residence and occupation to the extent that it does not interfere with the public welfare. Freedom for all persons to move to a foreign country and to divest themselves of their nationality shall be inviolate.

Hence it becomes a constitutional problem that the State regulates the entry, departure and re-entry of foreigners.

Restriction on freedom of entry

Whilst Article 22(1) of the Constitution guarantees freedom of residence and movement in Japan, it does not guarantee freedom of entry for foreigners. According to customary international law, a state can decide the kind of conditions under which it will accept a foreigner, as long as there is no special treaty (Supreme Court judgement, 19 June 1957).

Japan's immigration control system generally guarantees temporary visitors freedom to stay for less than 90 days without a visa, but a stay of 90 days or longer is subject to strict screening. At the beginning of 1998 there were visa exemption agreements with 55 countries[18] but these were suspended with Pakistan, Bangladesh and Iran in order to prevent frequent illegal overstaying by persons from these countries.[19]

Types of residence status

There are 23 types of residence status under which activities and residential terms are restricted. These are: diplomat; public services; professor; artist; religious activities; press; investor/business; legal/accounting; medical services; researcher; teacher; engineer; humanities/international services; intra-company transferee; entertainer; skilled labour; cultural activities; temporary visitor; college student; pre-college students; trainee; family stay; and designated activities. These types of residence status are known as 'Annexe Table I'.

In addition, there are four types of residence status under which activities are unrestricted. Among them, quasi-permanent residents,[20] spouse or child of a Japanese national, and spouse or child of permanent residents require renewal of the residence period. Only permanent residents are unrestricted as regards both activity and residence. These four types of residence status are known as 'Annexe Table II'. To clarify the difference between the former 23 types of residence status and the latter four, they are categorised as 'permissible intake' and 'permissible establishment' groups respectively.[21]

The Immigration Control and Refugee Recognition Act, which is modelled on the US Immigration and Nationality Law, sets down these conditions in Annexe Tables I and II and regulates the fair administration of immigration control. Japan does not have a system for granting an immigrant a permanent resident permit at the time of entrance, but some persons who enter the country with limited residence status can become permanent residents after a fixed period of residence. In this respect, the Japanese immigration system resembles European systems.

Requirements for permanent residence status

Under Article 22(2) of the Immigration Control and Refugee Recognition Law, permission to change status to permanent residence is granted at the discretion of the Ministry of Justice when the applicant adjusts to the citizen benefits of Japan and fulfils three requirements. The first legal condition is that the alien must have demonstrated good behaviour and conduct. The second legal condition is that the alien must have sufficient assets or skills to make an independent living. There is another practical condition. According to the administrative interpretation of 'the interests of Japan', in cases of the child or spouse of Japanese or permanent residents, a one or three-year residential term is required. Otherwise, a ten-year continuous residential term is necessary to be allowed a permanent residence permit.[22]

Re-entry rules and fingerprinting in the alien registration procedure

Freedom of departure is guaranteed to foreigners, but not freedom of entry. However, according to one judgement (Supreme Court judgement, 25 December 1957), it is not reasonable that freedom of emigration guaranteed in the Constitution – 22(2) – is limited for foreigners by restrictions on re-entry. Indeed some take the view that the Japanese entry requirements are too strict. It is also a matter of debate whether the alien's freedom of departure should be guaranteed more firmly than that of Japanese nationals. However, many researchers broadly agree with the existing precedents on freedom of departure and entry.

The third point to be discussed is the controversial question of procedure for re-entry, in other words temporary overseas travel. There is a view that withholding permission for re-entry based on an individual's refusal to provide their fingerprint is unconstitutional. There has always been strong criticism of the stipulation in the Alien Registration Law that resident aliens must at all times carry with them, as confirmation of their identity, an alien registration card bearing their fingerprint.[23] In the face of a number of cases involving foreigners refusing to be fingerprinted, the Japanese government has been forced to amend the Alien Registration Law numerous times. Initially, most foreigners were required to provide fingerprints of all ten fingers at each renewal. Since 1993, like permanent residents, foreigners residing for one or more years must provide a fingerprint of one finger at their first registration. In 1999 the amendment bill of the Alien Registration Law demanded the entire abolishment of fingerprinting duties. However, the obligation to carry an alien registration card remained in the amended Law.[24]

Under these circumstances, problems have arisen in some cases of permanent residents who refused fingerprinting and were subsequently refused re-entry into Japan after travelling abroad. The American spouse of a Japanese national, *Catherine*, became a plaintiff in such a case. According to the Supreme Court judgement, the Constitution does not guarantee aliens the freedom to travel abroad temporarily, and the Minister of Justice may use his discretionary right to refuse permission to re-enter (Supreme Court judgement, 16 November 1992). This judgement differed from the former district court judgement on the case of a permanent resident North Korean. This case recognised the freedom of re-entry as the freedom of temporary overseas travel that Article 22 of the Constitution guarantees, and assumed that the re-entry permission was not a matter for discretion by the Minister of Justice (Tokyo District Court judgement, 11 October 1968).

Another case concerned a permanent resident South Korean, *Che Sonhe*, who had planned to study abroad but could not receive permission for re-entry because of her refusal to be fingerprinted. She then lost her special permanent residence qualification when she left Japan. The Appellate Court judgement states that Article 22(2) of the Constitution does not guarantee the freedom of travel abroad for aliens. However, the status of the special permanent residents based on the Japan–Korea status agreement is hardly different from that of Japanese nationals. Hence the appellate court judged that non-permission of re-entry is illegal because it is an abuse of the Minister's discretion (Fukuoka Appellate Court judgement, 13 May 1994). Finally, the Supreme Court rejected the decision of the abuse and judged it legal (Supreme Court judgement, 26 March 1998). Indeed the recent precedent does not recognise the freedom of re-entry for a foreigner, but the overriding opinion of academics is that the freedom of re-entry is affirmed in the case of settled alien.[25]

Discrimination according to country of origin

Basically, there is no discrimination between aliens, whatever their originating countries may be. Indeed the former colonial Koreans and Taiwanese are given the status of special permanent residents. However, newcomer Koreans and Taiwanese are not given this status. Although Japanese origin second and third generations coming mainly from Brazil and Peru are given the status of 'quasi-permanent residents', the granting of this status is not limited to persons returning from Brazil or Peru.

Social rights

Let us now examine some issues and problems regarding social rights. Article 25(1) of the Constitution stipulates that 'all people shall have the right to maintain the minimum standards of wholesome and cultured living'. According to the former dominant theory, the term 'people' here means 'nationals' and the state of each person's nationality should guarantee social rights because they have the nature of 'post-state'.[26] However, the Japanese government ratified the International Covenants on Human Rights in 1979 and the Refugees Convention in 1981. Both treaties aimed for equality of social rights between nationals and non-nationals. As a result of Japan's accession to these treaties, nationality clauses were eliminated from such laws as the National Pension Law, the Child Rearing Allowance Law and the Child Allowance Law. Recently, according to the dominant opinion, there is no constitutional impediment to legislate for the security of social rights for settled aliens.[27]

Limitations for permanent residents

There still remains a problem with the national pension system. If foreigners were 35 years or older at the time of revision of the National Pension Act (1981), even if they have paid their insurance charge, they cannot receive the old-age pension because they still lack enough contributory premiums. Thus, some foreigners may not be able to enjoy the result of the abolition of the nationality clause. There might be a need for the courts to lend a helping hand in the future. For example, even though a disabled Korean resident, Mrs. Shiomi, regained Japanese nationality by naturalisation in 1970 before the National Pension Law was amended, she cannot receive the handicap welfare pension because she was a Korean when her disablement was determined on 1 November 1959 when the Law entered into force.[28] The Supreme Court confirmed a large legislative discretion for social security policy (Supreme Court judgement, 2 March 1989).

The Livelihood Protection Law did not clarify the nationality clause until the social section's chief issued a notice which limited the Law's application to Japanese nationals owing to the interpretation of the term 'national'. However, it applied *mutatis mutandis* to persons registered through alien registration and provided them with medical care. In effect, this was similar to the application of the Livelihood Protection Law because the central government paid the expenses for the local governments. However, the Immigration Control and Refugee Recognition Law was amended in 1990, when the Ministry of Health and

Welfare also issued a new directive. Now, the *mutatis mutandis* application covers only foreigners of the Annexe Table II, namely, permanent resident, spouse or child of a Japanese national, spouse or child of a permanent resident and quasi-permanent resident. Foreigners of the Annexe Table I are allowed to stay in Japan under the condition of not becoming a burden on the Japanese government, and they often leave their property and family in their home country.

Limitations for temporary residents

Temporary visiting foreigners are excluded from the National Health Insurance Law. Originally this Law did not have a nationality clause, but its enforcement regulation had laid down a clause concerning nationality until 1986. At present, Article 5 of this Law stipulates that persons insured are 'those who have a domicile in communes or special wards'. However, according to the administrative interpretation since 1992, these 'domicile (*Jûsho*)' must have a residence period of one or more years or they have to reside for one or more years by renewing their temporary visas. Temporary visiting foreigners are also excluded from the application of the National Pension Law.

Limitations for irregular residents

In the case of an irregular resident, she was not covered under the National Health Insurance Law (Tokyo District judgement, 27 September 1995), since an irregular resident is not allowed to have a 'domicile', even if she has paid the insurance for her Japanese child covered under the Insurance. However, in the case of an irregular resident married to a Japanese national, she is covered under the Insurance (Tokyo District judgement, 16 July 1998). The previous Medical Treatment of Atomic Bomb Victims Law has a character of humanity and national compensation, so this Law is applied to illegal immigrants (Supreme Court judgement, 30 March 1978). In practice, free maternity leave is guaranteed for over-staying persons (Article 22 of the Child Welfare Law), as is medical treatment for their physically handicapped children (Article 20 of the Child Welfare Law) and medical treatment for their premature babies (Article 20 of the Maternal and Child Health Law).[29] If a company employs more than five workers, over-stay workers are entitled to health insurance. Legally the worker's compensation insurance will be paid regardless of nationality, but in the case of over-stay workers, employers and employees are not willing to apply it for fear of the disclosure of the illegal employment. Furthermore, in the case of illegal foreign worker's accidents, the accounting of the lost benefit has a serious problem because of the difference between the standard of Japan and the standard assumed for a third world country. The Supreme Court based the calculation on a wage earner who had been in Japan for three years (Supreme Court judgement, 28 January 1997).

In cases involving temporary visitors or irregular residents, some local governments have to pay for the emergency medical costs of foreigners who may fall down by the roadside during their visit, according to the Law concerning the Treatment of Sick Wayfarers and Wayfarers Found Dead. Working residential status is required in order to be covered under employee's health insurance. Even if a foreigner has such a working status, small companies (less than five persons) and temporary workers are excluded from this insurance system. Additionally, some foreign workers are not willing to join this insurance system because they must at the same time join the welfare pension scheme, from which they cannot receive the benefits in the future. Foreigners who work or reside in Japan, however, cannot be classified as 'wayfarers'. Recently some local governments and NGOs have had to provide for their own expenditures.[30] Since 1996 the state has paid towards the expenditure for emergency medical care, on the condition that the illness is serious.[31]

Situation of former military personnel

A major problem to solve today is war compensation regardless of present nationality. Neither Taiwanese who were Japanese soldiers, nor their bereaved families, can be compensated because the Law concerning the Relief to Invalids and the War-Bereaved and the Civil Servants' Pension Law contain nationality clauses. The Supreme Court ruled that it is not contrary to Article 14 (the equal protection clause) of the Constitution (Supreme Court judgement, 28 April 1992). However, the Appellate Court judgement pointed out that there is an immediate need to correct the situation of remarkable loss compared with Japanese in similar circumstances. Therefore, the Law on Money of Condolence to Taiwanese Killed in Action and the Serious War Wounded Person was established in 1988. On the other hand, Korean soldiers and army families are not compensated.[32] The reason is the Japan and Korea Agreement of 1965, which concluded request rights between the people of both countries (Supreme Court judgement, 15 July 1994). Yet according to the research of the Ministry of Foreign Affairs, the USA, the UK, Germany, France and Italy have compensated foreign soldiers. The report of the human rights committee of the United Nations has pointed out nationality discrimination in Japan regarding war compensation, and the new war-related compensation law was established in 2000.

Multicultural education

For resident aliens in Japan, the opportunity to acquire an ethnic education is very limited. The General Association of (north) Korean Residents and the (south) Korean Residents Union run their own schools, which have a bilingual Japanese and Korean curriculum.[33] The Japanese government has refused to accredit these schools and therefore these students could not take the entrance examination for national universities until 1999. Few public schools have 'ethnic education classes' and most Korean students (86.5% in 1988) attend Japanese school without bilingual education.[34] Furthermore, there is a serious problem for newcomers. According to the survey of 1997, 16 835 children in compulsory schools (elementary schools and junior high schools) needed additional language training. Their native languages were Portuguese (43.1%), Chinese (30.8%), Spanish (10.1%) and so on.[35] Under the present conditions, it is difficult for foreign students to learn even the Japanese language. Moreover, if these children keep moving between Japan and their home countries at regular intervals, both the acquisition of the Japanese language and native language maintenance will become difficult.[36] Gradually, there is a growing awareness of the problems regarding multiethnic education. Most schools do not take any measures for their native language education, although a few cities the local governments have hired part-time Portuguese and Spanish teachers to teach Japanese origin (*Nikkei*) Brazilian and Peruvian students.[37]

Economic rights

Property rights

In general, there are no legal restrictions on aliens acquiring property rights. However, the Alien Land Law stipulates reciprocity for ownership of land, but such restrictive regulations have never been put into concrete action by cabinet ordinances. Also the Ship Law prohibits aliens from owning Japanese ships. The laws such as the Patent Law do stipulate reciprocity for patent and patent-related rights, unless aliens do not have domicile or permanent residence in Japan. A copyright of a work by an alien, unless otherwise provided for in treaties, is protected under the Copyright Law if the work is published first in Japan (or published first in places where the law is not in force but published in Japan within 30 days from the first publication). There are some restrictions to holding stocks issued by broadcasting and telephone companies.[38]

Self-employment

For aliens, there remain some limitations to their rights of self-employment. The Mining Law prohibits aliens from having mining rights. Indeed the nationality requirement was abolished for an advocate, but reciprocity remains for a patent attorney. An alien can not be a notary public. The Port Piloting Law prohibits aliens from being port pilots.

In Japan, work permits are included in the determination of status of residence. The status of the Annex Table I permits can be roughly classified into work visas[39] and non-work visas. Although Japan keeps the traditional policy of not admitting foreign workers for unskilled jobs, non-work visas have some exceptions. College students can work for four hours (eight hours in July and August) a day in order to make up for the cost of school and living. Pre-college students also can work for four hours a day. Indeed trainees' programmes were established to promote international transfers of skills and technology, but the practice of employers was to use these as a channel for recruiting unskilled foreign workers.

Public employment at the state level

It is important to note that the Constitution has not determined the nationality clause on the access to public jobs. The nationality clause for employment appears only in Article 7 of the Diplomat Law. Additionally, Article 10 of the Election Law stipulates the eligibility for a 'Japanese national'. Also, Article 67 of the Constitution lays down that the Prime Minster is elected from among Diet representatives. Yet the Constitution and many statutes do not impose the condition of nationality for general service public officials. Nevertheless, in 1953, the Cabinet Legislation Bureau and the National Personal Authority presented the 'Nationality Postulated Doctrine about Public Servants'. It imposes the requirement of Japanese nationality on public servants who 'participate in the exercise of public authority or formulation of national public will'. Likewise, the Ministry of Home Affairs explained that aliens can not be allowed to apply for the examination to become local public servants who would 'participate in the exercise of public authority or formulation of local public will'.

Recently, however, reflecting changes abroad,[40] the door to public service employment has gradually opened wider. In the first place, a national and public university professorship was opened to foreigners in

1982. Secondly, aliens can become national officials such as doctors, nurses and postal delivery workers.

Local authority employment

In contrast, some local governments abolished the nationality requirement for some specific positions, including doctors and manual labour, namely bus-drivers. Aliens can serve only as lectures, not ordinary teachers in elementary, junior and senior high schools. They are therefore not allowed promotion to management posts. However, in 1992, approximately 30 per cent of communes abolished the nationality requirement for general administrative officials. In 1996, Kawasaki City abolished the nationality requirement for posts in general office work for the first time as a large city. However, this effort excludes firemen and prohibits promotion to management posts. The District Court refused a Korean public health nurse, *Chon Hyan-Gyun*, the right to apply for section chief. Nevertheless, it confirmed that the constitutional principle of national sovereignty prevents foreigners from gaining employment in positions with direct governing functions such as Ministers and Judges, but it does not prohibit enacting a law for employment in indirect governing positions (Tokyo District Court judgement, 16 May 1996). Then the Appellate Court decided that plaintiff was right and confirmed that the principle of national sovereignty does not prevent foreign residents (especially permanent residents) from gaining employment in management posts without decisive competence (Tokyo Appellate Court judgement, 26 November 1997). According to the speech of the Minister of Home Affairs in November 1996, the interpretation of the 'Nationality Postulated Doctrine about Public Servants' should be left to the discretion of each local government. Therefore, the code is ultimately a matter of administrative discretion. For example, the Kanagawa prefecture has abolished the nationality requirement since 1997.

Data on aliens' governmental posts

Many local governments are now reviewing their current employment practices. In 1997, about 80 per cent of large local governments opened the door for some employment but only 20 per cent of local governments opened every type of job.[41] In a 1997 survey, there were 776 alien local governmental officials.[42]

Distinction between different national origin groups

Some local governments have opened the door to permanent residents or alien residents with permission for 'establishment' only because they do not have any limitation for activity. Originally, it was a desirable principle to gather talented persons from a wider range. No distinctions are made on the basis of national origin except for special residence status of former colonial or Japanese-origin people. The essence of the right to employment for public servants is the freedom to select an occupation as a public employee. As long as these rights have political duties, they assume the character of political rights such as voting rights.

Political rights

The last debate concerns electoral rights.[43] Precedents tend to vary in national and local elections.

State electoral rights

According to the *Alan* National Suffrage Case, the Election Law, limiting suffrage for the national Upper Chamber to Japanese nationals, was constitutional (Supreme Court judgement, 26 February 1993). On the other hand, in the *Kim* Local Suffrage Case, the Constitution does not guarantee local suffrage for permanent residents. However, the Constitution neither prohibits nor requests it. It is left as a matter of legislative adjustment (Supreme Court judgement, 28 February 1995). This decision is epoch-making, giving a signal to the Diet that the introduction of local suffrage of permanent residents is possible by statutory amendment without implying constitutional amendment.

The traditionally dominant opinion was 'Both Prohibition Theory', which denied national and local voting rights to foreigners. There were three reasons for this:

1 Article 15 of the Constitution stipulates that 'the people have the inalienable right to choose their public officials' and the 'people' refers to only Japanese nationals;
2 the sovereign is 'a body of nationality holders' in the principle of national sovereignty;
3 aliens can not be given voting rights from the point of 'functions' in the 'Dual Doctrine', which explains the nature of suffrage from the right and function of nationals.

In contrast, a recent proposal called a 'Both Request Theory', requests total suffrage to settled aliens who are members of Japanese society. There are three grounds for this:

1 the 'people' are not only nationals but also permanent residents;
2 the sovereign is 'those who are affected by political decisions' or 'a body of participants of a social contract' in the principle of people's sovereignty;
3 the 'Right Doctrine' of suffrage does not consider its aspect of functions. Furthermore, there is a moderate opinion, the 'Both Allowance Theory', that the Constitution neither prohibits aliens from voting nor requests them to vote in either national or local elections. According to this theory, it is possible for aliens to vote in both elections through a legislative amendment.

Local electoral rights

Currently, many scholars support the 'National Prohibition and Local Allowance Theory', which prohibits national suffrage because of the national sovereignty principle, but allows local suffrage because of the principle of local autonomy which implies self-governing by the inhabitants. In this respect the intention of nationals is enacted as a statute through a Diet, and the intention of inhabitants (implying some foreign residents) is enacted as a local ordinance through a local assembly. Hence the first democratic legitimacy from above and the second one from below are consistent. That is why Article 94 of the Constitution stipulates that local governments enact their local ordinance within the law.

There have been more than 1,400 resolutions in the local assemblies asking for a change in the law to introduce alien's political rights at the local level in Japan. Some local governments are investigating whether to allow voting rights in local referendums for alien residents. The Liberal Democratic Party government has not been willing to introduce the bill regarding aliens' voting rights, but the opposition parties have concerns about aliens' votes. After the reform of the Lower House election system in 1994, Japan's political climate was difficult to forecast. In any case, the constitutional hurdle appears to be slightly lowered. Public opinion and the opinion of the representatives of the national Parliament are on balance in favour of the denizen vote.[44] Furthermore, since the President of South Korea came to Japan in 1998, the political climate of Japan changed. Governmental parties submitted a bill to introduce local voting suffrage for permanent residents in 2000.

Voter participation and representation of aliens

At present, there are no local voting rights for aliens in Japan but it should be noted that the Supreme Court maintained that there is no constitutional prohibition and the bill on local suffrage is under Parliamentary discussion. Therefore, there is no representative of national and local parliaments in Japan. Only a few local governments have established consultative parliaments of alien residents.

Eligibility to stand for office

After the President of South Korea came to Japan in 1998, the political climate changed in South Korea and Japan. The South Korean government is preparing to introduce local voting suffrage for foreigners residing for five and more years. Japanese opposition parties submitted the bills. One bill will grant to denizens only local suffrage, the other will grant them local suffrage and eligibility. The Japanese coalition government, including former opposition parties, is submitting the bill to grant permanent residents local suffrage.

There is also a debate about making a distinction between representation on local councils and the position of mayor. It is argued that the right to stand for local councils involves political functions and policy and so in particular the position of mayor is prohibited for aliens because the mayor represents the state at the local level. As most of the powers at prefectural level and half at the commune level are delegated by the central government, if aliens were elected at these levels they would be involved in national politics, which should be reserved for citizens. However, decentralisation in Japan abolished these delegated functions and so made it easier to allow foreigners to participate in local politics.

Restrictions to political freedoms for aliens

Even if there are no electoral rights for resident aliens in Japan, there is a political party that consists only of resident aliens. This *Zainichi-tô* (the Foreign Residents' Voting Rights Party) asked for the right to stand for the national Parliament. As for the establishment of a political party and freedom of electoral campaigning, the government does not prohibit these to resident aliens. There was a long-established milestone judgement that rights of expression for political matters are not guaranteed for resident aliens (*McLean* case; Supreme Court judgement, 4 October 1978). An American language teacher, Mr McLean, had his request to prolong his residence permit rejected due to his involvment in the anti-Vietnam War movement. As a consequence, the judgement agreed with the decision of the Minister of Justice. However, now the discretion of the Minister should be regarded as being as narrow as possible and permanent resident aliens especially should enjoy all political rights other than electoral rights.

Concluding remarks

Permanent resident aliens have special status distinct from that of other aliens, especially as to re-entry rights, rights for a minimum standard of living, employment as civil servants and so on. Residential rights are divided into many categories and it is extremely difficult to acquire permanent residence status in Japan. Therefore, people are often classified as settled aliens (*teijû gaikokujin*) including long-term or quasi-permanent residents.

Social rights and economic rights are not fully guaranteed to temporary alien residents, but settled aliens are equal to nationals regarding social rights. While there are some restrictions to economic rights which apply to aliens, rights to employment, especially as local civil servants, have a tendency to be guaranteed to settled aliens. Moreover, there is huge support in public opinion for settled aliens to be granted local voting rights. Their residential, social, economic and political rights are considered as citizenship rights that are distinct from the formal citizenship, that is, nationality.

In addition to electoral rights for alien residents, it should be noted that some countries allow dual nationality in cases of international marriages and for second generation children of immigrants.[45] Persons who have dual nationality can of course vote at national and local levels. The Japanese Constitution declares the principle of international co-operation, and Articles 11 and 97 stipulates that fundamental human rights are guaranteed to the people of this and future generations (directly translated from its Japanese official text: present and future nationals). While it is necessary to review the meaning of 'future nationals' it should be emphasised that they are not only descendants of present Japanese nationals but also settled aliens (denizens) who can be naturalised if they wish. However, it should be noted that if the alien residents are naturalised they will become present nationals. In that case, who are the future nationals? Behind the concept of human rights for 'future nationals', we can find a clue to the nature of denizenship.

This can be illustrated by the concept of escalation. Even alien residents with a short-term residence permit have some chance of becoming nationals, but their human rights are not fully guaranteed in Japan. Citizenship rights such as residential rights, social rights, economic rights and electoral rights especially are limited for temporary alien residents.[46] On the other hand, there is a probability that denizens will become nationals, and their human rights need to be guaranteed as far as possible. As already pointed out in this chapter, the right to re-entry and many social rights are guaranteed for denizens as well as nationals; access to employment of public jobs are gradually opening to denizens and there is strong public support for granting electoral rights for denizens.

In order to satisfy this constitutional demand, however, there is an alternative way to make naturalisation easy, namely by admitting dual nationality. In this respect, we also need to deal with the amendment of the Election Law, the Local Government Law, the National Civil Servants' Law, the Local Civil Servants' Law, the Immigration Control and Refugee Recognition Law and the Nationality Law.

Notes

1 Hiroshi Tanaka, *Zainichi Gaikokujin* [The Settled Aliens in Japan] New. Version, (Tokyo: Iwanami Shoten, 1995), pp. 152–5, 164

2 Japan colonised Taiwan in 1895 and Korea in 1910 and established the puppet state of Manchuria (north east of China). This was basically considered an internal migration, not immigration, as all migrants were considered Japanese subjects. On the other hand, migration within the Japanese Empire was very restrictive and regulated. For instance, some of the Korean migrants chose to move to Japan, while others were forced to do so, in some cases against their will. There is still an on-going litigation regarding never received payment for such forcible work of Koreans.

3 Takamichi Kajita, 'The Challenge of Incorporating Foreigners in Japan: "Ethnic Japanese or Sociological Japanese"', in Myron Weiner and Tadashi Hanami (eds), *Temporary Workers or Future Citizens?* (London: Macmillan Press – now Palgrave, 1998), p. 120.

4 There are various opinions on the standard for settled aliens (*teijû gaikokujin*) in Japan. One is 3–5 years residence based on the standard of naturalisation or the standard of the normal 4-year election period. Another is the requirement of permanent residence. The other is aliens whose status are permanent resident, spouse or child of a Japanese citizen, spouse or child of a permanent resident and quasi-permanent resident.

5 Tomas Hammar, *Democracy and the Nation State*, (Aldershot: Avebury, 1990), pp. 12–18.

6 Japan Immigration Association, *Zairyû Gaikokujin Tôkei* [The Statistics of Foreigners in Japan] (Tokyo: Nyûkan Kyôkai, 1999), p. 3.

7 According to the estimate made by the Immigration Bureau, the Ministry of Justice in 1999. See http://www.moj.go.jp/PRESS/990924/990924-1.htm; *Nihon Keizai Shinbun* (28 March 1999).

8 Georg Jellinek, *System der subjektiven öffentlichen Rechte*, 2nd edn, 1919 (Tübingen: Scientia Verlag Aalen, 1979), p. 193.

9 Danièle Lochak, 'La citoyenneté: un concept juridique flou', in Dominique Colas *et al.* (eds), *Citoyenneté et nationalité*, (Paris: Presses universitaires de Paris, 1991), p. 205.

10 Japan Immigration Association, *op. cit.*, note 6, p. 5.
11 The similar clause is regulated in France, Italy and Spain. See Yasuhiro Okuda, *Kazoku to Kokuseki* [The Family and Nationality] (Tokyo: Yûhikaku, 1996), p. 63.
12 There are exceptions according to Article 4(2). If the alien has a family relationship with a Japanese citizen or special circumstances, such as when (for example a refugee's) home country will not allow relinquishment of nationality, the alien may retain his or her existing nationality on a temporary basis.
13 In Europe, there are usually three reasons to admit dual nationality: 1) International marriage; 2) refugees whose home country do not admit loss of their initial nationality; 3) *jus domicili* of second-generation immigrants. The Japanese system only admits cases 1) and 2).
14 John C. Maher and Yumiko Kawanishi, 'Maintaining Culture and Language: Koreans in Osaka', in John C. Maher and Gaynor Macdonald (eds), *Diversity in Japanese Culture and Language*, (London: Kegan Paul International, 1995), p. 170.
15 For the history of Japanese nationality, see Yoshio Hagino, 'Recent Developments of the Nationality Law of Japan', *Nanzan Hôgaku*, vol. 8, no. 2 (1984), pp. 1–9; Chikako Kashiwazaki, 'Citizenship in Japan: Legal Practice and Contemporary Development', in T. Alexander Aleinikoff and Douglas Klusmeyer (eds), *From Migrants to Citizens* (Washington, DC: Carnegie Endowment for International Peace, 2000), p. 438.
16 Tadamasa Kuroki and Kiyoshi Hosokawa, *Gaijihô and Kokusekihô* [Foreign Affairs Law and Nationality Law] (Tokyo: Gyôsei, 1988), pp. 251–2.
17 1994 and 1996 SOPEMI, *Trends in International Migration* (Paris: OPEC, 1995 and 1997), p. 60.
18 Japan Immigration Association, A Guide to Entry, Residence and Registration Procedures in Japan for Foreign nationals, 5th edn (Tokyo: Japan Immigration Association, 1998), pp. 53–5.
19 Hidenori Sakanaka and Toshio Saito, *Shutsunyûkoku kanri oyobi nintei hô. Chikujô kaisetsu* [The Immigration Control and Refugee Recognition Act. Commentary], (Tokyo: Nihon Kajo Shuppan, 1994), p. 304.
20 Officially, it is translated into the Long-term residents but this status is able to be given just after arriving at Japan and has to be renewed every 6 months, 1 year or 3 years even if the renewal is with ease. Its special nature is the possibility to work without restriction as well as permanent residents.
21 Hiromi Mori, *Immigration Policy and Foreign Workers in Japan*, (London: Macmillan, 1997), pp. 10–11.
22 Nobuyuki Koyama, *'Zairyû Shikaku "Eijûsha" ni tsuite'* [On the Status of Permanent Residents] *Kokusai Jinryû* [The Immigration Newsmagazine] no. 138 (1998), p. 26. Previously, it was reported the general requirement of a 20-year residence. See Ryoichi Yamada and Tadamasa Kuroki, *Wakariyasui Nûkanhô* [An Easy Textbook of Immigration Law] 4th edn, (Tokyo: Yûhikaku, 1997), p. 89; Shôtarô Takeuchi, *Shutsunyûkoku Kanri gyôsei Ron* [The Theory of Immigration Control] (Tokyo: Shinzansha, 1995) p. 244.
23 Yasuaki Ônuma, 'Beyond the Myth of Monoethnic Japan', in The Committee to Commemorate the Sixtieth Birthday of Prof. Suh Yong-Dal (ed.), *Ajia*

Shimin to Kan Choôsenjin [Asian Citizens and Koreans in Japan], (Tokyo: Nihon Hyôronsha, 1993), pp. 576–8.

24 *Asahi Shinbun* (13 May 1999).

25 Yoshio Hagino, *Kenpô Kôgi: Jinken* [The Lecture of the Constitution: Human Rights] (Kyoto: Hôritsu Bunkasha, 1994), p. 205.

26 Toshiyoshi Miyazawa, *Kempô* [Constitution] I (Tokyo: Yûhikaku, 1974), p. 241.

27 Nobuyoshi Ashibe, *Kempô* [Constitution] (Tokyo: Iwanami Shoten, 1997), p. 91.

28 Yuji Iwasawa, *International law, Human Rights, and Japanese Law* (Oxford: Clarendon Press, 1998), pp. 171–4.

29 Emiko Miki, '*Gaikokujin no Iryô* [Medical care for aliens]', in Nihon Bengoshi Rengôkai Henshû Iinkai (ed.), *Teijûka jidai no Gaikokujin no Jinken* [Aliens' Human Rights in the Permanently Domiciling Time] (Tokyo: Akashi Shoten, 1997), pp. 88–9.

30 Akira Hatate, '*Gaikokujin no kodomo to iryô* [Foreign children and their medical care]', in Japan Civil Liberties Union (ed.), *op. cit.*, pp. 87–91, 99–102.

31 Toshi Murata, '*Gaikokujin no rôdo kankyô wo meguru hôritsu mondai* [Legal problems on the aliens' labour environment]', in Nihon Bengoshi Rengôkai Henshû Iinkai (ed.), *op. cit.* note 29, p. 109.

32 If Mr. Sok Song-Ki had been Japanese, he would have received a cumulative total of 60 million yen for his injury (the loss of an arm). See Hiroshi Tanaka, 'Why is Asia Demanding Post-war Compensation Now?', *Hitotsubashi Journal of Social Studies* vol. 28, no. 1 (1996), p. 10.

33 The Association has 1 university, over 150 elementary, junior and senior high schools enrolling about 20 000 students. The Union has 4 schools with three levels and less than 2,000 students. George Hicks, *Japan's Hidden Appartheid* (Aldershot: Ashgate, 1997), p. 135.

34 Min Guan-Shik, *Zainichi Kankokujin no Genjô to Mirai* [The Present and Future of Koreans living in Japan] (Hakuteisha: Tokyo, 1994), p. 34; Ri Vol-Sun, '*Zainichi Chôsenjin no Minzoku Kyôiku* [Ethnic Education for Koreans living in Japan]', in Pak Chon-Myon (ed.), *Zainichi Chôsenjin* [Koreans living in Japan] (Tokyo: Akashi Shoten, 1999), p. 168.

35 Nihon Keizai Shinbun [Nihon Keizai Newspaper], 28 February 1999.

36 Takamichi Kajita, 'Nature de l'immigration au Japan', *Perspectives asiatiques*, no. 1 (1996), p. 116.

37 Kazuyuki Azusawa, '*Gaikokujin no Jinken no Genzai* [The present situation of alien's human rights]' in Nihon Bengoshi Rengôkai Henshû Iinkai (ed.), *op. cit.*, note 29, p. 14; Emiko Yukawa, '*Bairingaru Kyôiku no iru kodomotachi* [Children in Need of Bilingual Education In Japan]', *Japan Journal of Multicultural and Multiculturalism* vol. 4, no.1 (1998), pp. 9–13.

38 Akio Shimizu, Japan, in Dennis Campbell (ed.), *International Immigration and Nationality Law*, vol. 2, (Dordrecht: Kluwer, 1996), JAP – VIII-2.

39 diplomat; public services; professor; artist; religious activities; press; investor/business; legal/accounting; medical services; researcher; teacher; engineer; humanities/international services; intra-company transferee; entertainer; skilled labour.

40 See Astrid Auer *et al.*, *Civil Services in the Europe of Fifteen*, 1996, p. 40; M. Niedobitek, 'Das Recht des öffentlichen Dienstes in den Mitgliedstaaten der EG', in Siegfried Magiera and Heinrich Siedentopf (eds), *Das Recht des*

öffentlichen Dienstes in den Mitgliedstaaten der Europäischen Gemeinschaft, 1994, pp. 33–6.

41 *Asahi Shinbun* [Asahi Newspaper], 25 August 1997.

42 There were about 2 850 000 local government personnel in 1995.

43 For further details, see Atsushi Kondo, 'Electoral Rights for non-Citizens', Report at the 5th World Congress of the International Association of Constitutional Law in 1999 (Rotterdam); Atsushi Kondo, Gaikokujin sanseiken to kokuseki [Aliens' Electoral Rights and Citizenship] (Tokyo: Akashi Shoten, 1996), pp. 109–40; Atsushi Kondo, 'From "Mono Ethnic State" to Cultural Pluralism in Japan', in Janina W. Dacyl and Charles Westin (eds), *Governance of Cultural Diversity* (Stockholm: CEIFO, 2000), pp. 132–4.

44 Takashi Ebashi, '*Gaikokujin shimin no chihô sanseiken* [Local voting rights for alien citizens]', Nihon Bengoshi Rengôkai Henshû Iinkai (ed.), *op. cit.*, note 29, pp. 114–15.

45 Dilek Çinar, 'From Aliens to Citizens: Rules of Transition', in Rainer Bauböck (ed.), *From Aliens to Citizens* (Aldershot: Avebury, 1994), p. 59.

46 In the cases of irregular residents, there are serious problems regarding medical care and so on. It is estimated that approximately 270 000 overstayers are living in Japan. In 1999, A group of overstayers asked the Minister of Justice to give them special permission to live in Japan. Some of them work and live with their children who attend to Japanese schools for several years. Regularisation for the long-term irregular resident families is important for the 'Right of the Child.'

2

Access to Citizenship for Aliens in the Netherlands

Gerard-René de Groot

Introduction

This paper will deal with the access to citizenship for aliens in the Netherlands. Traditionally the Netherlands are liberal in respect of granting residence rights and finally citizenship to foreigners. Already in the sixteenth century the Republic of the United Netherlands granted residence rights to a large number of Sefardic jews, who had to leave the Iberian Peninsula (Spain and Portugal) because of the measures of persecution undertaken by the Kings of Spain. At the end of the seventeenth century many Huguenots coming from France went to the Netherlands; in the beginning of the eighteenth century a considerable number of Mennonites had to leave Switzerland and went to the Netherlands. During both the seventeenth and eighteenth centuries many migrant workers went to the Netherlands, coming mainly from the different German states. During the same period a lot of Jews from Middle and Eastern Europe arrived in the Netherlands. At the end of the nineteenth century again a considerable number of (Catholic) Germans arrived in the Netherlands as a consequence of the so called 'Kulturkampf' in Germany.

From the end of the sixteenth century the Republic of the United Netherlands built up a colonial empire. All colonies were occupied by England during the Napoleonic Wars. In 1814 only a part of the colonies were given back to the Netherlands: the Netherlands Indies, Suriname and six islands in the Caribbean. Directly after World War II the Netherlands Indies tried to get independence. A new state, Indonesia, was proclaimed. The Netherlands recognised this independence in 1949. Suriname became an independent republic in 1975. The six Caribbean islands (Aruba, Bonaire, Curaçao, Sint Maarten, Sint Eustasius and Saba) are still part of the Kingdom of the Netherlands. Aruba is a 'country' within the Kingdom, the other Caribbean islands together form another country: the Netherlands Antilles.

As a consequence of the independence of Indonesia a considerable number of people migrated from Indonesia to the Netherlands during the late 1940s and the 1950s. As a consequence of the independence of Suriname many inhabitants of Suriname settled down in the Netherlands during the months directly before the independence of Suriname on 25 November 1975. The vast majority of both groups of migrants already possessed nationality of the Netherlands before they came to the European part of the Kingdom. This was mainly the consequence of treaties concluded with the new independent states. With Indonesia the '*Overeenkomst betreffende de toescheiding van staatsburgers tussen het Koninkrijk der Nederlanden en de Republiek der Verenigde Staten van Indonesië*' (Treaty on the allocation of citizens between the Kingdom of the Netherlands and the Republic of the United States of Indonesia) was concluded in 1949. In 1975 another Convention to allocate citizens was concluded between the Netherlands and Suriname: '*Overeenkomst betreffende de toescheiding van staatsburgers tussen het Koninkrijk der Nederlanden en de Republiek Suriname*' (Treaty on the allocation of citizens between the Kingdom of the Netherlands and the Republic of Suriname).

During the 1930s, groups of Germans (mainly of Jewish origin) came to the Netherlands. Some stayed in the country even after the restoration of democracy in Germany. In the sixties and seventies large groups of migrant workers came from the Mediterranean area to the Netherlands. The most important countries of origin were Turkey and Morocco; Spain, Italy, Greece and former Yugoslavia should also be mentioned. Especially since 1985, many migrant workers and their family members have acquired Netherlands nationality by naturalisation.

A considerable number of people have requested asylum in the Netherlands. In recent years, the annual number of asylum seekers was as follows: 1992: 20 300; 1993: 35 400; 1994: 52 600; 1995: 29 300; 1996: 22 900; 1997: 34 400. Only a relatively low percentage of asylum seekers receive official refugee status (between 12 and 15%), a considerably higher percentage (more than 30%) receives another status, which allows the persons involved to stay in the Netherlands, at least until they can return to their country without risk for their safety. In 1996, 51 464 illegal immigrants had to leave the Netherlands: 16 481 of them were asylum seekers, whose requests for asylum were rejected.

Origin of aliens

In 1997 the Netherlands had 15 600 000 inhabitants, 680 000 of whom (around 4% of the population) did not possess Netherlands nationality. Of these aliens living in the Netherlands 126 000 were born on Netherlands territory, 149 000 in other EU states, 96 000 in Morocco, 91 000 in Turkey.[1] The Netherlands have a strong tradition of granting nationality to aliens under liberal conditions, if they apply for naturalisation. Of the total population of the Netherlands, 1 434 000 (more than 9% of the population) were born abroad. Although most of them were not of Netherlands origin, the majority possess Netherlands nationality at the moment. To illustrate:

- 175 000 persons were born in Indonesia/Netherlands East Indies. Of these persons only 8,000 do not possess Netherlands nationality. The total Indonesian population living in the Netherlands (including Indonesians born in the Netherlands) is also around 8,000;[2]
- 182 000 persons were born in Suriname. Of these persons only 11 000 do not possess Netherlands nationality. The total Surinamese population living in the Netherlands (including Surinamese born in the Netherlands) is around 12 000;
- 128 000 persons were born in Germany. Of these persons 48 000 do not possess Netherlands nationality. The total German population living in the Netherlands (including Germans born in the Netherlands) is around 54 000;
- 143 000 persons were born in Morocco. Of these persons 97 000 do not possess Netherlands nationality. The total Moroccan population, i.e. without Netherlands nationality (comprising Moroccans born in the Netherlands and those born in Morocco) is around 139 000;
- 169 000 persons were born in Turkey. Of these persons 92 000 do not possess Netherlands nationality. The total Turkish population living in the Netherlands (including Turks born in the Netherlands) is around 127 000).

From these numbers it can be concluded that almost 400 000 people living in the Netherlands came from the former colonies (Indonesia and Suriname, and also Netherland Antilles and Aruba). A considerably higher number of people are descended from people who were living in the former colonies. Nowadays almost all these people possess Netherlands nationality.

Of the migrant workers who came to the Netherlands some decades ago, a considerable percentage acquired Netherlands nationality by naturalisation or (for the first generation of descendants born in the territory of the Netherlands) by lodging a declaration of option (art. 6 sub b Nationality Act). Now the children of these migrant workers are giving birth to children in the Netherlands. If the parents of these children were born when their father or mother was already living in the Netherlands, the now newborn children acquire Netherlands nationality at birth (art. 3 para. 3 Nationality Act).

Constitutional provisions

Article 2 paragraph 2 of the Constitution of the Netherlands emphasises that the admission of aliens to the Netherlands, their right to stay in the Netherlands, and their expulsion have to be regulated by an act of parliament. Based on this constitutional provision the *Vreemdelingenwet* (Aliens Act) was enacted. This Aliens Act, however, gives only a framework, which is elaborated in the *Vreemdelingenbesluit* (Aliens Decree) and the *Vreemdelingencirculaire* (Guidelines on Aliens).

One might hesitate to say whether the elaboration of the Aliens Act in a Decree and by Guidelines is perfectly in conformity with the Constitution, because the Decree and the Guidelines are definitely not acts of parliament.

The Constitution does not grant specific rights to aliens, but most rights guaranteed in the Constitution are guaranteed for all persons (citizens and other persons living in the Netherlands). Exceptions are articles 3, 4 and 19. Article 3 states that all Netherlands nationals shall be equally eligible for appointment to public service. But this does not imply that aliens can not be appointed as officials. Article 4 mentions that every Netherlands national shall have an equal right to elect the members of the general representative bodies and to stand for elections as a member of those bodies, subject to the limitations and exceptions prescribed by act of parliament. But again, this provision does not exclude aliens from participating in some elections.

A further exception is the right on free choice of labour, which is guaranteed in article 19 paragraph 3 for all Netherlands nationals. But it has to be emphasised that this guarantee is a rather weak one for Netherlands nationals as well, because the article makes it possible to restrict this right by or pursuant to an act of parliament.

Nationality and citizenship

Acquisition and loss of nationality

The nationality of the Netherlands is regulated by the Kingdom Act of 19 December 1984, which entered into force on 1 January 1985. This act replaced the Nationality Act of 12 December 1892. A total revision of the nationality law of the Netherlands was necessary in order to realise equal treatment of men and women in this field of law and to enable the Netherlands to ratify three international treaties: the New York Convention on the reduction of statelessness of 30 August 1961, the Strasbourg Convention on reduction of cases of multiple nationality and military obligations in cases of multiple nationality of 6 May 1963, and the Bern Agreement on the reduction of the number of cases of statelessness of 13 September 1973.

The Netherlands law of nationality is based on a system of *jus sanguinis a patre et a matre*. A legitimate child acquires Netherlands nationality if the father or the mother is a Netherlands national at the time of its birth or is a Netherlands national who died before the birth of the child (art. 3 para. 1 Nationality Act 1984). Illegitimate children acquire Netherlands citizenship *jus sanguinis* if the mother is a Netherlands national (art 3 para. 1 Nationality Act). If the child is recognised subsequently by a foreigner and therefore acquires another nationality, it retains the Netherlands nationality. If a foreign minor is recognised by a man with Netherlands nationality, the minor acquires Netherlands nationality (art. 4 para. 1 Nationality Act). In this context it is important to stress that in the Netherlands family law the recognition of an illegitimate child by a man is a juridical act. It is not necessary that the man who recognises the child is the biological father of the child. In case of a judicial establishment of paternity of a Netherlands man the foreign child involved acquires Netherlands nationality as well, although this is not expressly mentioned in the Nationality Act. This acquisition is a consequence of the retroactivity (until the moment of birth of the child) of such a judicial establishment of paternity. A minor who is legitimised by a Netherlands national without previous recognition (e.g. in case of letters of legitimisation given by the King) acquires Netherlands nationality as well. Netherlands citizenship can also be acquired by adoption. If a foreign child is adopted pursuant to a judicial decision he acquires Netherlands nationality, provided that the adoptive father or adoptive mother is a Netherlands national on the day that the decision becomes final and that the child is a minor on the day of the decision at first instance (art. 5 Nationality Act).

Netherlands nationality can also be acquired at birth *jus soli* or *jus domicilius*. An acquisition which comes close to an acquisition *jus soli* only applies for foundlings. According to article 3, paragraph 2 of the Nationality Act a foundling shall be deemed to be the child of a Netherlands national if it was found on the territory of the Netherlands, the

Netherlands Antilles or Aruba or on a ship or aircraft registered in one of these countries. In this case it also obtains Netherlands nationality on the basis of article 3 paragraph 1 of the Act. This presupposition (*praesumptio jus sanguinis*) is not absolute. If it becomes apparent within five years from the day on which the child was found, that it does not possess Netherlands nationality, but only a foreign nationality by birth, Netherlands nationality will be lost. But in the case of potential statelessness it keeps Netherlands nationality.

Very important for the nationality integration of families of foreign origin living on Netherlands territory is the provision of article 3, paragraph 3 of the Nationality Act:

> a child shall be a Netherlands national if it is born to a father or mother who is residing in the Netherlands, the Netherlands Antilles or Aruba at the time of its birth and if this father or mother was born to a mother residing in one of these countries at the moment of the birth of her child.

This is the so-called third-generation rule. The provision of article 3, paragraph 3 does not contain a strict *jus soli*-regulation. The provision does not demand that the child was born on Netherlands soil, only that the father or mother resides in the Kingdom. It can therefore be described as an acquisition *jus domicilius* (i.e. based on 'domicilium' in the continental European sense of habitual residence).

Some categories of foreigners can obtain Netherlands nationality by making a declaration of option. This is the case with aliens, who are of full age and who were born in the Netherlands and had their domicile or habitual residence there since their birth, provided that they have not attained the age of 25 years. Persons born stateless in the Netherlands and with domicile or habitual residence here can acquire Netherlands nationality after a period of three years. Other foreigners can acquire Netherlands nationality by naturalisation, if they fulfil the conditions mentioned in the Nationality Act (articles 8 and 9). In principle an applicant possessing a foreign nationality has to renounce that nationality or has to promise to do that after his naturalisation, unless this cannot reasonably be expected of him (art. 9 para. 1(b)). From 1992 the government tried to abolish the condition of renunciation of a previous nationality, but parliament finally agreed only to increase the number of categories in which a renunciation can not reasonably be expected from the applicant. Between 1992 and 1998 the condition of renunciation of a previous nationality was not applied in practice. Since 1998 this condition has been reintroduced but with many more exceptions than before 1992.

Netherlands nationality is lost by a major in the case of voluntary acquisition of a foreign nationality (art. 15 lit. a), by making a declaration of renunciation (art. 15 lit. b), or if he, after coming of age, has his place of residence for a continuous period of ten years outside the Netherlands, the Netherlands Antilles or Aruba, in the country of his birth and of which he is a national as well, other than in the service of the Netherlands, the Netherlands Antilles or Aruba, or of an international organization at which the Kingdom is represented, or as the spouse of a person in such service (art. 15 lit. c Nationality Act). Finally article 15(d) lays down as a ground for the loss of Netherlands nationality the revocation of the decree granting Netherlands nationality. However this may only take place if the person concerned fails, after his naturalisation, to make every effort to divest himself of his original nationality. This article is a sanction against not fulfilling the requirement laid down in article 9 para 1 lit. b. However Netherlands nationality can never be lost on any ground whatsoever if this would lead to statelessness. The grounds for loss of nationality by minors are regulated by article 16 of the Nationality Act. The main principle is that no minor shall lose Netherlands nationality, as long as one parent still possesses Netherlands nationality.

In 1998 a bill amending the Nationality Act was sent to parliament (draft nr. 25 891 (R 1609)). The bill provides for the abolishment of recognition and legitimation as grounds for acquisition of Netherlands nationality, but the judicial establishment of paternity can cause the acquisition of Netherlands nationality. The bill proposes to introduce more cases where a foreigner can acquire Netherlands nationality by lodging a declaration of option. However the legal construction of the option will be altered as well. Under the law in force a foreigner acquires Netherlands nationality by using his option right immediately, if he fulfils the conditions which give to him the option right involved. In the future Netherlands nationality will be acquired after the confirmation by the competent authorities that the conditions for the option right were fulfilled at the moment of use of the option right.

The bill describes in article 9 para. 3 those cases in which renunciation of a previous nationality is not requested as a condition for naturalisation. What is remarkable, is that according article 15 voluntary acquisition of a foreign nationality is no longer a general ground for loss of citizenship. In some cases a foreign nationality can be acquired without losing Netherlands nationality. The bill proposes to introduce a new ground for loss of Netherlands nationality: deprivation of nationality should be made possible in the case of fraudulent conduct or the concealment of any relevant fact during the naturalisation procedure. In such a case deprivation is even possible in cases where statelessness would be the consequence.

'Nationality' and 'citizenship' distinguished

The legal system of the Netherlands does not distinguish between the concept of 'nationality' (nationaliteit) and the concept of 'citizenship' (burgerschap). Nevertheless the term 'burgerschap' is often used in order to indicate the right to exercise political rights. But it has to be emphasised that in principle every adult who possesses Netherlands nationality also has the right to exercise political rights. Moreover permanent residents can exercise political rights on the municipal level (see below). The word 'burgerschap' is not often used in legal texts, but can often be found in texts written by political scientists.

Following the modification of the EC Treaty by the Maastricht Treaty, publications on European Community law deal with the scope and content of European citizenship (Europees burgerschap) and the rights linked to European citizenship. Because nationals of the Member States of the European Union possess European citizenship (under Article 8 EC Treaty), all nationals of the Netherlands possess the rights linked to European citizenship.

Stateless persons

The Netherlands ratified the New York Convention on the reduction of statelessness of 30 August 1961[3] and the Bern Agreement on the reduction of the number of cases of statelessness of 13 September 1973.[4] In order to avoid cases of statelessness article 6(b) Nationality Act 1984 gives an option right to Netherlands nationality to stateless persons born on Netherlands territory after a residence in the Netherlands of at least three years. The granting of Netherlands nationality to those persons immediately at the moment of birth was refused. There were two reasons for this refusal. Some political parties argued that in case of such a regulation perhaps many women due to give birth to a potentially stateless child, would travel to the Netherlands. Another – more convincing – reason was that such a regulation would attribute Netherlands nationality to the children of stateless South-Moluccan persons, who live in the Netherlands since the occupation of the South Moluccan Republic by Indonesia in the early fifties, and who expressly do not want to acquire Netherlands nationality, because they are still hoping for a new independent South Moluccan Republic.

Another consequence of the aim to avoid statelessness is the provision of article 14 Nationality Act 1984, which states that Netherlands nationality is never lost, if this would cause statelessness. At the time of writing, a bill proposing an amendment of art. 14 is in the Second Chamber of Parliament. If the bill is accepted, Netherlands nationality may be lost by a Government decision, if the nationality was acquired by naturalisation or option declaration based on fraudulent information, even if such a loss of Netherlands nationality would cause statelessness.

Dual nationality and naturalisation rate

The Netherlands ratified the Strasbourg Convention on reduction of cases of multiple nationality and military obligations in cases of multiple nationality of 6 May 1963.[5] Obviously, the Netherlands legislator deemed the realisation of sexual equality in the law of nationality much more important than the avoidance of plural nationality. In the Nationality Act of 1984 the reduction of cases involving plural nationality is embodied in just five provisions (art. 9 para. 1(b) and the four paras of art. 15) and only one of these provisions was really new in comparison with the previous legislation. The Netherlands ratified the 1993 Second Protocol to the 1963 Convention, which allows some exceptions to the main principle of the Convention embodied in article 1: the loss of a nationality in case of voluntary acquisition of a foreign nationality. Because of the fact that Netherlands nationals, who also possess another nationality, are registered exclusively as Netherlands nationals, no statistical data on the amount of such dual or plural nationals are available.

A considerable number of foreigners have acquired Netherlands nationality in the recent past by declaration of option, naturalisation or adoption. The figures are as follows:

1985: 34 700; 1990: 12 800; 1994: 49 400; 1995: 71 400; 1996: 82 700

The relatively high figure in 1985 can be explained by the fact that in 1985 the equal treatment of men and women was realised in Netherlands nationality law. Minor children of a foreign father and a Netherlands mother, who did not acquire the nationality of the mother before 1985, could acquire the nationality of their mother by lodging a declaration of option between 1 January 1985 and 1 January 1988. The enormous increase of naturalisations between 1994 and 1997 can partly be explained by the fact that in these years naturalisation was possible without renunciation of a previous nationality.

Rights of nationals and rights of aliens

The rights of nationals differ from rights of aliens in several respects:

Electoral rights

Only Netherlands nationals may participate in the national elections (arts 4 and 56 Constitution) and in the elections on the provincial level (art. 129 Constitution). On the municipal level both citizens and (permanent) residents can participate (art. 130 Constitution and art. B 3 (Elections Act) *Kieswet*): the right to participate in the municipal elections is granted to all Netherlands nationals, EU citizens and, finally, all aliens residing at least five years in the Netherlands and possessing a residence permit based on articles 9 or 10 Aliens Act.

Access to some (public) functions

The Netherlands want to restrict the functions reserved for nationals as far as possible; a list with so-called '*vertrouwensfuncties*' (confidence functions) reserved for nationals is published in the Staatscourant 1988, 248.

Some 'financial' rights

Although permanent residents are almost in all cases equally treated; having Netherlands nationality is often not enough in order to be entitled to certain financial benefits (rights to a pension, social benefits); very often residence is an additional requirement. See, for example, article 56 National Old Age Pensions Act (*Algemene Ouderdoms Wet*): 'The advantages of art. 55 can exclusively be enjoyed by a person, who is Netherlands national and resides in the Netherlands.' Moreover, very often some groups of aliens and Netherlands nationals are treated equally. See, for example, article 56 National Social Assistance Act (*Algemene Bijstandswet*), which determines that an alien living in the Netherlands with a permit based on articles 9 or 10 Aliens Act enjoys the same rights as a Netherlands national.

Other rights

An example to the right on free choice of labour, guaranteed by article 19 para 3 of the constitution, although it has to be emphasised that this right is not really enforceable for nationals as well.

Applicability of Netherlands or foreign private law

The application of Netherlands private law is determined by conflict rules; in some of these conflict rules the nationality of persons involved is a connecting factor.

Applicability of Netherlands criminal law

Again nationality is sometimes used as a connecting factor.

Residential rights

Restriction on freedom of entry and departure

The freedom of entry for foreigners is restricted. The possibility of entry of EU citizens is governed by EU law. Other citizens must fulfil the conditions of international treaties, for example, the convention on refugees of 1951, or of Netherlands immigration law (arts 6–10 Aliens Act). A right to enter the country may exist because of international obligations, or may exist where there is a special Netherlands interest, for example when it concerns business people or medical specialists with particular expertise. A right of residence may also be obtained on humanitarian grounds, for example reunion with family members or urgent need of medical assistance. Netherlands citizens always have the right to enter the territory.

Aliens and citizens have in principle the freedom of departure. This freedom is restricted if they are sentenced to imprisonment or a criminal action is commenced against the persons involved.

Types of residential status

The Netherlands know an enormous variation of residential status for foreigners living in the Netherlands. The main categories are:

a) Temporary stay permit for aliens, without the obligation of a visa (EU citizens and the nationals of some other countries). Maximum period of stay: three months (art. 8 Aliens Act). The person must possess valid documents for crossing the border, for example a passport. Aliens who are not nationals of a European Union or European Economic Area country must also have enough financial means to support themselves during their stay and enough money to pay for their departure from the Netherlands. EU/EEA nationals are, during their temporary stay, not eligible for state benefits, such as national assistance benefits.

b) Temporary stay permit for aliens, with visa obligation. The visa has to be applied for at the Netherlands diplomatic representation in the country of origin or the country of residence. Maximum period of stay: three months (art. 8 Aliens Act).
c) Authorisation for temporary stay (*machtiging tot voorlopig verblijf*). Nationals of most countries for which a visa is required, who want to stay in the Netherlands for a period longer than three months must, in principle, have an authorisation for temporary stay. The authorisation must be requested at the Netherlands embassy or consulate in the country of origin, or the country of residence. The authorisation is a sticker which is placed inside the passport of the person involved. Within three days after arrival in the Netherlands the alien involved has to apply for a residence permit at the Aliens Police (*Vreemdelingenpolitie*).
d) Temporary residence permit (*vergunning tot verblijf*), valid for one year. A temporary residence permit must be taken each year to the Aliens Police for extension. After five years, an alien can apply for a permanent residence permit (*vergunning tot vestiging*).
e) Conditional temporary residence permit (*voorwaardelijke vergunning tot verblijf*).
f) Permanent residence permit (*vergunning tot vestiging*), valid for an indefinite period (art. 10 para 1 lit. a Aliens Act).
g) Admission as a refugee (so-called A-status under art. 15 Aliens Act); valid for an indefinite period (art. 10 para. 1 lit. b); no time limit is attached to this status.
h) Permit for residence on humanitarian grounds, granted because of individual circumstances; valid for one year, but may be extended (art. 9, 12a Aliens Act). After five years they can apply for a permanent residence permit. They are allowed to work.
i) Provisional temporary residence permit (art. 12b Aliens Act); given to asylum seekers who did not receive refugee status or a residence permit on humanitarian grounds, but whose compulsory expulsion is not possible because of the situation in the country of origin. When the situation in their country of origin improves, these asylum seekers can be sent back to their home countries. If the situation does not improve within three years, they can receive a normal temporary residence permit. During the first year of residence these persons are only allowed to take temporary jobs; during the second year they can take vocational courses in addition to temporary jobs. In their third year they can allowed to work without restrictions. A provisional temporary residence

permit is valid for one year, but may be extended twice with one year.

If an alien lives in the Netherlands on any permit for a period of three years, in principle a normal temporary residence permit is granted. After a period of residence of at least five years application may be made for a permanent residence permit. After the same period of residence, five years, an application for naturalisation is possible (art. 8 Nationality Act).

Except for the already-mentioned residence requirement of five years, the alien who applies for a permanent residential status must fulfil the following requirements:

1 he must have sufficient assets, and
2 he must not constitute serious danger to national security (art. 13 para. 3 Aliens Act).

If a permanent resident moves his main habitual residence to another country, he loses his permanent residence status in the Netherlands (art. 14 para 2 Aliens Act). It is not always clear whether a person has already moved his main habitual residence. If a person stays abroad for an uninterrupted period of nine months within one year, he is deemed to have moved his main habitual residence to another country.[6]

It follows already from the previous paragraphs that citizens of other Member States of the European Union have a better residence position in the Netherlands than other aliens. The same applies for nationals of the Member States of the European Economic Area. Citizens of States with an Association Treaty with the European Union are also privileged, if they want to work in the Netherlands independently. The citizens of Belgium and Luxembourg are immediately entitled to a permanent residence permit (without the condition of five years of residence and without the requirement of sufficient assets). This privileged position is based on the Benelux Treaty. The citizen of Indonesia and Suriname (former possessions of the Netherlands) no longes have a privileged position.

The Netherlands do not have particular problems with the alien registration procedure. Aliens can be requested by the border control authorities to provide fingerprinting and to be photographed (art. 65 Aliens Decree).

Social rights

Some social rights differ for citizens and aliens, but it has to be mentioned that often citizens only enjoy certain social rights if they are residing in the Netherlands, and that often aliens residing in the Netherlands enjoy the same social rights as citizens. The principle formulated above applies in particular to the national pension system.

Not all aliens residing in the Netherlands can ask for social assistance if they do not have enough money to support themselves. Aliens having a temporary residence permit are often not entitled to social assistance.

Illegal aliens (i.e. persons who reside illegally in the Netherlands) are excluded from the use of public facilities, with the exception (in certain circumstances) of education, health care and legal assistance. In order to enforce this exclusion the databases of the institutions involved are linked with each other and with the databases of the immigration authorities.

The Netherlands do not have a special war-related compensation scheme for alien residents in the Netherlands. It may theoretically happen that foreigners are entitled to war-related compensation, but the number of such persons will be negligible.

The children of some groups of aliens living in the Netherlands have a right to follow some lessons in the language of their parents during their primary and secondary school education.

Economic rights

The Netherlands does not limit property rights for aliens.

If an alien has a residence permit for the Netherlands and has a labour permit, in principle there are no limitations to the right of self-employment. As already mentioned above, no '*vertrouwensfuncties*' (confidence functions) can be fulfilled by aliens.

Limitations do apply to work according to status. The right to work is very restricted for asylum seekers (see above).

As already mentioned above only a very restricted number of so-called '*vertrouwensfuncties*' (confidence functions) are reserved for nationals. Therefore an alien can be appointed as, for example, university professor, doctor, nurse, or civil servant of a ministry, province or municipality. The reason for reserving some functions for nationals is normally because of national sovereignty, and in some cases national security.

Aliens may not join the Netherlands police force. The reason for reserving this function for nationals is the exercise of public authority.

No statistical data are available on the amount of aliens working in governmental posts.

An EU citizen may be appointed as a government official under the same conditions as a Netherlands national. EU citizens are only excluded from the so-called *'vertrouwensfuncties'* (confidence functions). Other aliens may be appointed as government officials, if they have a labour permit. If an alien does not have a labour permit, such a permit will only be given, and therefore the person involved can only be appointed, if no qualified EU citizen can be found for the job concerned.

Political rights

As already mentioned above, aliens can participate in municipal elections, but do not have electoral rights for the national parliament or provincial parliaments. The reason that they are excluded is national sovereignty. There is, however, a bill in parliament proposing to grant the right of participation in the elections of the provincial parliaments to aliens residing in the Netherlands.

Requirements for aliens in order to participate in elections on municipal level are set as above. No official statistics are published regarding the turn-out of aliens at municipal elections of (i.e. those living in the Netherlands for at least five years or being EU citizens); and no official statistics are published regarding the elected foreign members of municipal councils.

There is no obligation to vote on persons who have the right to vote. In the past an obligation to vote did exist, but this was abrogated some 25 years ago.

Is it true that the Netherlands do not make a distinction between a right to vote and a right to stand in respect of the participation of aliens in the elections on municipal level? Compare Article B 3 Elections Act mentioned above at p. 40 with art. 10 of the Statute on Municipalities. In this context it has to be mentioned that, unlike some other states, the mayors of municipalities are not elected, but directly appointed by the Queen on proposal by the Minister of Internal Affairs. The position of a mayor is classified as a *'vertrouwensfunctie'* and therefore reserved for Netherlands nationals.

The political freedoms are not restricted for aliens. Restrictions would violate the Constitution, in particular article 7–9.

Notes

1 Source of the statistical information in this paragraph: *Statistisch Jaarboek 1998* (Centraal Bureau voor de Statistiek: Voorburg/Heerlen, 1998).
2 It has to be mentioned that the Indonesian community in the Netherlands has lived there for almost fifty years. Most children born within this community have as Indonesian parents persons who themselves were born in the territory of the Netherlands. Therefore most new born children acquire at birth Netherlands nationality as a consequence of the provision of art. 3 para. 3 Nationality Act. They are no longer counted in Netherlands statistics as Indonesian citizens.
3 UNTS, Bd. 989, 175; Tractatenblad 1967, 124.
4 Tractatenblad 1974, 32.
5 UNTS Bd. 634, 221; Tractatenblad 1964, 4; ETS, No. 43.
6 Aldo Kuijer/Hanneke (J.D.M.) Steenbergen, *Nederlands vreemdelingenrecht*, 4th edn (Nederlands: Centrum voor Buitenlanders, 1999), pp. 194, 195.

3
Citizenship Rights for Aliens in Sweden

Elena Dingu-Kyrklund

Introduction

Country of old bureaucratic traditions, Sweden was among the first in the world where citizenship became an established concept with a clear legal content, even though its significance and rules subsequently evolved in time. Initially, an absolute requirement for citizenship was being a Lutheran protestant. Consequently, changing one's religion could be equated with loss of one's citizenship. The king had the authority to allow a foreigner to stay in the country and to grant the status of subject to the king, in practice having the same significance with becoming a citizen nowadays. On the other hand, Sweden seems to have been among the first to introduce a passport obligation for foreigners, already by the beginning of the 1800s, even though this was abolished in 1860, not to reappear until 1917, under the influence of historical events. However, the first modern Aliens Act dates from 1927, followed by changes and subsequent new Acts in 1938, 1945, 1954 and 1980.[1] The Act now in force dates from 1989[2] and has constantly been modified. Nordic and EU citizens benefit from privileges deriving from conventions applying to them.[3]

Citizenship rights as well as legal and practical implications of citizenship can be inferred from a number of other laws, among which the most important provisions are to be found in the Swedish Constitution (RF kap.2 § 22).

Citizenship and nationality

Acquisition/loss of citizenship

In Sweden, the main laws regulating aspects of citizenship are the Swedish Citizenship Act (1950:382),[4] periodically revised,[5] and the

Citizenship Ordinance (1969:235).[6] The Swedish citizenship law is based on *jus sanguinis*. The main rule of automatic acquisition is *by birth*:

- when the mother is a Swedish citizen (1§1);[7]
- when the father only has Swedish citizenship and is married to the child's mother (1§2), even if the father is deceased at the time of the child's birth (1§3).

A foundling is to be considered a Swedish citizen as long as the parents remain unknown and some other identity to contradict this assumption has not been established (1§3).[8]

A child under 12 years of age also becomes a Swedish citizen automatically through *adoption* by a Swedish citizen (1a§). A child under 18 who is still unmarried also receives Swedish citizenship automatically when the child's mother marries the child's father who is a Swedish citizen through *legitimatisation*[9] (2§) or when the child's parent becomes a Swedish citizen[10] and the child (also) is domiciled in Sweden (5§).

A child acquires Swedish citizenship *by notification* if the Swedish father is not married to the non-Swedish mother, but he legally has custody of the child. The child's consent is required from the age of 15 (2a§).

A foreigner living in Sweden at the age of 16 who has continuously been domiciled here for at least five years can apply for Swedish citizenship from the age of 21 but before the age of 23, *by increscens*.[11] This rule also applies for stateless persons with the same requirements (i.e. five years' domicile condition), with the difference that the person can apply for Swedish citizenship already from the age of 18 (3§). A Nordic citizen[12] domiciled for (at least) five years in Sweden and who has reached 18 years of age acquires Swedish citizenship by notifying his wish to the local authorities[13] of his domicile (10b§). This automatically applies for the person's unmarried minor children (under 18 years of age) in accordance with the rules in 5§ (see above). In such a case, the child must make an *option* for Swedish citizenship between 19 and 22 years of age, as an expression of own choice, under the penalty of otherwise being deprived of it (7a§).[14] A former Swedish citizen by birth who has uninterruptedly been domiciled in Sweden until the age of 18, has lost his citizenship and has later returned, can after two years' stay *regain* Swedish citizenship by written notification (4§). Loss of former ('intermediary') citizenship is required (law 1984:682).[15]

Swedish citizenship may be acquired by naturalisation (6§) under the following conditions: (i) they can prove their identity;[16] (ii) they are over 18 of age; (iii) they have been domiciled in Sweden for five years, or two years for Nordic citizens;[17] and (iv) they fulfil the good conduct requirement.[18] The National Board of Immigration[19] has a discretionary right to decide whether a person shall be granted the right to acquire Swedish citizenship or not, which is by no means a guaranteed right, even if the person fulfils all the requirements. Further requirements than the above-stated may be made by the authorities as a condition for granting Swedish citizenship.[20] Naturalisation can also be granted as a matter of exception from the above conditions if: the applicant's becoming a Swedish citizen is considered as a benefit, a gain for the country;[21] the applicant has previously been a Swedish citizen or is married to a Swedish citizen;[22] or there are other special reasons to grant the applicant Swedish citizenship.[23] Also, naturalisation can exceptionally be granted, based on exemption from, for example, *the residence duration condition*, applicable to refugees[24] after four years in Sweden, and to non-Nordic spouses of a Swedish citizen after three years' residence in Sweden and two years' marriage.[25]

Swedish citizenship can be lost when acquiring another citizenship, by application or consent (7§1); by entering another state's public service office (7§2); and, in the case of unmarried children under 18 years of age, when the parents with custody become foreign citizens (7§3).

Swedish citizens born abroad who have never lived in Sweden or maintained kinship relations with Sweden,[26] lose their Swedish citizenship by prescription at the age of 22 if no option application has been filed before their 22nd birthday (8§). This rule does not apply however if the person lived in a Nordic country for at least seven years (10§a 3rd line). If a Nordic country is involved, this option age limit depends on the terms of the Convention with the respective state and can vary between 19 and 22 (see above corresponding rules on acquiring citizenship according to 7a§). Children supposed to make an *option* (7a§) between the age of 17–22, who have not done so as required, lose their citizenship accordingly. In this case, even the children of such a child consequently lose Swedish citizenship automatically, unless they would thus become stateless (8§). This latter rule applies equally to Swedish citizens born abroad, who have neither been domiciled in Sweden nor otherwise maintained a distinct relationship with Sweden. If not deprived of Swedish citizenship in accordance with 7a§ above, they lose their citizenship unless they apply to preserve it before their 22nd birthday, when they otherwise automatically lose their Swedish citizenship (8§).

A Swedish citizen wishing to become a citizen of another state can renounce his Swedish citizenship by applying for that (9§). If the person lives in another state, he cannot be denied this right. However, if the person does not already have another citizenship, a time limit for acquiring this will be imposed as a prerequisite for loss of the Swedish citizenship (law 1984:682), a rule intended to prevent the occurrence of cases of statelessness.[27]

Distinctions between nationality and citizenship

Nationality and citizenship are two closely related concepts in the Swedish language. They are used in somewhat different ways, especially in specialised contexts, even though they are considered synonymous in dictionaries and encyclopaedias. Both terms depict a relationship between the state and its subjects i.e. citizens. However, the term 'nation' preserves more accentuated initial connotations of unity based on common geographical territory, and also of a common ethnical background, defined as a community of origin and culture i.e. language, religion, etc., apart from the unifying community of territory.[28] In this latter sense, the term nationality, *nationalitet* in Swedish, is related to a political use and connotation, referring to the 'fatherland', *'nation'* in the above-mentioned sense, as the spring and confirmation of 'nationality': a two-way relationship between country and subject. An ethnic community according to the nationality principle is at least indirectly assumed. Much of this is common to both interpretations leading however, in the end, to a specialised use of two different terms.

Citizenship, *medborgarskap* in Swedish, derived from *'medborgare'*, 'citizen', is rather related to the other sense of the term 'nation', i.e. referring to the relationship between state and citizen as a two-way legal–administrative and political one, irrespective of ethnic origin and (cultural, etc.) background. According to Tomas Hammar, in the legal and political meaning, citizenship signifies membership of a state. However, in the social and cultural meaning, it signifies membership of a nation. Most states claim they are nation-states or strive to become nation-states through nation-building efforts. Citizenship is therefore often conceived as nationality, as membership of the dominant cultural group in a particular state.[29] That results in the fact that the use of the term *'nation'* preserves a certain ethnic connotation and, on the other hand, it is *not* as a rule used in purely legal or administrative contexts in Sweden. Whenever citizenship is involved with reference to persons, the term is not replaceable with 'nationality'. Therefore, the legal provisions related to this aspect are called in Swedish *medborgarskapslagen*, the Citizenship

Act, and *medborgarskapskungörelsen*, the Citizenship Ordinance, respectively. As this is directly related to the (contents of this relationship, i.e. the) fact that specific rights and duties are derived from the quality of being a citizen, the same term, *medborgare*, is used in this sense in the Constitution.[30]

On the other hand, one may refer, e.g. to an international ship's or aircraft's nationality, if not using another reference, such as 'under (a country's) flag', instead.

The concept of citizenship

As yet, the term 'citizenship', as already explained above, has not altered its basically constitutional meaning of 'rights and duties' assumed on the basis of the bilateral relationship between a state and its citizens, as embodied by the very concept. That implies that, in this context, neither have the implied citizenship rights, which characterise this relationship of belonging, undergone sweeping modifications. As citizenship, once acquired, is/becomes[31] an absolute right, that cannot (even according to the latest changes proposed[32]) be withdrawn. Which in fact means that, once a citizen, even a naturalised Swedish citizen, a person becomes/is in all respects equal to all other citizens, irrespective of how citizenship was acquired.[33] Even though minted in modern acceptation by a Swede,[34] the term 'denizenship' does not have a counterpart in Swedish. Even the terms 'permanent residents' or 'long-time (term) residents' lack as yet an established counterpart in the Swedish language. However, the essence of this reality is present in the very immigrant policy of Sweden. Non-Swedish citizens domiciled in Sweden have, generally speaking, about the same rights as the Swedes themselves, with very few exceptions.

In accordance with the provisions in the Swedish Constitution (RF[35] kap.2 § 22, first part, specifically regulating the foreigners' legal status), a foreign citizen is equal to a Swedish citizen in most respects. The rights listed under this article 22 almost entirely reproduce the correspondent list of rights and freedoms granted by the Constitution (RF kap.2 §§ 1–21).

These rights are guaranteed for foreigners under the same conditions as for Swedish citizens, actually corresponding to the similar provisions for the latter.[36] Rights listed in the second part of the same article 22 are granted to foreigners as equal rights with Swedish citizens, unless *no special laws prescribe otherwise*. In practice, this only means that these rights *may* be limited for non-Swedish citizens, yet only by special legal provisions adopted for the purpose (i.e. under exceptional circumstances, as for instance in case of war[37]). Which means that, within these distinct limits, a certain limitation of rights to the non-citizens' disadvantage can occur.[38]

On the other hand, by comparing the respective lists of rights for Swedish and non-Swedish citizens, from § 22 *e contrario* it can be inferred that foreigners are not constitutionally protected against registration of opinions,[39] banishment[40] and limitations to one's freedom of movement otherwise than by deprivation of liberty,[41] nor are they protected against restrictions as to entering or leaving the country, or movement within the country or, according to Szabó, against loss of their citizenship.[42]

Stateless persons

Provisions in the Citizenship Act aim at preventing statelessness in citizenship matters, a consideration that can, as seen above, be decisive, especially when children are involved. However, at the end of 1997, there were 6,139 stateless persons in Sweden and a number of 6,590 persons counted as 'with unknown citizenship' in the annual statistics,[43] out of a total of 522 049 persons of foreign origin living in Sweden.[44] This can, among others, be inferred from the fact that, between 1984–96, only 3 per cent of the asylum-seekers in Sweden, i.e. a number of 10 693 persons of a total of 320 954 persons, were according to figures presented by the National Board of the Police[45] and the National Aliens Board[46] and reported by the National Board of Statistics[47] considered stateless, alternatively having 'unknown citizenship'.[48] It was however mentioned that most of these persons were Palestinians.

Generally, stateless persons are equalled/equated to citizens, the decisive element in their case being their permanent domicile. A person domiciled in Sweden and officially having this status of permanent resident generally enjoys the same rights as a Swedish citizen or as any other foreign citizen/alien in the country. In practice, statelessness may even result in a paradoxical advantage in some cases, such as when an entry refusal or expulsion cannot be executed due to the fact that no land will agree to receive a person and no obligation on the part of a state to do so can be established.[49] These cases are very rare.

A 1992 precedent[50] case established a possibility for stateless Palestinians to be granted travel documents and refugee status, which also implies a right to be granted a permanent residence permit. This precedent has been invoked a number of times since, including in an extreme case from 1992 (UN 66/92), as follows: A stateless Palestinian born in Gaza and raised in Kuwait arrives in Sweden through a third country that rejects him. Despite of an application based on a false pretence, a fact normally sufficient to forfeit any chance of getting a positive decision, the Aliens Board acting as an Appellate Authority confirms the Immigration Authorities' ruling, agreeing that although there are no grounds for asylum in this case, a permanent residence permit should be granted, mostly taking into account the obvious difficulties that the contrary decision would entail. The fact that UNRWA corroborated the story and the above-mentioned precedent regarding Palestinians were also invoked.

Dual nationality

The question of double citizenship has been discussed over a long time[51] both on a domestic and on an international plan, due to the complex problems that the existence/acceptance or prohibition of dual citizenship may raise both for those involved and for the countries whose citizens they are. As a general rule, in the Swedish legislation both statelessness and double citizenship are to be, in principle, avoided. Consequently, as mentioned before, in the naturalisation procedure, a condition may be attached by the National Immigration Board that the applicant be released from his/her earlier citizenship as a condition for being granted Swedish citizenship, according to § 6 section four of the Citizenship Act (1950:382). However, in practice it is impossible to make this request an absolute rule, because in certain cases it would be impossible for such a legal effect to become effective, for example, in cases when the land of origin does not or will not liberate its citizens from that state's citizenship or when children born in a mixed marriage are involved and the different rules of acquisition of citizenship in the parents' countries automatically lead to a double citizenship for the child. As shown before, Swedish legislation resolved this latter question to a certain extent by demanding a choice to be made by a child in this position, when he reached a certain age, by opting for one citizenship, with, in some cases, lack of such a declaration of choice leading to the loss of the Swedish citizenship.[52]

The issue of dual citizenship has been under investigation in Sweden for a number of years, specifically on the agenda of the so-called Citizenship Committee. A first Official Committee Report on 'Dual Citizenship' (DsA 1986:6) analysed its multiple consequences with a starting-point in the fact that the contemporary development of international migration patterns leads to an increasing frequency of dual citizenship cases. The phenomenon, ascertained as a growing tendency, makes the issue more and more actual in time. The Committee's conclusions were that, on the one hand, the question ought to be further discussed on an international level, not in the least within the Nordic countries, with the idea of adopting similar regional solutions. On the other hand, the Commission recommended a certain relaxation of jurisprudence, allowing a dispensation from the requirement of renouncing one's previous citizenship as a condition for being granted Swedish citizenship. Another question to be further analysed was an eventual change of the Citizenship Act, limiting the requirement to renounce an earlier citizenship as a condition for becoming a Swedish citizen for long-term residents. A similar rule for Swedish citizens domiciled abroad was also to be considered.

The above-mentioned inquiry has not as yet led to any substantial modifications of the Citizenship Act: being forced to renounce an earlier citizenship to become a Swedish citizen is not compulsory, but remains a possible requirement for the competent authorities to decide.

In the Government's writ 1995/96:193 regarding a report on the activity within the European Council's Committee of Ministers during 1995, reference is made to the Committee of Experts on Dual Citizenship (CJ-PL), subsequently named the Committee of Experts on Citizenship Matters (CJ-NA), whose draft convention on dual citizenship concluded that the signatory states oughtn't to be forced to accept multiple citizenship. Instead, the convention ought to state general principles regarding citizenship, analyse the question of whether or not discrimination among born and naturalised citizens ought to be accepted, with the possibility of withdrawing citizenship for the latter, etc. A unanimous decision was reached in favour of a general rule granting long-term residents/denizens a chance of being naturalised.[53]

Recently, the 1997 Citizenship Committee, assigned to analyse a multitude of actual aspects of citizenship,[54] received a new directive[55] to a special inquiry on the question of dual citizenship. The consequences of dual citizenship were being analysed from both the state's and the individuals' points of view, both regarding immigration and emigration. Special aspects studied were: voting and elective rights in several countries; consular assistance; military duty and security aspects; as well as possible implications of an eventual deviation from the principle now in force of avoiding double citizenship. The general issues of citizenship were also analysed in another inquiry on Swedish citizenship. The Committee's Reports were presented in February–March 1999.[56] According to SOU 1999:34 (p. 214), there are about 300 000 persons with double citizenship in Sweden, which indicates that the

Swedish legislation and practice is already rather generous today, accepting a number of exceptions from the general rule prohibiting dual citizenship. The Committee's recommendation is that the conditioned naturalization[57] i.e. the demand of renouncing one's previous citizenship in order to achieve Swedish citizenship should be abolished,[58] consequent to the changes in Article 16 of the 1997 European Convention on Citizenship. Another reason for this is the high administrative costs of the old procedure. A new Citizenship Act thus modified is proposed to enter into force on 1 July 2001, according to recommendations.

As yet, apart from the general principles mentioned above, the only specific reference to concrete consequences of double citizenship is made in the Ordinance on Conscription (1995:238),[59] stating in § 4 regarding dual citizenship that persons who also are citizens of another state, not domiciled in Sweden, may satisfy their military duty only on request.

As things are now, there are no real disadvantages attached to having a double citizenship, apart from eventual taxation problems if the permanent residence aspect is unclear. Also, internationally, there are some discussions regarding aspects attached to it, like double voting and elective rights. A major advantage for those concerned is that a dual citizen does not need a visa to travel to the other country, is able to preserve inheritance and property rights reserved for national citizens and, for some professions, is allowed/free to work on equal terms in both countries.

On a personal level, another advantage in preserving one's former citizenship is often to give emotional expression to one's old loyalty, interest, identity, etc. for the 'old' country. However, this very same aspect may as well be considered a problem by the new state, that can feel the new citizen's double loyalty as a possible latent problem or even threat, and very difficult to deal with; for example in a case of conflict between the two states, an argument that still cannot be dismissed under the present circumstances in international relations.

Residential rights

The right to enter, stay and reside in Sweden is regulated by a number of special laws, among which the most important are the Aliens Act (1989:529) reprinted (SFS 1994:515) and the Aliens Ordinance (1989:547) reprinted (SFS 1995:254). Apart from these, related provisions to be found in a number of other laws will only be mentioned when relevant.

Due to the special relationship between the Nordic countries[60] on the one hand and that with EU, consequent to Sweden's membership,[61] on the other hand, citizens coming from these countries have a status that in several respects is privileged, on a reciprocity basis, as compared to other countries' citizens. Other special provisions regarding citizens from other countries may also apply based on reciprocity according to bilateral conventions in this sense.

Restriction on freedom of entry for foreigners

Thus, Nordic citizens are exempted from the pass-request since the 1957 Passport-Union[62] and consequently they also do not require a visa, residence or working permit.[63] By comparison, EU citizens need to have a passport when travelling within the EU and EEA countries, including the non-EU member Nordic countries, but they benefit from a visa-exemption and favoured status when it comes to a residence or working permit due to the freedom of movement of persons/workers.[64] As said before, the government may decide on other exceptional status rules for other countries' citizens based on bilateral agreements that may have occurred in this sense, usually based on reciprocity.[65]

Otherwise, the general rule in force is the obligation to have a valid passport and visa:[66]

- a tourist-visa up to three months (Aliens' Act, Ch. 2 § 1); and
- a residence permit for longer periods of time (*ibid.* Ch. 2 §§ 2–5) i.e.
  - a temporary one,[67] for 6–12 months as a rule, possibly renewable under certain circumstances to a maximum total of two years;[68] or
  - a permanent one,[69] normally automatically renewed every fifth year.

Special rules may apply to both types of residence permit in special cases (see also above in this chapter).

As can be inferred from the above, there are virtually no restrictions in the 'freedom of movement' over borders for Nordic and EU/EEA citizens. As mentioned above, a certain comparable freedom of movement may also apply to citizens of other countries, based on reciprocity agreements. However, an increasing number of restrictions apply to citizens of other countries, whose right to enter and reside in Sweden is comparatively very limited and strictly regulated by law. In contrast, there are no restrictions regarding the freedom of departure for foreigners, as long as there are no specific hindrances (such as: committed crime, searched by the police, etc.). Re-entry after a departure may however be a problem for certain categories of foreigners, whose residence permit may not be renewed if they have stayed outside Sweden longer than a certain period of time, or if their (prolonged) presence abroad may cast a doubt on their established relationship to Sweden or their need to return there, depending on the grounds on which they were permitted to stay [70] Permanent residents do not normally encounter problems of re-entry, at least as long as their stay abroad doesn't exceed six months in a row or their prolonged stay abroad does not contradict their need of protection, for example as former asylum-seekers.[71]

Types of residence status

The conditions governing the issue of a residence permit will depend on the grounds on which one was allowed to stay and thus reflect and be limited by these grounds and status, as follows: (1) students;[72] (2) seasonal/temporary workers; (3) professionals, representatives of the free professions and artists; (4) self-employed and representatives of the free professions; (5) persons officially delivering or receiving a service; (6) close relatives to Swedish citizens and permanent residents; (7) persons having a close relationship to Sweden, other than the above;[73] (8) persons in need of protection such as asylum-seekers and refugees; (9) other persons in need of protection; (10) persons of own means or who were granted a work permit; (11) sailors.

Requirements for permanent residence status

Depending on the grounds on which it is based, a permanent residence permit, PUT, is issued under different conditions for the various categories to which it may apply, e.g.:

- *Spouses* to Swedish citizens are granted a PUT at the end of the two-year trial period.
- *Children* of persons granted a PUT also receive that automatically, together with their parents. [*Close relatives* to Swedish citizens and permanent residents may be granted a PUT, as persons having a close relationship to Sweden, other than the above (see above).]
- *Convention refugees/acknowledged refugees*, accepted asylum-seekers, are granted a PUT consequent to their status. (Mass refugees granted temporary protection normally receive a temporary residence permit (TUT), prolonged for six months at a time, in case the protection need continues.)
- *Some persons having received a residence permit on humanitarian grounds* are granted a PUT, others are granted a TUT strictly depending on their grounds for staying.

- *Self-employed and professionals* having resided and worked sufficiently long time in Sweden (1–3 years, depending on category) and fulfilled other related conditions may receive a five-years automatically renewable residence permit, under certain circumstances even after they ceased their activity because of permanent work invalidity, retirement or even movement to another EEA country[74] but continues to reside in Sweden and return to their residence at least once a week.

A permanent residence permit is never automatically granted or prolonged, with the exception of spouses,[75] but it remains at the discretion of the authorities, who can raise objections to one's application. Conditions of good behaviour, duration of residence or, when applicable, sufficient own means can be taken into consideration or imposed as a condition, in order for any residence permit to be issued, as said before, depending on the grounds invoked, but the fact of receiving/renewing a permanent residence permit is strictly based on the structure described above.

Illustrative of the intricate question of residential rights is the debated case of an Iranian physician having lived in Sweden for ten years, also married in Sweden with children born in Sweden. In spite of these facts, after applying for a regular residence permit, he received a decision of immediate expulsion. The motivation was that he had been mostly working as a guest researcher and had never been granted any other status. His application for a residence permit was considered as lacking sufficient motivation and, moreover, the main argument was that he was considered a security risk for the country. This last argument couldn't be combated as, according to the rules, the Security Services SÄPO didn't have to give any information on the nature of the objection as it was considered classified information. In the end, however, also under the pressure from the Media, he was allowed to stay because of his family in Sweden.

As said before, the freedom of (re-)entry is only restricted by the very conditions upon which a residence permit was granted. Otherwise, no special restrictions apply.

Nordic and EU/EEA citizens benefit from the freedom of movement and work based on the Nordic Agreements and the EU Treaty.

Alien registration process

Aliens' registration procedure is directly related to their status and grounds of presence in the country, as well as their nationality. As said before, Nordic citizens are equated/equal to Swedish citizens, i.e. have comparable full residential rights, and consequently only need to register in the National Population Register at the Tax-authorities[76] as sole requirement. EU citizens benefit from a special, simplified registration procedure, according to the rules established within the Union, i.e. consequent to the freedom of movement. Otherwise, for other countries' citizens, normally a passport and, if applicable, a visa or a residence permit is required. Other documents and information considered of importance for exerting national control over the right to enter or stay (reside) shall also be provided on request, from case to case.[77] The police have the right to body search and check on an alien's personal effects, transport means, etc. Fingerprinting and taking of photos may be imposed if an asylum-seeker cannot prove his/her identity; in addition, he or she may eventually be taken into custody. Differences in treatment may of course arise from bilateral treaties based on reciprocity.

Normally, no other special registration procedure applies, apart from registration at the Tax-authorities for residents. Once officially an (accepted) resident of Sweden, consequent to this registration, every person is allotted a so-called *personal number*,[78] formed of ten digits of which the first six represent the person's birth date. The personal number will then function as a unique identification tool, used in all contacts with authorities, banks, etc., and implicitly playing the role of proving one's residential rights. An ID-document is therefore only required when an explicit ad-hoc identification control is necessary, for example, when visiting a bank for executing certain financial operations, when making a purchase by using a credit card, or when picking up a registered letter at the post-office.

Social rights

First of all, there is no war-related compensation for alien residents, unless some special agreement with other states exists.

Limitations for permanent residents

There are almost no restrictions regarding social rights for permanent residents. Once granted such a resident status, aliens benefit from about the same rights as citizens, with a minimum difference arising mostly out of the duration of their stay and (if applicable) work in Sweden, which is usually the basis on which some social rights and their extent are being established. I must underline the fact that the Swedish social system is constantly being modified, which also triggers modifications upon the rules that apply for various rights. The main principle for granting social rights to a person is the domicile principle i.e. persons officially domiciled in Sweden, Swedes or aliens, are as a rule entitled to social benefits.

Old-age pension rights are covered by two different pensions: a national basic pension and a national supplementary pension, directly related to the time worked and related income.[79] All persons who are resident in Sweden, citizens and aliens alike, irrespective of nationality (as long as they are legal immigrants) are entitled to a national basic pension, *folkpension*, on condition that they have been residing here for at least three years or have three years of ATP-points i.e. 'national pension-points'.[80] A person having less 'Swedish years' than required may be credited with time insured in some other country i.e. according to the EU/EEA agreement, or based on a bilateral agreement with the person's country of origin.[81] The main laws governing old-age pension rights are: Law (1962:381) on general social insurance; Law (1959:551) on calculating pension-founding income according to the Law (1962:381) on social insurance[82] and Law (1998:674) on old-age pension based on income. Other pension rights, e.g., disability, survivor's, adjustment,[83] child's or widow's pension, etc. are paid under the same conditions to all people, based on the domicile principle, i.e. if and as long as they are permanent residents in Sweden (see above).

All components of the social benefit system are granted under the same conditions to all people residing in Sweden, Swedes and aliens alike, as long as they are registered permanent residents. Everybody residing in Sweden is registered with a social insurance office when reaching 16 years of age or, for immigrants, the moment they were allowed to reside in the country. The minimum time limit to be registered is a year, supposing permanent residence in the country. Even EU/EEA citizens coming to Sweden based on the freedom of movement of workers are being registered. In some cases, one is required to have already lived in Sweden a minimum period of time, varying up to two years, in order to benefit from certain rights, such as study allowance, while in other cases no such time limitation is imposed, e.g. health care, social welfare, etc. The normal retirement age is 65. Age-related changes structurally follow in the social benefit system as applicable after retirement, which is of course adapted to the specific requirements of this particular category.

Limitations for temporary residents and irregular residents

Temporary visitors do not benefit from the same social rights as mentioned above under the same circumstances, unless the visitors are covered by a special agreement as, e.g., Nordic, EU/EEA citizens or when a bilateral agreement between Sweden and the home country exists. Temporary visitors are normally required to have a health insurance.[84] Foreign students are limited by the conditions of their presence in the country.

Some assistance is however offered to everybody while being in Swedish territory, under certain circumstances, e.g. emergency assistance, under the general conditions of the Social Welfare Law (1980:620).

Persons not having a valid residence permit (irregular/illegal/over-stay aliens) are not entitled to any rights, as their presence in the country is not legal. However, there are people and unofficial networks that do sometimes offer medical and other assistance to illegal refugees.

Multicultural education

The Swedish system ensures possibilities to both maintain one's cultural heritage, not in the least by a number of rights related to mother-tongue instruction, and help immigrants integrate by appropriate Swedish language training.

According to the age and personal prerequisites, immigrants, once granted the right to stay, are entitled to an entire integration programme normally estimated to last for about two years, with individual variations. All immigrants are entitled to special Swedish language courses – SFI[85] – free of charge, organised as intensive studies equating a full-time occupation. Children are entitled to similar classes organised in schools as intensive Swedish, as a second language classes.

Children having a mother tongue other than Swedish are, according to the latest changes in the Swedish integration policy, to be encouraged to develop it in parallel to improving their level in Swedish.[86] During their school-time, children are entitled to up to seven years of instruction in their mother tongue, under certain conditions. This rule is valid for all children whose parent(s) have a mother tongue other than Swedish, used as a communication language at home, if a minimum of five pupils/students are require that kind of language instruction. However, there are some groups that benefit from special rights in this sense, even if the above-mentioned condition is not fulfilled.

Children speaking Saami-language, Finnish, Tornedalfinnish,[87] Yiddish and Romani or Romanese are entitled to education in their own language under all circumstances, even when adoptive children are involved. Also the seven-years limitation does not apply to them.

For historic reasons, and as there is a larger number of Finnish speakers, Finnish has a special position in the whole Swedish education system, resulting in the possibility of studying in this language up to high-school level, without needing to pass any Swedish language test in order to continue studies on university level. For other Nordic languages speakers different rules apply, based on the special relationship between their respective countries and languages, to a large extent both reciprocally intelligible and even taught to a certain extent in each other's schools, as a part of their mother-tongue education.

Economic rights

There are no limitations to property rights for aliens in Sweden.

There are no specific limitations to the right of self-employment for aliens, depending on their nationality and grounds to stay (i.e. those grounds on which their residence (& work) permit was issued).

Working rights are specifically limited in Sweden, as already stated above, and are strictly related to the right to reside. Only persons having the right to reside in the country, having obtained, when required, a residence and working permit[88] are allowed to work. As a general rule, with the exception of Nordic and EU/EEA citizens, (for whom special rules apply, due to the reciprocal freedom of movement of workers), only aliens granted a work permit are allowed to work under strict conditions (see above). That implies that only permanent residents have a virtually unlimited right to work in Sweden, with few exceptions of classified jobs requiring Swedish citizenship. Otherwise, persons granted a temporary work permit are prohibited from taking jobs exceeding the conditions under which their permit was issued. Seasonal workers, for example, are only allowed to do that work for which they were admitted into the country; persons allowed to work for a specific employer who applied on their behalf are not allowed to stay longer than the time for which they preserve that specific job. Professionals, artists and specialists/experts are bound by the conditions of their employment. Students and other temporary visitors are prohibited from taking employment, under sanctions for both themselves and their potential employer.

The Nordic Agreement on a common labour market[89] established the equality of rights between Nordic citizens, implying a virtually total non-discrimination between the participants' citizens in all respects. In Government Bill 1995/96:33, preceding the latest modification of the Helsinki Agreement, a comprehensive equal treatment principle was introduced, from which the only exceptions mentioned are cases when the citizenship condition is imposed by the Constitution, international agreements, or if special reasons impose it.

The Swedish Constitution states in Ch. 5 § 2 that Swedish citizenship is a condition for the position as chief of state i.e. king or regent, and in Ch. 11 § 9 that Swedish citizenship is a condition for working as a judge, a civil servant directly subordinated to the government, the head or member of an authority directly subordinated to the parliament or government, government officials or governmental civil servants and such like, central elective positions as well as any other positions on central or local level where special laws may impose this. Such laws are mostly related to the Swedish Secrecy Act, *Sekretesslagen* (1980:100), stating the limits of access to classified information for national security reasons. All Nordic citizens are eligible for any position in the Nordic Council.

EEA citizens have the right to work in Sweden for three months without any permit, but they need a residence permit in order to work longer. Their access to the above-mentioned positions is equally limited. EU citizens are, however, eligible for positions at Community level.

For all other resident aliens entitled to work the same limited restrictions apply as above. There is no comprehensive list of public positions only accessible to Swedish citizens,[90] but in cases when this is a condition, that may either depend on stated constitutional limitations or on the fact that a certain personal 'clearance' is required for a job implying access to classified data. There are no specific figures in this sense based on nationality, as this would be considered a discriminatory registration ground.

Political rights

As stated above, *electoral rights* in the national elections are prohibited to aliens by the Swedish Constitution. That relates both to eligibility and to the right to vote.

The Electoral Law (1997:157) states in Ch. 1 § 3 that local electoral rights are granted to all registered residents at the age of 18. Most aliens get the right to vote in the local elections after three consecutive years of registration as residents in Sweden. This right is unrestricted for Nordic citizens and immediate for EU citizens i.e. as soon as they have registered as residents with the tax authorities.[91] This discrimination is directly related to the reciprocity principle in the Nordic Agreement mentioned above on the one hand and the EU Treaty on the other.

Participation in elections is lower among immigrants than among Swedes, but efforts are being made to encourage them to engage themselves in the political life of the community. Representation of aliens is very low. Thus, the participation ratio during the most recent elections was as shown in Table 3.1.

Table 3.1 Turnout in Swedish elections, 1976–98

Election year	*Immigrant voters (%)*	*Swedish voters (%)*
1976	60	90
1994	40	87
1998	34	81

Eligibility follows the right to elect: once entitled to vote, one is also entitled to be elected. In the case of EU citizens, eligibility rights for the European Parliament are also governed by their voting rights according to their home-country rules as well as by eventual conflicts of rules between European and national positions and rules: Ch. 1 § 8.

Representation of aliens again is rather low. However, a study of the latest elections by Umeå university,[92] quoted by the daily *Svenska Dagbladet,*[93] pointed out that the amount of locally elected politicians of immigrant origin has increased by 25 per cent in comparison with the former elections, at least in the 20 immigrant-dense local regional elections studied.

For restrictions and extent of political freedoms for aliens, see 'The concept of citizenship' (p. 51).

Conclusions

In a comparative perspective, Sweden offers rather generous conditions to aliens, once their immigrant status has been established, both regarding social rights and as access to citizenship. Non-citizens benefit from similar social, economic and political rights as citizens, practically only pension rights differing – in practice, this applies for citizens also, as pension rights always depend on one's working years in the country and income level. Otherwise, economic, as political, rights are formally almost unrestricted, the few limitations that apply referring to access to classified positions in such specific national interest fields that hardly any state allows unlimited access to non-nationals. On the other hand, in most cases, most of these positions would normally be very few and difficult to attain for practically anybody, thus even less so for immigrants. Sweden imposes rather liberal conditions for granting citizenship (five years residence; no compulsory language competence; proven identity; good conduct), even providing a number of exceptions from these (2–3 years residence; 'probable' identity; time-limits for criminal deeds). Recent trends to be expressed by the new Citizenship Act, to be enacted in 2001, only confirm continuation of this tendency, also present in the 1997 European Convention on Citizenship. The proposed increased acceptance of dual citizenship (an integration incentive for long-time residents!), or the intention to facilitate acquisition of citizenship by children living in Sweden,[94] by enlarging the currently restricted scope of the simplified administrative procedure (see 'Acquisition/loss of citizenship', p. 47 above), illustrate, perhaps, a tendency towards a more realistic, future-oriented approach of the Swedish integration policy. In the European context, this may serve as an implicit example for a comparable pan-European solution, badly needed (as hardly unproblematic!) in a future harmonised Union, or Schengenland.

Notes

1 SFS (1927:333), SFS (1937:344), SFS (1945:315), SFS (1954:193), SFS (1980:376).
2 SFS (1989:529).
3 Nordic Passport Convention, other Nordic Conventions, the EU Treaty.
4 *Lagen om svensk medborgarskap, Medborgarskapslagen,* in Swedish, from: *medborgare* = citizen and *lag* = law.
5 An official commitee report, SOU 1997:162 *Medborgarskap och identitet,* 'citizenship and identity', presented a number of changes in the present law. The proposition based on this report, prop. 1997/98:178, accepts one proposed modification and rejects another. The main modification refers to the demand to prove one's identity as a foremost condition in order to achieve Swedish citizenship, proposing that even persons unable to prove their identity may exceptionally receive it by naturalisation, if their identity can at least with certain probability be inferred and no contradictory pieces of information occurred, through a dispensation that may be given after eight years of legal residence in the country. This time span is to be counted from the time a residence permit has been issued i.e. eight uninterrupted years of residence, or, where a change in the identity data occurred, eight years from the date when the change was registered. This modification came into force on 1 January 1999. A proposed possibility of withdrawing citizenship once granted, if based on false premises, was rejected.
6 *Medborgarskapskungörelsen* (1969:235) republished (SFS 1979:140). Completes the Citizenship Act with application rules and regulations regarding detail aspects in citizenship matters.
7 According to a change proposed to come into force on 1 July 2001 (Proposition 1999/2000:147), descent from a Swedish father shall have the same effect on a child's citizenship as the mother's, if the child is born in Sweden. If the child is born abroad, s/he will be able to acquire Swedish citizenship by simple application.

8 At the end of March 1999 a newborn child was found abandoned on the premises of a hospital in Stockholm. Efforts were made to find the parents, and in less than a fortnight they were identified. However, if that hadn't happened, the child would presumably have been considered a Swedish citizen, under the implicit reservation of a change when the mother/parents (if married!) were identified, in which case *jus sanguinis* would have retroactively applied, i.e. the mother's eventual other citizenship, if different from Swedish, would also have automatically become the child's citizenship.

9 In Swedish, *legitimation*.

10 The child is considered a *bi-person*, a dependant to his parent(s).

11 *increscens (inväxande) vid*, 'to grow up (in/into the society)'. Considering that the person has been domiciled in the country during his/her childhood, consequently integrating in the Swedish society i.e. forming a strong (personal) relationship with this country.

12 Other than naturalized citizens.

13 In this case *länsstyrelsen*, the County Administrative Board.

14 See further on in this section on loss of citizenship.

15 This was the situation until 1999, when I revised this chapter, consequent to the release of SOU 1999:34, the Official Committee Report on Swedish Citizenship. According to its new law proposal (Proposition 1999/2000:147), loss of former citizenship as a condition of regaining Swedish citizenship will be abolished in favour of accepting double citizenship. The provisions in the new law will come into force on 1 July 2001.

16 In force from 1 January 1999 (modification by law 1998:1453). Dispensation can exceptionally be granted (see note 17 below).

17 Other exceptions: spouses of Swedish citizens (three years); persons with unclear identity may also apply after eight years (from 1 January 1999).

18 The good conduct clause, *att föra en hederlig vandel* (litt. 'to lead an honest life/conduct'). According to proposition 1997/98:178, a new condition imposed from 1 January 1999 is that of having an (officially) confirmed identity. However, the same document provides the exception to the rule in the form of a delayed procedure involving a waiting time of eight years instead of five, provided that the presented data/documents regarding one's identity aren't contradictory and the identity can be at least with some degree of probability assumed to be correct (see also previous notes).

19 *Statens Invandrarverk*, SIV, is the competent authority regarding immigration and citizenship matters in Sweden.

20 Proposition 1975/76:136 p. 36, SOU 1997:162 pp. 63 et seq., prop. 1997/98:178 p. 6.

21 e.g. elite sportsmen, outstanding artists, etc. An example is Ljudmila Engqvist, who became a Swedish citizen according to this speedy procedure in order to be able to represent Sweden at the 1994 Winter Olympic Games. Queen Sylvia also benefited from this procedure in 1976 when marrying the King of Sweden Carl Gustaf Bernadotte.

22 See further on the specific time-requirement dispensation for a spouse to a Swedish citizen.

23 *särskilda skäl*, special reasons, for instance taking into consideration the applicant's special relationship to Sweden.

24 Convention-refugees, *konventionsflyktingar*, having refugee status according to the Geneva Convention.
25 For further exceptions see prop. 1997/98:178 p. 7; Official Committee Report, SOU 1993:120, *Uppehållstillstånd och avvisning. Vilket betydelse skall en utlännings vandel tillmätas?*, 'Residence permit and expulsion. What importance is to be attached to (good) conduct?' SOU 1994:33 *Vandelns betydelse i medborgarskapsärenden m.m.*, 'The importance of good conduct in citizenship matters and others'; prop. 1993/94:159, Act 1994:515 both on the same subject; Westin and Dingu-Kyrklund, *Reducing immigration, reviewing integration*, 1997, CEIFO, Stockholm University, pp. 39, 40, 43, 46.
26 In the original, *samhörighet* = 'kinship/sense of belonging'.
27 See note 15 on proposed acceptance of double citizenship from 1 July 2000, with implications even in this case.
28 From e.g. Fichte's and Herder's nationalism to its various 'patriotic' variants of today's still war-steering ones.
29 T. Hammar, 'State, Nation, and Dual Citizenship', in S.A. Reinans and T. Hammar (eds) *'Citizens by birth and naturalisation'* (Stockholm: CEIFO, 1993, p. 82).
30 *nationalitet* as well as *medborgarskap* are actually not much used as terms in the daily language. Instead, to specifically ask somebody about his/her nationality as 'land of origin', the question will refer directly to 'what land/ where are you coming from' and not 'what is your nationality', which would probably sound rather odd as a question for most of the people. Often, the two concepts are rather freely used in each other's place.
31 at least in the actual Swedish context.
32 See above reference to the Official Committee Report, SOU 1997:162 Medborgarskap *och identitet*, 'citizenship and identity'. Prop. 1997/98:178, based on it, rejects a proposed possibility to withdraw citizenship.
33 i.e. by birth, by naturalization, etc.
34 Tomas Hammar.
35 *Regeringsformen*, RF, 'the government form', reprinted (SFS 1998:1437). The Swedish Constitution is formed of four distinct parts, of which RF is the most important. The other components are: *Successionsordningen*, SO, 'the succession form', reprinted (SFS 1979:935); *Tryckfrihetsförordingen*, TF, 'ordinance on the freedom of printing', reprinted (SFS 1998:1701); *Yttrandefrihetsgrundlagen*, YGL, 'the constitutional law of freedom of speech', reprinted (SFS 1998:1439).
36 See above.
37 Laws or ordinances, e.g. as wartime provisions referred to in RF 13:6.
38 H. Strömholm, *Sveriges författning*, (Lund: Studentlitteratur, 1995, p. 84). See also SOU 1999:34 pp. 112–13.
39 *åsiktsregistrering.*
40 *(lands)förvisning.*
41 Strömholm – *op. cit.*, same page (p. 84).
42 M. Szabó, *Vägen mot medborgarskap*, (Stockholm: Arena, 1997, p. 31).
43 According to the Annual Statistic Bulletin of Population, SCB *Befolkningsstatisktik, del 3, 1997*, p. 19.
44 See also table in Statistics Sweden, 1997.
45 *Rikspolisstyrelsen, RPS*, 1984–June 1987.

46 *Statens Invandrarverk, SIV*, July 1987–96.
47 *Statistiska Centralbyrån, SCB* (1997).
48 See note 47 above regarding the amount of stateless persons respectively persons of unknown citizenship (cf. SCB 1997).
49 An article in Sweden's largest morning newspaper, *Dagens Nyheter*, commented recently (19 April 1999) on 'loopholes' in the legislation, allowing immigrant criminals to avoid expulsion by voluntarily becoming stateless.
50 Decision of the Aliens' Board – *Utlänningsnämnden*, UN, from 20 March 1992 (UN 47/92).
51 A recent investigation on dual citizenship has recently been completed (towards the end of 1998), as well as a more general discussion on the question of immigration and citizenship (SOU 1999:008), issued at the end of February 1999 and a more complex investigation on issues regarding Swedish citizenship (SOU 1999:34). A main conclusion is that it ought to be made easier for immigrants to acquire Swedish citizenship, even without being compelled to renounce their initial citizenship, as the main rule required until now.
52 See above provisions related e.g. to option (*optionsrätten*).
53 The revision of the text of the Convention was to be completed during 1996.
54 See above e.g. references to the recent Committee Reports 'Citizenship and Identity' and 'Swedish Citizenship'.
55 Civildepartementet – Dir. 1997:5 *Översyn av lagen om svenskt medborgarskap* – 'Revision of the Swedish Citizenship Act'. Among other things, it states that double citizenship and statelessness should as a principle be avoided. *Jus sanguinis* is to remain the basic principle of acquiring citizenship. However, it is possible that a larger number of situations of double citizenship may be accepted. The extent of the actual occurrence of double citizenship is to be analysed. In the attempt to reduce the extent of the cases of statelessness, the Committee is to analyse further measures that may increase the possibility for stateless persons to become Swedish citizens.
56 See note 51 above regarding the recent completion of this report (SOU 1999:008 *Invandrarskap och medborgarskap* – Immigration and citizenship) and the general report on citizenship (SOU 1999:34, *Svensk medborgarskap* – Swedish citizenship). See also SfU 1998/99:03 *Medborgarskap och identitet* (issued 9 December 1998).
57 *villkorad medborgarskap*.
58 SOU 1999:34, p. 278 et seq.
59 *Förordning (1995:238) om totalförsvarsplikt.*
60 The Nordic free labour market and Passport Union.
61 Sweden became a member of the European Union in 1994.
62 See also Aliens' Ordinance § 1.
63 See also Aliens' Act Ch 1 §§ 2–5.
64 Aliens Ordinance Ch. 3 § 8, according to Ordinance (EEG) nr. 1612/68, Directive 68/360/EEG and Ordinance (1998:153). Also, exception from the obligation of having a working permit is granted to the same category i.e. EEA citizens according to Aliens Ordinance Ch. 4 § 1 and Ordinance (1998:153) mentioned above.
65 A list of exceptions in this sense is to be found in the Aliens' Ordinance Ch. 2 § 1.

66 Other ID-documents may under certain circumstances be accepted, according to Aliens Ord. Ch. 1. §§ 6–9.
67 TUT, *temporärt uppehållstillstånd*, temporary residence permit.
68 Additionally two years may exceptionally be granted to persons having received a temporary residence permit as persons in need of protection according to Aliens' Act Ch. 3, integrated in an already initiated repatriation programme, according to the Aliens' Ordinance Ch. 2 § 4a.
69 PUT, *permanent uppehållstillstånd*, permanent residence permit.
70 Asylum-seekers having received a residence permit due to their assumed need of protection are a specific example in this context. The very fact of their voluntarily travelling abroad, especially to the land they needed to escape from, may automatically cast a shadow of doubt over the authenticity of their need of protection and thus their very grounds of being permitted to stay in Sweden.
71 See note 70 above.
72 An Algerian was granted a residence permit for studies. After marrying an asylum-seeking countryman a renewal of the residence permit alternatively pleading to either be granted a residence and work permit, on humanitarian grounds because of penalty risks in the home country due to the marriage and subsequent conversion to Christianity, or as a student, was denied on both counts invoked. The reason was that humanitarian grounds did not apply, while a prolonged residence permit for studies could not be granted because basic requirements for that were not fulfilled i.e. *capacity to support herself* and *intention to return*. This shows that attempts to change status after arrival made the applicant unreliable as to invoked reasons and actual intentions, resulting in immediate rejection. UN/41/94, decision of the Aliens Board (*utlänningsnämnden, UN*).
73 e.g. former Swedish citizens or their relatives having lived abroad, etc.
74 Special requirements apply (Aliens Ordinance Ch. 3 § 5a).
75 A permanent residence permit is normally renewed or prolonged (almost) automatically, yet this never becomes an undisputed or unconditional right. The authorities always have the possibility of reassessing a concrete case and asserting a certain discretionary power in their decision. It must however be stated that such 'permanent' residence permits are normally prolonged (almost) automatically, unless special reasons for the contrary occur.
76 *Skattemyndigheterna*.
77 See above on other details.
78 *personnummer*.
79 The pension system is under reform, partially implemented since 1998 but still under debate.
80 ATP points, from *'allmän tilläggspension'* – general supplementary pension, calculated on the basis of 15 out of 30 working years' income (according to the new system, life-long annual income, minimum 40 working years giving full pension rights). One must have earned at least a minimum sum exceeding the so-called 'increased base amount for the income year' (37 100 SKr for 1998) and normally have worked for at least three years in order to benefit from the ATP system i.e. to also be entitled to a national supplementary pension, calculated on the basis of life-long working years and income. Normal retirement age is 65 in Sweden (1999).

81 Ordinance (1979:131) on calculating national basic pension in certain cases, stating that pension according to foreign legislation is equal to Swedish provisions when calculating basic pension rights in accordance with the Swedish law.

82 Replaced by SFS 1998:675 but still valid to a variable extent until 1999, when the new law (1998:675) entered into force. The old law was still applicable until the end of 1998.

83 Payable when the spouse has died, under certain conditions, normally for six months, possibly longer, as long as one has a child under 12 years of age.

84 Ordinary tourists however are advised, but not compelled to have one, as a matter of own risk.

85 *Svenska för invandrare* – Swedish for foreigners.

86 Proposition 1997/98:16 *Sverige, framtiden och mångfalden – från invandrarpolitik till integrationspolitik,* Sweden, the Future and Multiculturalism – from Immigration Policy to Integration Policy, pp. 60–62.

87 *Tornedalsfinska* or *mienkiele* is a local variety of Finnish, considered as a distinct minority language.

88 Normally, a residence and work permit is to be applied for and obtained prior to the entrance in the country.

89 SÖ 1954:34 Överenskommelse mellan Sverige, Danmark, Finland och Norge om gemensam arbetsmarknad and 1962 Helsingforsavtalet – Samarbetsöverenskommelsen mellan Danmark, Finland, Island, Norge och Sverige.

90 Such a list was recently (March 1999) made available by SOU 1999:34, pp. 119–22.

91 In practice, they must register at least before November the year preceding the year of the election in order for the authorities to have time to register them in the Electorate Register and consequently be able to vote.

92 *Demokratiundersökningen,* 'Inquiry on Democracy'.

93 16 November 1998.

94 which could in a way be defined as a 'surrogate' *jus soli,* to apply to children either born or living/having lived in Sweden all/most of their life, or some sort of incremental *jus domicili,* relating to the close personal relations to the country children get while living here for a longer time, as today's *increscens,* 'growing-up' in the society, in itself a simplified procedure valid today.

4

Citizenship Rights for Aliens in France

Benoît Guiguet

Introduction

The immigration tradition which characterises France involves primarily the fall in birth rate starting from the middle of the eighteenth century. Until the Second World War, the situation of France differed from that of the other European countries which experienced a strong birth and emigration rate.

The crisis of the thirties and the 1939 war slowed down immigration in France distinctly and involved an important backward flow. The first measures taken by the public authorities to reduce the installation of immigrant workers and to encourage departures date back to 1931. The law of 10 August 1932 aims at protecting national manpower and lays down the principle of limitation of foreign manpower in each sector.[1] After the Second World War, France officially encouraged immigration to cope with the needs for rebuilding, but wanted also to control it better. Foreigners' rights became governed, on a principal basis, by the regulation (*ordonnance*) of 2 November 1945, enacted in reaction against the acts of the Vichy government,[2] as well as that of 19 October, which determined the conditions of access to nationality. The Immigration National Office (*ONI*) was created in order organise the recruitment of foreign workers. Family immigration was also encouraged. In 1952, France signed the Geneva Convention on asylum and created the French office for the protection of refugees as stateless people (*OFPRA*).[3] The end of the *'Trente Glorieuses'* led the government in 1974 to decide that immigration should be stopped, except within the framework of family reunion and specific requests emanating from employers. The last decades mark the hardening of immigration policies, depending however on the swing of the pendulum according to the governmental majorities in power. But as D. Lochak emphasises, the image of the pendulum should not be misleading: the movement of the pendulum never goes as far as the end and so, each time, part of the provisions adopted by the previous majority remains.[4]

Generally, in addition to the traditional dichotomy between Community and third country nationals, the doctrines usually distinguish between the immigrants of the first generation and the children from the second and third generations, the latter not being included in the category of immigrants because they were born in France. The immigrants of the first generation correspond to those who have no right to French nationality as persons born abroad to foreign parents. To be a member of the national Community, the persons concerned will have to follow the naturalisation procedure unless they obtain nationality incidentally by means of marriage. The children of the second generation refer to the children born in France to foreign parents who were not born there. They were at the heart of the last reforms of nationality law. Lastly, the said children of the third generation are the children born in France to foreign parents one of whom at least was also born there. They refer to the concept of dual *jus soli*, attributive of French nationality at birth. A new 'category' has appeared in recent years, in a context of strong collective mobilisation: it concerns the movement of the '*sans-papiers*' constituted by the emergence of a category of foreigners who cannot be deported but remain illegals as a result of the inconsistencies of legislative and administrative mechanisms which were however conceived in order to fight against situations of unlawful residence.

It is well-known that the constitutional texts maintain a certain ambiguity regarding their range of application. This is in particular the case of the Declaration of Man and the Citizen which does not establish any clear distinction between man and the citizen. Moreover, one cannot ignore that the foreigners' civil rights still raise some problems, since the constitutional standards sometimes declare equality of *all* men (article 1 of the Declaration) and sometimes equality only of the *citizens* in the eyes of the law (article 6 of the Declaration and new article 1 of the 1958 Constitution). The latter again is confusing, because if it guarantees equality in the eyes of the law of all citizens, it omits to define what a citizen is. There would be actually only be two series of provisions reserved for the nationals: the exercise of political rights (article 3 of the 1958 Constitution) and 'the solidarity and equality of every Frenchman which result from the national calamities' (Preamble of the 1946 Constitution to which that of the 1958 Constitution refers). In contrast, the Preamble of 1946 contains a right addressed to aliens only: 'Any man persecuted because of his action for freedom is granted the right of asylum in the territory of the Republic'.[5] The constitutional status of aliens was outlined recently in several decisions of the *Conseil constitutionnel*, and in particular that of 13 August 1993 (no. 93–325 DC.). It establishes clearly that foreigners are placed in a different situation from that of the nationals and that it is advisable to distinguish, for the granting of certain rights, between legal aliens and illegal aliens.

Citizenship and nationality

The *Code civil* of 1804 made filiation the principal criterion of 'nationality' thus sanctioning the principle of *jus sanguinis*. Conversely, the individual born in France to foreign parents is not French. He will only be able to request French nationality during the year following his majority if he fixes his residence in France. Some authors consider this technique of nationality to be a consequence of the exaltation of national feeling caused by the wars of the Revolution.[6] *Jus sanguinis* also seemed best capable of corresponding to the idea according to which nationality is connected with personality. Moreover, it is true that the demographic situation of France at that time put up with this primacy of *jus sanguinis*. The development of the demographic data, with its consequences as regards manpower and national defence, will have had some influence on the reappearance of *jus soli* during the nineteenth century, even if this is only a partial factor of explanation.

The law of 7 February 1851 marked a turning point in the history of our nationality law.[7] France introduced the notion of dual *jus soli*, conferring citizenship automatically *ab initio* on a child born in the country to a foreigner also born there. It is frequent to associate this reform with some demographic and military concerns in France. Those who consider that the reasons for reform were rather matter-of-fact were numerous.[8] But as W.R. Brubaker showed, demographic and military concerns were not so decisive in 1851. For Brubaker, one should rather lay the emphasis on the social resentment of the nationals against the exemption of military obligations from which aliens could benefit even if they were long-term residents in France. Indeed, the *Code civil* provided the possibility for the persons born in France to foreign parents becoming French at the age of majority, but only a few of them wanted to take advantage of such a possibility, in order to escape from military obligations.[9] The extension of *jus soli* can be perceived as a corollary of republican egalitarianism which would tend not only to eliminate the privilege constituted by the military service exemption but also to avoid the appearance of nations within the nation.

W.R. Brubaker seemed sceptical about the possibilities of reform of nationality proposed by the Chirac government at the time of the first *cohabitation* in 1986, by virtue of the aforesaid *jure soli* assimilationist characteristics of the nation. Under the previous arrangement, provided for by the law of 26 June 1889, the child born in France to foreign parents born abroad became French at the age of majority. The requirements were to be resident in France, to have lived there during the five years preceding the declaration and not to have declared to decline the *qualité de français* in the year preceding the age of majority (articles 44 ff.). There was therefore the possibility of expressing a negative choice. Article 52 of the Nationality Code also enabled this child, assisted or represented by his parents, to anticipate at any time the acquisition of French nationality, by a declaratory procedure subject globally to the same conditions.

Initiated by the Conservative government, as opposed to the French tradition, the law of 22 July 1993 provided for the acquisition of French nationality by expression of wish (*'manifestation de volonté'*) for persons born in France to non-French parents (article 21-7 C. civ.). These second generation aliens could acquire French nationality by simple declaration made between the ages of 16 and 21. Apart from the five years residence requirement, the new law required that the applicant should have no conviction resulting in a prison sentence of more than six months for serious criminal offence committed after the age of 18. The country therefore passed, for almost five years, according to the terms of D. Lochak, from a system of *'contracting out'* to a system of *'contracting in'*.[10] Moreover, as the system corresponded to a voluntary acquisition, the person concerned could run the risk of losing his/her nationality of origin at the same time, particularly if this nationality involved a State party to the Convention of 6 May 1963.[11] Indeed, at first sight, this reform seems to conform to the pattern of the elective conception of the nation, but the scope of this theoretical link should not be overestimated. It is advisable to defend an elective model that allows the inclusion of foreigners in the nation, and not that which, in practice, is likely to force the latter to remain with alien status. One reproached the law of 22 July 1993 with not bringing sufficient guarantees, without stressing the context of suspicion against non national elements in which it was adopted.[12]

Article 21-7 of the civil Code is the keystone of the new mechanism of acquisition of French nationality according to birth and residence in

France. The new law (*loi Guigou*) adopted on 16 March 1998 restores the principle of automatic acquisition at the age of majority, such as it had occurred since the law of 1889, and makes the condition of usual residence more flexible. Henceforth, any child born in France to foreign parents acquires French nationality at his majority if at that time he is resident in France and if he lived there continuously or intermittently for at least five years, from the age of eleven. The re-establishment of full acquisition does not exclude, however, any recognition of individual will. Thus, article 28-1 of the *Code civil* leaves the young person who meets the conditions in order to acquire automatically French nationality at eighteen years, the ability to reject this position within a six-month period preceding his majority or, as envisaged in the 1993 legislation, within the following twelve months. The silence of the person concerned will be taken as acceptance of nationality. The logic is therefore reversed in relation to the 1993 reform, even if it takes up again certain contributions that are still considered to be relevant. The idea described in the *Weil Report* submitted to the Prime Minister[13] is that one should not become French without wishing nor knowing it. In this connection the possibility of anticipating one's acquisition is provided by the new law (art. 21-11 C. civ.). On the contrary, the old mechanism according to which the foreign parents of a child born in France could call for French nationality on behalf of their child under age, if they had had their usual residence in France for at least five years, has not been taken up again. Regretting this gap in the initial text, the Commission of constitutional laws adopted an amendment enabling the foreign parents of a child of at least thirteen years old, born in France and having his usual residence there for at least five years, to call for French nationality on his behalf and with his personal assent (art. 21-11 al. 2).

Acquisition and loss of nationality

First of all one distinguishes between attribution of nationality owing to filiation and attribution of nationality owing to birth in France. Legitimate or natural children born to one French parent are French as from their birth (article 18 C. civ.). According to article 19-3, France confers her citizenship on an alien child born in the country to a foreigner also born there. Such a rule of dual *jus soli* in France is well anchored in French nationality law. It derives from a particularly strong presumption of integration into the French community: the birth in France of both children and parents can hardly be a pure coincidence. The child born in France to two parents who were born there as well is not given the option to renounce French nationality. On the other hand, if only one of the parents was born in France, the French child, under the provisions of article 19-3, can renounce this French nationality within six months preceding his majority and within the following year. This faculty is lost if one of the parents becomes French during the minority of the child.

Regarding *acquisition* of nationality as such, one has to distinguish between *ex lege* acquisition and naturalisation. *Ex lege* acquisition embraces the principal methods of acquisition by birth and residence (see *supra* the principal provisions of the law of March 1998 amending the civil Code) and acquisition by marriage. Marriage has no effect on nationality (article 21-1 C. civ.). The foreign spouse can choose to acquire French nationality. This acquisition is subject to certain conditions. New article 21-2 reduced from two years to one year the period which has to separate the date of marriage and that of the claim for French nationality. The previous legislation (before 1993) had fixed a period of six months. The period is suppressed when there is a child whose filiation is established to both spouses, whether the child was born before or after the marriage.

As for naturalisation, the foreigner who requests it has no right to become French. On the other hand the acquisition is not subject to the renunciation of the former nationality. The abrogation of the incapacities of the naturalised person is relatively recent (December 1983). Similarly, the administration has been required to state the reasons for refusal in writing since the law of 22 July 1993. With the coming of age a person may apply for nationality (art. 21-22 C. civ.). As far as the residence requirements are concerned, no-one can be naturalised if he is not resident in France at the time of the signature of the naturalisation decree (art. 21-16). Moreover, the person concerned has to prove usual residence in France during the five years which precede the submission of the application (art. 21-17). According to the *Conseil d'Etat*, within the meaning of article 21-16, aliens shall have their principal source of income in France, in particular by having a job. Foreign students are therefore excluded even if they are considered to have lawful residence in France. There is a certain number of cases for which the duration of probation period is reduced[14] or suppressed.[15] In order for his request to be admissible, the foreigner is required to prove that he is assimilated into the French community, in particular by sufficient knowledge of the French language, according to his level of education (article 21-24). Health is no longer a condition of admissibility of the request, but it still remains an element to be taken into account, as far as the appropriateness of naturalisation is concerned. Finally good conduct is not to be belittled: article 21-23 stipulates that no one can be naturalised if he is not 'of good life and manners' ('*de bonne vie et moeurs*') or if he cannot show a 'clean criminal record' according to article 21-27.

There are no longer cases of *ex lege* loss of French nationality. Today, French nationality can be lost by declaration by the person concerned[16] or a decree taken by government (articles 23 ff). Article 23-4 C. civ. stipulates that the French, even under age, who have a foreign nationality, may be authorised, upon their request, by the French government, to lose the French nationality (*qualité de Français*). The law only requires the possession of dual nationality so that it will be possible to reduce, without creating any case of statelessness. Deprivation of French nationality involves a sanction which consists in withdrawing French nationality from an individual who had acquired it, due to unworthiness or of lack of loyalty. Withdrawal of a naturalisation decree may take place in two instances (article 27-2 C. civ.): when the applicant did not meet all the required legal conditions; and when the decision was obtained by lie or fraud. A long-term settlement abroad can involve the loss of nationality too. Globally, the question will thus not apply to the first generation of emigrants but to French people *jure sanguinis* who have never had their habitual residence in France and whose parents have not had their residence there for half a century. The loss of nationality implies a decision of the *tribunal de grande instance*, but it seems that in practice that the nationality of the descendant of the emigrant is considered to be lost after 50 years, without awaiting the decision mentioned above according to article 23-6 C. civ.

Distinction between citizenship and nationality

This distinction refers to a very French specific character that appeared after the revolutionary period marked by some confusion mainly due to the predominance of politics at the time.[17] Citizenship used to play what I have called a *double semantic function* because, on the one hand, the word *citoyen* identified those who were allowed to exercise political rights, but on the other hand, it was also the term used to identify the rest of the people, whether or not they had such rights. Despite the fact that the term nationality only appeared somewhere in the middle of the nineteenth century,[18] the conceptual distinction was clearly confirmed in the *Code civil*. Thus, article 7 distinguished between the exercise of the civil rights, determined by the Code, and the status of citizen, determined by the Constitution: 'The exercise of civil rights is independant from the status of citizen, which can only be acquired and retained in conformity with constitutional law'. The article remained unchanged until 1889, when by the law of 26 June, *la qualité de citoyen* was replaced by *l'exercice des droits politiques*. Although the civil rights, at that time, were far from being well-defined, this provision put an end to the ambiguity which resulted from the previous period.

New acceptations of the term citizenship

Citizenship is understood in many ways, but none of them exists in terms of positive law. The underlying idea is to conceive a new form of citizenship, a kind of social citizenship that would be really participative and capable of strengthening the civil society vis-à-vis the State and transcending the borders of the policy. In this connection appeared the – rather fuzzy – thematics of the 'new citizenship' (*nouvelle citoyenneté*) developed by the left-wing parties at the beginning of the 1980s and that has so far remained at the level of political speech.

Problems relating to statelessness

On this question, the law of 16 March 1998 tried to eliminate certain risks, in situations which remain however very marginal. The deprivation of nationality planned in cases of attacks to the fundamental interests of the nation or terrorism acts shall not generate situations of statelessness (new article 25 al. 1 C. civ.).

With regard to the attribution of nationality by birth in France, the child born to unknown parents is granted French nationality only provisionally. The same aim that consists of avoiding statelessness accounts for the attribution of French nationality to the child born in France to stateless parents (article 19-1 C civ.). But here, the retroactive disappearance of nationality was not envisaged. This involved a legislative gap which was filled by the *loi Guigou*.

Dual nationality

France is characterised by the weakness of the reducing mechanisms of dual nationality. A whole series of factors – not specific to France – accounts for situations of dual nationality.[19] Despite such legal recognition of plural nationality, some traditional opposition can still be found in the doctrine. Some scepticism with regard to dual nationality will sometimes be noted, insofar as it produces legal complications and brings about uncertainty for the old concepts of loyalty or allegiance. The increase in the situations of dual nationality often gave rise to concerns on the part of the State, as it may still be considered a danger for the nation. For some people, Proudhon's famous maxim according to which 'one cannot have two fatherlands as one cannot have two mothers', would still be relevant. Sometimes hardly dissimulated by technical problems that may be generated, only the mistrust of aliens would account for the refusal of dual nationality. On the contrary, one may be of the opinion that the advantages derived from dual nationality override the drawbacks, by allowing the formation of a transnational identity and by optimising personal freedoms in the host country. In France, the exercise of political rights once depended on the seniority of naturalisation, but dual nationality was never considered as an obstacle. With the laws of 8 and 20 December 1983, all the electoral incapacities attached to naturalisation were dismantled.

Among the technical disadvantages likely to be caused by dual nationality, certain points have to be stressed. The national service was traditionally regarded as being a major source of difficulties, insofar as dual nationals could remain subjected to dual military obligations. The reformation of the French national service as well as the conventional solutions in force in many countries – according to which dual nationals shall fulfil their military obligations in the state in which they have their habitual residence – have led to acceptable solutions.[20] One can regret however – on behalf of the idea of social integration – that the Convention of 11 October 1983 between France and Algeria made it possible for their dual nationals resident in France to serve in the Algerian army.

Another difficulty concerns the criterion of determination of the law applicable in the event of positive conflict of nationalities in matters of civil majority, marriage, divorce, filiation, successions. In France, the Courts have developed a solution which consists of ignoring the existence of the other nationality, and in allotting logically to the dual nationals all the effects attached to French nationality. This method, favourable to aliens' integration can nevertheless lead to unsatisfying situations, for example in the case where a decision of a foreign court would not be recognised in France. This is why the so-called functional approach makes it possible, to a certain extent, to take account of the other nationality. It seems that there is no contradiction in retaining one of the nationalities of a dual national in a determined hypothesis, and the second nationality for the solution of a legal question of another kind.[21]

Factors affecting the naturalisation rate

The number of naturalisations mainly depends on the nature of the legislation concerning the acquisition of nationality.[22] In France, one must take into account the liberal nature of nationality law with respect to the second and third generations of immigrants (see *supra*), as well as the open-minded attitude towards dual nationality. Indeed the different reforms of nationality law have consequences on the number of naturalisations. But contrary to what is commonly asserted, we are not sure that they strictly depend on the political and ideological orientations of the governments in power. It seems that a better administrative organisation (the number of requests largely differing from one *préfecture* to another) with an increase in staff, skills and computerisation, as well as efficient 'decentralisation' of the relevant services, are of greater influence than a political will aiming at controlling the volume of naturalisations.[23]

Residential rights

In its decision of 13 August 1993 (no. 93-325 DC), the constitutional Council stated clearly that no principle or any rule of constitutional value ensures aliens of general and absolute rights of abode and residence on the national territory.

Restrictions on freedom of entry for foreigners

Under article 5 of the *ordonnance* no. 45-2658 of 2 November 1945, entry will be considered lawful only insofar as the foreigners possess certain documents that make it possible to assess the nature of their stay: this involves in particular passports, visas and (apart from the persons concerned with family reunion) information concerning the reason for and the conditions of the stay, the means of subsistance of the person concerned and plans for his/her return home.

The following rules do not apply to nationals of the European Union or of the European Economic Area, which benefit from free movement measures.

Two main categories of visas allow the right of entry:

1 Short stay or tourism visas: these are granted for visits of less than three months. They can allow one or several admissions to France. There are also what are called *visas de circulation*, the validity of which can range between one and three years, but which permit only visits of less than three months,[24] and *transit visas* which concern the foreigners who are crossing the territory. Forty-eight countries are now exempted from the obligation of tourism visas.[25]
2 Visas of establishment or of long stay: these are granted to foreigners coming to France for a long period (students, workers, relatives, visitors).

A considerable exception to the general obligation to substantiate unfavourable individual administrative decisions concerned the refusal to grant a visa.[26] The law of 11 May 1998 (*loi Chevènement*) restricted the scope of that exception. Article 1 stipulates that refusal of a visa shall state the reasons on which the refusal is based (unless it is subject to considerations dealing with the safety of the State) for given categories of foreigners, like certain relatives of Community nationals; the spouses, children of less than 21 years old; children more than 21 years old but still dependent; ascendants of French nationals; recipients of an authorisation of family reunion; workers allowed to carry on their trade in France, persons registered on the *Schengen Information System* file; or students coming to France to continue higher studies there.

The question of the accommodation certificates (*certificats d'hébergement*) gave rise to much political debate, in particular in the context of the law of 24 April 1997 (*loi Debré*). Created by a decree of 27 May 1982, the accommodation certificate, was originally devised to check that a foreigner coming to France in the context of a private visit could find suitable accomodation. At the beginning of the 1990s, it started to be used as a pretext to strengthen the control of immigration flows. The law of 24 August 1993 conferred legislative value to the provisions concerning the certificate (article 5-3 of the *ordonnance* of 2 November 1945): the latter had to be established by the person with whom the foreigner resided and to receive the consent of the mayor of the commune in which the signatory resided. In spite of the critics of the *Conseil d'Etat* (31 October 1996), the *loi Debré* of April 1997 went further by creating a kind of file of the hosts and by establishing the obligation for the foreigners to give their certificate to the police before leaving France.[27] Article 5-3 was finally repealed by article 2 of the *loi Chevènement*.

By the law of 6 July 1992 adding an article 35 *quater* to the 1945 *ordonnance*, the legislator envisaged the creation of 'waiting zones' for foreigners denied the right to enter French territory. At the same time, it gave the Ministry of the Interior the opportunity to sort among the asylum applicants with the aim of refusing entry to those whose request he considered to be obviously unfounded. By this 'politically correct' euphemistic formulation of 'waiting areas', the idea was to permit and organise the retention of non-admitted foreigners who, as a matter of fact, had already stepped onto French soil. These areas are located in certain railway stations open to international traffic, harbours and airports. Retention in such areas cannot exceed forty-eight hours, but can be renewed for the same duration. It is pronounced by a decision containing the written reasons of the head of department of the frontier control or of an official appointed by the latter. A new extension can only be decided, for a maximum of eight days – renewable in exceptional circumstances – by the president of the *tribunal de grande instance* or by a judge that he nominates. The maximum duration of retention in such zones cannot exceed twenty days. Beyond this, the alien concerned is admitted to enter French territory under cover of an eight-day regularising visa, after which he will have to leave the territory or obtain a temporary residence permit. The alien concerned shall benefit from a number of rights and guarantees during the retention. He is free to leave the waiting area at any time for any destination located out of France. Nevertheless, it is necessary that he be accepted by another country. Generally speaking, the adoption of the waiting areas did not put an end to highly criticised administrative practices which partly depend on the mode of transportation used to reach French soil.

Categories of foreigners according to their residence status

Under article 6 of the *ordonnance* of 2 November 1945, any foreigner who remains in France after the expiry of a three-month deadline since his entry into French territory, shall be provided with a residence permit. Apart from the temporary residence permit, in 1984 a new residence document was introduced: the '*carte de résident*', also called '*carte de dix ans*'.

The temporary residence permit is delivered to those foreigners who do not meet the necessary conditions to obtain a residence card. Its period of validity cannot exceed one year, like the validity of the documents and visas provided for entering the country. Its issue is subordinated to the fact that the presence of the foreigner does represent any threat to the public order, including not living polygamously. The card is not renewable *ex lege*. It is therefore a precarious title, all the more as the administrative courts only exercise a restricted control on the negative decisions of the administration.[28] Various types of temporary residence permits can be identified.[29] Whether one can regret that the law of 11 May 1998 multiplies the issues of temporary cards to the detriment of the resident's status, the contribution of the new legislation lies precisely in taking into account private or family life to reach the right of abode, including also the health of the foreigners who require medical assistance (the *loi Debré* of 24 April 1997 had only stipulated that these foreigners could not be deported from the French territory). According to article 12 *ter* inserted by article 6 of the *loi Chevènement*, the foreigner who has been granted territorial asylum (*asile territorial*) is also given a residence permit *ex lege* which also allows the exercise of a professional activity.

The residence document (*carte de résident*) is valid for ten years and grants access to all employment and independant professional activities (article 17 of the ord. of 1945). It is renewable *ex lege* every ten years, except if the foreigner has been living polygamously (article 15 *bis*) or left the French territory for more than three years (article 18). The residence document grants access to all employment and independant professional activities. But it does not provide special protection against expulsion. This residence card may be issued to an alien with at least three years of lawful residence in France and sufficient income (article 14).[30] But certain categories of aliens (13 in total) have a statutory right to this document.[31] The law of 11 May 1998 suppressed the condition of lawful entry which was a requirement of the *loi Pasqua* of 24 August 1993 (for foreigners referred to in §§ 1 to 5 of article 15) but it maintains paradoxically the condition of lawful residence in order to be granted the statutory right to the ten years residence card. Therefore, the foreigner will need first a temporary residence permit, which reduces the scope of the modification to nothing. In this respect, it must be stressed that the *loi Joxe* of 2 August 1989 opposed neither unlawful entry and residence nor public order considerations to the delivery of a residence card. In the same regulation, a new article 18 *bis* created a card with the word 'retired', so that the persons concerned could move freely between France and their country and be facilitated the perception of their pensions abroad. This card will enable pensioners to enter French territory at any time for periods not exceeding one year. It is valid for ten years and is renewable automatically.[32]

According to the decree no. 94-211 of 11 March 1994, the workers of the Member States of the European Union and equivalent categories received a residence permit valid for five years. It was then renewable *ex lege* for ten years (article 7). In accordance with the proposals of the *Weil report*, the *loi Chevènement* improved the status of those persons. The card is now valid for ten years *ab initio* and renewable once for good. However, it must not be forgotten that the residence permit is declaratory and therefore not constitutive of a right. This means that residence is acquired independently of the delivery of the document. But it appears that the absence of residence permit remains sanctioned in a way which is unjustified in relation to the fundamental principles of free movement.[33]

Re-entry rules

According to Article 18 of the *ordonnance* of 2 November 1945, the residence card of a foreigner who has left the French territory for a period of more than three consecutive years expires automatically, except upon special request either before departure, or during the stay abroad. This is why the card 'retired' was introduced recently.[34]

Registration Process

Under article 8-3 of the *ordonnance* of 2 November 1945 (inserted by the *loi Debré* of 24 April 1997), the fingerprints of all the foreigners (non-nationals of a Member State of the European Union) who ask to remain in France can be taken and registered in a file, as well as those whose situation is unlawful or who are concerned by an expulsion measure. The aim of the disposition is to prevent a foreigner from getting rid of his/her travel documents in order to escape from forced departure. The Ministry of the Interior will be able to consult this file in order to identify the foreigners concerned with a view to carrying out the measure of expulsion. Except for the cases of application for the status of refugees, the constitutional Council, in its decision of 22 April 1997 (no. 97-389 DC), considered that the legislator, on behalf of public interest considerations, had not impaired personal freedom in a way likely to ignore the Constitution.[35] It is to be regretted that the article does not differentiate according to the nature of the stay. In the wake of the *GISTI* (Group of information and support of migrant workers), it might be said that this provision falls under a police management of immigration. As from the request for a residence permit, one prepares for the possibility of deporting the migrant concerned.[36]

We have mentioned so far the description of the conditions of entry and residence on national territory. But the French example shows that the development of regulations contributed to generate situations of unlawfulness, by the effect of the law. Article 15 of the *ordonnance* of 2 November 1945 enumerates the categories of aliens that have a statutory right to the ten-year card. But, as we saw, this involves certain conditions which may raise, in addition to problems of consistency, real practical difficulties. In effect, it is not rare that the administration refuses a residence permit to foreigners, however protected from forced departure or who cannot reasonably envisage leaving French territory. Thus, the spouse of a Frenchman may be denied the delivery of a residence permit, because of unlawful stay at the time of the application, while according to the law, an alien married for at least a year to a French national, cannot be deported, provided that the couple still live under the same roof (article 25-4° of the *ordonnance* of 2 Nov. 1945). Contrary to its intentions, the *loi Debré* of 24 April 1997 did not eliminate the persistence of irregular situations. This is why the circular of 24 June 1997, aiming at putting an end to the intolerable or inextricable situation of certain foreigners, engaged the *préfets* to review the situation of the latter, by way of an exception; but the results did not appear convincing at all. We take up again the example of the foreign spouse who has entered French territory unlawfully: he or she will only be granted a temporary residence permit after a year of marriage. Therefore he or she will be forced to remain illegal throughout this period. In spite of certain improvements, the wording of new article 12 *bis* of the 1945 regulation (7°) does not *a priori* get rid of any ambiguity on the matter, a large power of interpretation being left to the *préfet*.[37] For the time being the category of *sans-papiers* is unlikely to disappear. The procedure of regularisation officially ended on 31 December 1998, but more than 60 000 *sans-papiers* have been denied a residence document so far.[38] This is still a thorny matter for the present government.[39]

Social rights

The state of foreigners' rights as regards social welfare was judged 'globally satisfactory' by the *Weil report*.[40] By and large, it is true that one can note in this field the disappearance of the conditions of nationality.[41] But the main discriminations reappear through residence requirements,[42] which the Constitutional Council did not consider as opposing the principle of equality – defined restrictively[43] – in its decision of 22 January 1990. Those rights are granted *ratione loci* more than *ratione personae*, and are more 'territorial rights' than 'human rights'. Accordingly, except for bilateral conventions, migrant workers' families that remained in the country of origin do not benefit, or not much, from those rights.

Pensions and allowances

The criteria retained for the calculation of the pensions are identical, whether the recipient is French or non-national. But some additional conditions of residence are specific to aliens. The foreigners shall justify lawful residence (article 161-18-1 of the *Code de la Securité sociale*: *CSS*) and shall reside in French territory at the time of the payment of the pension, with the exception of bilateral conventions of Social Security. Thus, in the absence of a special convention, the foreigner who is no longer resident in France is required to return there in order to liquidate his or her basic old-age pension paid by the Social Security. In its decision of 13 August 1993, the constitutional Council specified that, subject to requirements of public order, the foreigners concerned shall be granted a temporary permit, the duration of which shall be long enough to let them take the necessary steps (§ 116). Once liquidated, it will be possible to export the pension, to whatever country is required.[44] The person concerned will only be required to produce certificates showing that he is still alive. On the other hand, he will lose the benefit of health allowances, despite the fact that he contributed for all his working life. The new card *'retraités'* covers certain rights inadequately. The holder of such a card who benefits from one or more pensions paying insurance for at least 15 years is, according to the conditions laid down by law, entitled to the benefits of the health insurance of the pension scheme to which he was contributing at the time of his departure, for himself and his spouse, if, on the occasion of temporary visits to the metropolitan territory or overseas departments, their health happens to require immediate care (article L 161-25-3 new *CSS*). As far as supplementary pensions are concerned, they can be obtained directly from the country of origin.

Regarding non-contributive social security benefits (old age minimum), there were still some discriminations. They have just been eliminated by the law of 11 May 1998. To benefit from the allocation granted to old workers, one had to be of French nationality, a refugee, a stateless person, or a member of the European Union or European Economic Area, or of a State having concluded a reciprocity convention with France (article 811-1 *CSS*). It was the same for the special old age allowances (article 815-5 *CSS*). In the decision dated 22 January 1990 (no. 89-267 DC), the Constitutional Council considered, however, that the non-contributory benefits connected with old age or with disability could not, without ignoring the constitutional principle of equality, be subordinated to a condition of nationality. As the *Code de la Sécurité sociale* was not amended, many foreigners remained practically excluded from such benefits despite the fact that many of them could avail themselves of more favourable international agreements (EC–Third Country agreements; Convention no. 118 ILO). Article L 816-1 has recently been inserted into the Social Security Code. This change does not correspond to a real governmental initiative but rather is the result of EC institutions' proceedings and of numerous cases raised before the courts by individuals in order to put an end to the failure (*manquement*) of France in this respect. It suppresses the nationality condition to have access to non-contributory benefits connected with old age; but they remain subject to the condition of lawful residence in France.

As for allowances to disabled adults, the development is identical to that described in the previous paragraph. The condition of nationality has recently been withdrawn, but still to the profit of lawful residence in France (new article 821-9 *CSS*).

The unemployed migrant worker benefits from unemployment insurance under the same conditions as the French, if he holds a residence permit that grants access to employment activities (article R. 351-25 of the *Code du Travail*). The national employment agency checks the validity of the residence document at the time of the alien's registration on the list of job seekers (article L 311-5-1).

Set up in December 1988, the insertion minimum income (*revenu minimum d'insertion*: *RMI*) is a differential allowance intended to ensure suitable means of existence and to encourage social and professional reintegration. To claim *RMI*, it is necessary to be over 25 years old. No condition of nationality is required; it suffices to be lawfully resident in France. The recipient of a temporary residence permit allowing the exercise of a professional activity must show three years of lawful and continuous residence in France. This condition is attested by the presentation of a certificate drawn up by the *préfecture* on delivery of the card. Repeated stays exceeding three months abroad during the same year imply the withdrawal of *RMI*. The consequences that the perception such an allowance can have on residence must not be underestimated either: indeed, the temporary residence permit allowing the exercise of a professional activity is delivered or renewed on the ground of the production of an employment contract or balance-sheet (*bilan d'activité*). The problem is that these conditions are no longer satisfied when *RMI* is granted. So there is a risk of being refused when requesting the renewal of the residence permit.

Foreigners coming to France to receive care there

Aliens can be admitted to hospital in the event of foreseeable or non-urgent care, if they are in a position of producing evidence of financial means likely to cover health expenditure. Non-resident foreigners will (only in very few cases) be exempted from paying hospital expenses after presenting a request to the consular authorities of their country which will be forwarded to the various relevant ministries. Moreover, certain bilateral agreements envisage a possibility of coverage by the Social Security organisations of the country of origin. In such a case, it will occur within the limits of the local tariffs, which makes this solution rather illusory.[45]

Social security schemes and condition of residence

As a result of the *loi Pasqua* of 24 August 1993, foreigners can be affiliated to an obligatory Social Security scheme only if they are lawfully resident or have requested the renewal of their residence permit. In the case of affiliation of unlawful resident aliens, their contributions remain due. However, according to article L 161-8 of the *Code de Sécurité sociale*, access to social security benefits is extended for a year after the suspension of the situation which created them. As the Constitutional Council specified in its decision of 13 August 1993, the law of 24 August does not exclude unlawful resident foreigners from the benefit of these provisions.

In accordance with the suggestions of the *Weil report*,[46] the present government has maintained this requirement of regular stay in France, which is subject to some debate.[47]

As they can no longer be affiliated to Social Security, unlawful resident foreigners will now have to claim the benefits of social assistance (*aide sociale*), reserved for the the most needy people. The principle comprises two exceptions: irregular migrant workers who are victims of industrial injuries or occupational diseases shall benefit from the qualified allowances.

In addition, regarding urgent and unforeseen care, the foreigner, even in an unlawful situation, may always be admitted to hospital: otherwise it would be a case of 'non-assistance to person in jeopardy'. Certain bilateral conventions envisage the possibilty of coverage by the social benefit system of the country of origin. Failing this, the person concerned will be charged for the care. If he is not solvent, the bill can be sent only to those obliged to assist (*obligés alimentaires*).

Multicultural education

At the request of the parents, foreign children can receive extra teaching in their mother tongue, in school, either as public or private tuition (3 hours per week). This optional teaching is given under bilateral agreements negotiated between the French ministry of education and the corresponding ministry of the countries concerned (Portugal, Spain, Italy, Maghreb, Turkey etc.). The foreign teachers are appointed and remunerated by the government of origin. Considered as officials on mission, they are not subject to the provisions concerning the possession of residence and working authorisations.[48]

Economic rights

Situation of aliens with respect to private rights

According to Article 11 of the civil Code, 'foreigners will enjoy in France the same civil rights as those which are or will be granted to the French by the treaties of the nation to which these foreigners will belong'.

Taken literally, this article resulted in refusing the foreigners who did not benefit from such treaties the enjoyment of all civil rights. Actually, the restrictive drafting of article 11 was moderated by the doctrine and case law, in such a way that it led to a more satisfactory formula sanctioned by the reversal of the *'Cour de cassation'* in 1948, according to which foreigners in France enjoy the rights they are not specifically denied.

Restrictions regarding employment

Access to a number of occupations remains subject to a condition of nationality. P. Mayer mentions three reasons for this that are usually involved: fear of incompetence, influence and competition.[49] In France, every paid activity, including commercial or agricultural, requires an authorisation, except for the holder of a residence card.

Certainly, one must take account of the possibilities of legislative reciprocity or relaxation of rules resulting from treaties concluded with the host country[50] and, of course, of the influence of EC law. Nationality here loses a significant part of its meaning for EC nationals, with restrictions now occurring at the external borders of the Union,[51] as the Schengen agreements turned out to prove.

Working limitations regarding the status of immigrants

To carry on a paid activity, the foreign student has to request a provisional authorisation within the departmental Directorate of Work and Employment (*Direction départementale du Travail et de l'Emploi*). The job must be part-time under penalty of withdrawal of the residence permit and of penal proceedings. The student must give evidence of his registration in an establishment granting access to Social Security. An objection to the employment situation can be made at the time of the examination of the application. Some nationals benefit from a more favourable arrangement (EEC, EEA, Togo, Gabon, Andorra, Monaco, Algeria): they must be lawfully resident as students, but they do not require any work permit. Lastly, requests must be examined benevolently during university and school holidays, although the employment situation remains, in theory, open to objection, except for some nationalities.[52] Foreign students cannot register as job applicants in the *ANPE* (National Employment Agencies). On the other hand, they benefit from the employment opportunities offered by the students' representative bodies. The previous instructions according to which foreign students were required to get back to their country at the end of their studies and could not remain in France to carry on a job there have been cancelled (Circular of 5 March 1982 of the Ministry of the Interior and of Decentralisation).[53]

Asylum applicants are subject to common law rules applicable to migrant workers as far as the issue of a work permit is concerned. Since 1 October 1991, the receipt noting the submission of an application for the status of refugee (which corresponds to a three-month renewable residence permit) has no longer been equivalent to a work permit. However the persons concerned can benefit from specific allowances.

Occupations reserved for the nationals

One may wonder here about the lawfulness of certain effects traditionally established in the domestic system. It is well known that the criterion of distinction linked to the equality principle is based on the difference of situations.[54] But such a difference cannot account for all discriminations with which foreigners are confronted. Just let us mention the conditions of access to the public service, even when certain activities are independent from the safeguard of public interest and the exercise of State authority, while foreigners are enabled to perform the same tasks but only as assistants or contract workers.

From this point of view it appears that there is no consitutional necessity. Actually such position was adopted by the ECJ, interpreting restrictively article 48(4) EC, according to which the exception contained in this article does not apply to posts 'whilst coming under the State or other organisations governed by public law, still do not involve any association with duties belonging to the public service properly so called'.[55] The paradox applies not only to the major part of the public sector (including public firms)[56] but also to some posts in the private sector, far from the principles laid down by the Preamble of the Constitution of 1946. About 6.5 to 7 million positions would be closed to aliens, including 5.2 million in the public service, out of a working population estimated at 22.1 million (March 1998).[57]

Aliens can teach in higher education but they are denied access to secondary schools, except as modern language assistants, teachers appointed in exchange programmes and supply teachers, on the condition that there is no national who is able to perform those jobs. Upon authorisation of the higher council of Education and of the Minister for Education, aliens can teach in the private sector. On the other hand, they could not, until recently, teach in primary schools (law of 30 October 1886). The condition of nationality has just been suppressed for Community nationals and comparable categories.[58] If there was no nationality condition for doctors as wage-earners, aliens in the professions as a whole would not exceed 1 per cent.[59]

Percentage of aliens in the public service

Table 4.1 sets out the percentage of aliens employed in public service, according to the last census of the population (1990) by the national Institute of Statistics and Economic surveys (*INSEE*) calculated:[60]

Table 4.1 Aliens employed in public service (percentage)

Service	*1990 (%)*	*1982 (%)*
managerial staff	1.72	0.9
professors, scientific professions	3.6	2.6
teachers and equivalent	2.14	1.22
intermediate professions in the public service	0.5	0.2
employees	1.73	1.4

Political rights

General elections and condition of nationality

In France, nationality remains a necessary condition for the exercise of political rights. The reform resulting from Article 8 EC can be regarded as a minor departure from the law in force. The doctrine often stresses the traditional constitutional link between political citizenship and nationality. This approach does not resist historical analysis: citizenship conceived as a number of rights reserved to the French cannot stand up to close examination of the revolutionary constitutions. This involves much more a preconception which ended up in acquiring constitutional basis as from 1814–30 and even more clearly in 1848.[61]

Even if the right to vote was allotted to still broader categories of voters (end of the '*suffrage censitaire*', women's vote, lowering of the age of the majority etc.), foreigners always remained excluded from such developments. The lack of autonomy of citizenship in relation to nationality represented a permanent feature, a presupposition, or even eventually a kind of legitimation of the exclusion as shown by article 3 of the Constitution of 4 October 1958.[62]

The constitutional modification of 25 June 1992 connected with the ratification of the Maastricht Treaty did not radically refine the problem. Thus the bases of the exclusion of foreigners from voting still remain topical.

A first element of explanation for this exclusion rests on the – questionable – idea of national sovereignty. It results from the constitutional tradition that only the nationals can be entitled to vote, because only the nationals can formulate public will for the nation.[63] Aliens would form part not of the people but only of the population. A range of interpretations, no less debatable, is thus made possible, the foreigners representing a threat for the state, precisely because of their national membership. For the adversaries to the right to vote, foreigners would not be completely connected with the national community and with its destiny. Consequently, they would be likely, not only to vote in a less responsible way, but also to be granted a right without any counterpart (military service), some people seeing here an attack against the principle of equality, without bringing any proof of real allegiance. Foreigners would do nothing but ignore national aspirations!

A further explanation, more seriously, refers to the unity of the body politic. Today, some will consider that only the municipal polls, the decisions of which concern the inhabitants' daily life, justify that the electorate be widened to the non-nationals, while others claim that the development of national sovereignty is carried out at the first level of the politico-administrative organisation of the state and that the national body is indivisible. In its decision of 18 November 1982 (no. 82-146 DC) declaring unconstitutional the introduction of quotas for women in the lists of candidates at the municipal level, the constitutional Council removed any possible ambiguity in making no distinction between local elections and national elections. It considered that this results from article 3 of the Constitution and from article 6 of the Declaration of Man and the Citizen that these principles of constitutional value are opposed to any division by category of the voting or eligible citizens, for any political suffrage and in particular for the town councillors' elections. The real cleavage would be between political elections and professional elections, that is to say between political representation and representation of interests, as the dogma of homogeneity did not prevent the development of other representation authorities founded, outside the political representation, on a division by category.

The Maastricht Treaty inserting Article 8 EC will, however, introduce the fragmentation of the body politic refused hitherto, thus breaking the link between unity of the public power and people's political unity (*unité du peuple politique*). The obstacle of the unity of the body politic as accounting for the exclusion of foreigners from local voting rights disappears, without one being able to draw any conclusion from the point of view of general elections. The principal obstacle of national sovereignty remains, although it was affected indeed by the acceptance of local suffrage for 'privileged' aliens.

Voting rights limited to EC nationals

In its decision of 9 April 1992 (no. 92-308 DC), the constitutional judge modified his position in relation to his above-mentioned decision of 18 November 1982 and seemed to call into question the unit of the body politic, by ruling out a direct violation of article 3, considering that local voting rights for non-nationals are contrary to article 3 only because municipal elections are connected to senatorial ones, the Senate being elected through indirect suffrage.

In a climate of strong political tensions, article 88-3 was inserted finally in the Constitution (constitutional law of 25 June 1992).[64] The reference to *only* Community nationals confirms the exemption character of the reform on the right to vote. Senators were particularly attached to it. With more than two years of delay on the timetable envisaged, on 21 April 1998, the Parliament adopted the organic law mentioned in article 88-3, transposing Directive 94/80/EC of 19 December 1994.[65] The citizens of the Union are considered to be resident in France if they have their real *'domicile'* there and if their residence has been continuous (art. LO 227-1). There might be some problems of interpretation, considering the absence of definition in EC law of the notions of residence and domicile.

Parallel between active and passive voting rights

The constitutional reserve on the functions of mayor and of deputy mayor does not seem to derive from the provisions of Article 8B of the EC Treaty. One can indeed detect certain incompatibility with the phrase 'under the same conditions as the nationals of the state of residence', although the preparatory documents relating to the proposal for a Directive COM (89) 524 final make it possible to understand better the restrictions envisaged by the text of the constitutional revision and referred to in the Directive 94/80/EC (article 5-3).

In addition, the exclusion of the non-national representatives from the senatorial electors is not entirely satisfactory, for reasons dealing with the very nature of senatorial elections. According to C. Grewe, the desire to make it so that foreigners with the right to vote and to eligibility no longer take part in national sovereignty does not seem workable, since excluding the European citizens from senatorial elections does not prevent the latter from counting in the mass of local voters and elected citizens, from being as such represented by the Senate and thus from constituting a foreign expression in the heart of national sovereignty.[66]

Political freedoms

The condition of nationality is reduced, (cases of fundamental freedoms considered inherent in the human being: freedoms of thought, of conscience and of religion, for instance) but has not completely disappeared. Thus the freedom of the press is still subject to the control of the Minister of the Interior who can prohibit newspapers or texts written in a foreign language or of foreign origin (art. 14 of the law of July 1881). Indeed, the powers of the minister depend on law and order considerations which are now subject to the plenary control of the judge.[67]

Concluding remarks

In France, nationality law is quite open, favourable to foreigners' integration into the national community, even if one must admit that it has never been *a priori* synonymous with social integration. One of the priorities of the *Jospin government* on coming into power after the dissolution of the National Assembly in 1997 was to hark back to the 1993 reform of nationality law which had appeared estranged from the French tradition. The new law restores the rule of full acquisition for the second-generation immigrants, without however returning completely to the system in force before 1993. The situation of aliens was also appreciably modified by the law of 11 May 1998 which again replaces the previous legislation only partially. The few aspects stressed in this report mention some softening as regards entry and stay in France while maintaining or even strengthening the principle of control of immigration, according to a dual logic: the adoption of reasonably generous measures towards legitimate immigrants compensating for increased strictness against illegal workers.[68] The main dispositions regarding the social security system constitute a significant example.

As regards employment, one still wonders about the lawfulness of the activities reserved for the only nationals. The evolution is made under the influence of EC law, but at the price of a new dichotomy, between Community nationals and nationals of non-member States.

The question of political rights which will perhaps appear secondary in particular in the current context of the movement of the *'sans-papiers'* offers another illustration of such reality. The constitutional modification allowing the adaptation of the French law to the new Community standards relating to European citizenship proved to be limited to the bare minimum. Under certain aspects, aliens' rights in France still remain rather unimportant.

Notes

1 G. le Moigne, *L'Immigration en France*, 3rd edn (Paris: PUF, 1997) p. 7.
2 See P. Weil, *La France et ses étrangers. L'aventure d'une politique de l'immigration 1938–1991* (Paris: Calmann-Lévy, 1991) pp. 60 ff.
3 *Office Français de Protection des Réfugiés et des Apatrides.*
4 D. Lochak, 'Quand le droit court après la politique', *Plein Droit*, no. 29–30, Nov. 1995, p. 52.
5 X. Vandendriessche, *Le Droit des étrangers* (Paris: Dalloz, 1996, p. 5). See also P. Weil, *La France et ses étrangers, op. cit.*, pp. 7 ff.
6 See P. Courbe, *Le Nouveau droit de la nationalité*, 2nd edn (Paris: Dalloz, 1998) p. 34.
7 See *La Nationalité française. Textes et documents* (Paris: La Documentation française, 1996).
8 J.-P. Niboyet, *Droit international privé*, vol. 1 (Paris: Sirey, 1947, no. 129).
9 W.R. Brubaker, 'De l'immigré au citoyen', *Actes de la Recherche en Sciences sociales*, no. 99, Sept., 1993, p. 9.
10 D. Lochak, 'Usages et mésusages d'une notion polémique. La référence à l'identité nationale dans le débat sur la réforme du Code de la nationalité, 1985–1993' in Crispa–Curapp, *L'identité politique* (Paris: PUF, 1994) p. 313.
11 P. Lagarde, *La Nationalité française*, 3rd edn (Paris: Dalloz, 1997) p. 106.
12 Y. Loussouarn and P. Bourel, *Droit international privé*, 5th edn (Paris: Dalloz, 1996) § 543.
13 P. Weil, *Mission d'étude des législations de la nationalité et de l'immigration* (Paris: La Documentation française, 1997).
14 Article 21-18 C. civ. reduces the condition of residence to two years for the foreigners who achieved successfully two years of higher studies in a French higher educational establishment or for the foreigners who proved or may prove to be very useful to France.
15 Article 21-19 C. civ. suppresses the condition of residence for:

- the minor who did not benefit from the collective effect of acquisition of French nationality by one of his parents;
- the spouse and the child of full age of a person who acquires or has acquired French nationality;
- the foreigner who served in a unit of the French army or who joined the French or allied armies in wartime;
- the national or former national of the territories and states on which France exerted either sovereignty, protectorate, or mandate;
- the foreigner who rendered exceptional services to France or whose naturalisation represents an exceptional interest for the country.

NB: the law of 16 March 1998 (art. 8) also exempts refugees applying for naturalisation. Lastly, according to article 21-20, French-speaking foreigners can also be exempted from the period of probation.

16 Voluntary acquisition of a foreign nationality had been – until the law of 9 January 1973 – a case of loss of French nationality *ex lege*. Now, any French person of full age, usually resident abroad, who voluntarily acquires a foreign nationality, loses his nationality only at his initiative.

17 See B. Guiguet, *Citoyenneté et nationalité: limites de la rupture d'un lien*, PhD, Florence, EUI, 1997, pp. 22 ff.

18 *ibid.*

19
- the use of the various criteria concerning the attribution of nationality;
- the growing equality of treatment between men and women. In the past, there was indeed unity within the family but this always involved the husband's nationality. Since the 1973 reform, the acquisition of nationality by marriage has no longer taken on a unilateral character nor conditioned the loss of the previous nationality. There is therefore transmission of nationality by the mother as well as by the father;
- children of the second generation benefit automatically from the nationality of the host country at the age of majority and are not required to renounce their first nationality;
- it also is worth pointing out the cases of dual nationality which may result from state successions. Thus, *ordonnance* no. 62-825 of 21 July 1962 contemplated the possibility of retaining French nationality for a large number of persons originating from Algeria who also became Algerian according to the legislation of the new State;
- from the point of view of naturalisation, dual nationality involves a legislation of the State of origin that allows to retain its nationality. France has been in favour for this shared allegiance since 1973.

20 Cf. the 1963 Convention of the Council of Europe on the Reduction of Cases of Multiple Nationality and Military Obligations in Cases of Multiple Nationality, and the new European Convention of Nationality adopted on 6 November 1997.

21 See P. Lagarde, 'Vers une approche fonctionnelle du conflit positif de nationalités', *Revue critique de droit international privé*, vol. 77, no. 1, 1988, pp. 39 ff; G. de la Pradelle, 'Nationalité française, extranéité, nationalités étrangères', in *Mélanges dédiés à Dominique Holleaux* (Paris: Litec, 1990) pp. 135 ff.

22 See Sopemi, *Trends in International Migration*, OECE, 1997, pp. 59 ff.

23 See J. Costa-Lascoux, 'Devenir Français aujourd'hui . . . Réflexions sur la sociologie des naturalisations', in H. Fulchiron (ed.), *'Etre Français aujourd'hui'. Premier bilan de la mise en oeuvre du nouveau droit de la nationalité* (Lyon: PUL, 1996) pp. 140 ff.

24 Circular no. 86-347 of 28 November 1986 of the ministry of the Interior.

25 *OMI Classeur*, 1998, p. A-5.

26 Law no. 86-1025 of 9 Sept. 1986, art. 16.

27 The draft of the law even provided for a declaration/report from the host himself, thus not so far from painful periods of French history, under the Vichy regime . . . See J. Derrida 'Quand j'ai entendu l'expression *"délit d'hospitalité" . . .*', *Plein Droit*, no. 34, April 1997, pp. 3 ff.

28 P. Wachsmann, *Libertés publiques*, 2nd edn (Paris: Dalloz, 1998) p. 285.

29 'visitor'; 'student'; 'wage-earner', with mention of the permitted activity; article 4 of the law of 11 May 1998 created two new indications qualifying the residence permits, i.e. 'scientist' and 'artistic and cultural occupation'; and Article 12 *bis* of the *ordonnance* of 2 November 1945 modified by article 5 of the *loi Chevènement* sets out *ex lege* temporary residence permits which refer to 'private and family life' and give the right to the exercise of a professional activity.

30 At this stage, few aliens are granted a residence card, because at this moment it is at the discretion of the administration to grant or refuse the card (K. Gronendijk, E. Guild and H. Dogan, *Security of residence of long-term migrants* (Strasbourg, Council of Europe Publishing, 1997) p. 33.

31
- on the basis of a special relationship with a French citizen (being the spouse of a French national for more than one year under certain conditions or being the ascendants of a French national);
- after admission for family reunification with a foreigner holding such a residence document;
- the foreigners that have been lawfully resident for more than ten years, unless they have been students for the whole period;
- the recipients of the status of refugee.

The thirteenth case aimed at by this procedure was added to article 15 by the law of 11 May 1998. It concerns by and large the foreigners that have been lawfully resident for five years with a special permit for 'private and family life' or granting territorial asylum.

32 P. Weil, *Mission d'étude des législations de la nationalité et de l'immigration, op. cit.*, pp. 68–9.

33 See H. Gacon, 'Communautaires peut-être, mais étrangers surtout', *Plein Droit*, no. 35 Sept. 1997, pp. 21–4.

34 See *supra*.

35 See D. Turpin, 'La loi no. 97–396 du 24 avril 1997 portant diverses dispositions relatives à l'immigration: de l'ajustement au durcissement', *Rev. crit. dr. internat. privé*, vol. 86, no. 3, July–Sept. 1997, p. 462.

36 Gisti, Comments of the draft of the *loi Debré*, 27 Jan. 1997.

37 Article 12 *bis*: 'Unless his presence constitutes a threat to the public order, the temporary residence permit being marked "private and family life" is delivered *ex lege*: . . . : 7° to the alien who does not live polygamously, who is not included in the previous categories or in those which provide for family reunification, whose personal and family links in France are such that the denial of a residence permit would affect his right to private and family life in a disproportionate manner compared to the reasons for the refusal.'

38 *Libération*, 9 Dec. 1998.

39 See P. Wachsmann, *Libertés publiques, op. cit.*, p. 287.

40 P. Weil, *Mission d'étude des législations de la nationalité et de l'immigration, op. cit.*, p. 85.

41 See the Preamble of the 1946 Constitution and the Decision of the *Conseil constitutionnel* no. 89–269 DC. of 22 January 1990, especially *considérants* 34–35.

42 See D. Turpin, 'Le statut constitutionnel de l'étranger', *Les Petites Affiches*, 15 March 1991, no. 32, p. 14.

43 See new art. 1 of the 1958 Constitution.

44 On the contrary, the invalidity allowance liquidated in France is exportable only if it is envisaged by a bilateral agreement. It is also the case for industrial injuries (Convention no. 19 of ILO).

45 Gisti, *Le Guide de la protection sociale des étrangers en France* (Paris: Syros, 1997) pp. 205–7.

46 P. Weil, *Mission d'étude des législations de la nationalité et de l'immigration, op. cit.*, p. 87.

47 See A. Toullier, 'Fidélité à la logique Pasqua', *Plein Droit*, no. 36–37, Dec. 1997, pp. 48–51.

48 C. Barats (ed.), *Droit des étrangers. Le Guide* (Paris: Le livre de poche, 1994) p. 91. *OMI Classeur*, 1998, p. B-61.

49 P. Mayer, *Droit international privé*, 5th edn (Paris: Montchrestien, 1994) § 979.

50 *OMI Classeur*, 1997, p. 72.

51 C.A. Groenendijk, 'Le rôle changeant de la nationalité dans la condition juridique de l'étranger', in *La Condition juridique de l'étranger, hier et aujourd'hui*, Actes du colloque de Nimègue, 9–11 May 1988, Nijmegen, Faculteit der Rechtsgeleerdheit, 1988, p. 112.

52 Laos, Vietnam, Cambodia, the Lebanon (*OMI Classeur*, 1998, p. C-41).

53 *OMI Classeur*, 1996, pp. 111–12.

54 See G. Pellissier, *Le Principe d'égalité en droit public* (Paris: LGDJ, 1996).

55 Case 149/79, *Commission v. Kingdom of Belgium*, 17 Dec. 1980. Also 307/84, *Commission v. France*, 3 June 1986. In this frame of mind, the French law of 26 July 1991 suppressed (for some posts determined by decree) the condition of nationality for EC nationals for their getting tenure.

56 Only a few of them have modified their status and abandonned the nationality requirement. See A. Math and A. Spire, 'Sept millions d'emplois interdits', *Plein Droit*, no. 41–42, April 1999, pp. 4 ff.

57 *ibid.*

58 *OMI Classeur*, 1998, p. B-55.

59 A. Math and A. Spire, 'Sept millions d'emplois interdits', *op. cit.*, p. 5.

60 *INSEE, Population active immigrée en 1990 et 1982*, no. 577, Oct. 1997, p. 43. The present figures refer to aliens as a whole and not to immigrants, the latter comprising the French who have acquired French nationality.

61 See art. 1 and art. 25 of the Constitution.

62 'National sovereignty belongs to the people, which exert it through their representatives and via referendum (al. 1). All major French nationals of both sexes, enjoying their civil and political rights, are entitled to vote, under the conditions determined by the law (al. 4)'.

63 This approach, far from being contradicted by international agreements, comes close to the one according to which aliens, by retaining their nationality of origin, would hardly express the 'solidarity' or the 'reciprocity of rights and duties' which characterise nationality according to the International Court of Justice. See the *Nottebohm* case (*Liechtenstein v. Guatemala*), ICJ Reports, 6 April 1955.

64 'Subject to reciprocity and according to the methods provided for in the Treaty on European Union signed on 7 February 1992, the right to vote and to be elected for the municipal elections can be granted to the only citizens of the Union residing in France. These citizens cannot exercise the functions of

mayor or deputy mayor nor take part in the senators' designation. An organic law voted in the same terms by both assemblies determines the conditions of application of this article'.

65 Directive supplemented by Directive 96/30/EC of the Council at its meeting of 13 May 1993, following the last enlargement of the Community.

66 C. Grewe, 'La révision constitutionnelle en vue de la ratification du traité de Maastricht', *Revue française de droit constitutionnel*, no. 11, 1992, pp. 428–9.

67 *Conseil d'Etat*, 9 July 1997, *Association Ekin*.

68 D. Fassin, A. Morice and C. Quiminal (eds), *Les Lois de l'inhospitalité* (Paris: La Découverte, 1997) p. 265.

5
Citizenship Rights for Aliens in Germany

Kay Hailbronner

Germany as a de facto country of immigration: some facts

By the end of 1998 there were 7.32 million foreign nationals living in Germany, accounting for 9 per cent of the German Population.[1] The largest groups of foreigners living in Germany came from Turkey with 2.11 million (28.8%), from the Federal Republic of Yugoslavia with 719 474 (9.8%), from Italy with 612 048 (8.4%), from Greece with 363 514 (5%), from Poland with 283 604 (3.9%), from Croaţia with 208 909 (2.9%), from Bosnia with 190 119 (2.6%) and from Austria with 185 159 (2.5%). Only 25.1 per cent of all foreigners living in Germany were nationals from EU Member States.

A survey of the foreign population shows that most of the foreigners living in Germany have been living there for a long time. By the end of 1997, approximately 30 per cent of all foreigners had been in Germany for 20 years or more, 40 per cent for at least 15 years and almost 50 per cent for more than 10 years.[2] The trend towards immigration is even stronger when we look at the nationals of the former 'recruitment' states. Almost two-thirds of all Turks and Greeks, 71 per cent of Italians and 80 per cent of Spaniards lived in Germany for more than 10 years. 8.59 million (21.7%) of all foreigners were already born in Germany; among those foreigners of less than 18 years of age, 1.11 million (65.39%) were born in Germany.

All demographic surveys forecast a substantial increase of the foreign population in Germany during the next 30 years.[3] Assuming net migration of approximately 190 000 foreigners per year on the basis of the average level of net migration witnessed for the past 35 years, the number of foreigners living in Germany will increase until 2030 to 12.6 million, making up 16.9 per cent in contrast to 8.9 per cent at present.[4] In the event of a substantial increase of naturalisations from 60 000 per year to 120 000 per year, the share of foreigners would increase to 14.6 per cent (in absolute numbers 10.9 million).[5]

The figures show a basic dilemma of German immigration policy: an increasing number of children of migrant workers are born in Germany and grow up in Germany, receive their schooling and professional formation in Germany, will eventually work in Germany and have children of 'foreign' nationality in Germany, although their foreign nationality has frequently become only an emotional attachment to the home country of their parents, and is sometimes considered a mere reassurance, a sort of 'alternative' nationality. There is in principle no dispute about the need to integrate large parts of the foreign population into Germany by inducing them to become German citizens. All German governments have declared that there is a public interest in the naturalisation of foreigners living permanently in Germany.[6] There is no consensus, however, on the ways and conditions under which German citizenship should be acquired. It is particularly the issue of acquisition of German citizenship by birth on German territory which would introduce an element of *jus soli* into the German citizenship conception which has given rise to a heated controversy between the major political parties in recent years, so far blocking any reform of the German Citizenship Law.

An attempt to solve the fundamental dilemma arising from the exclusion of a substantial part of the population from political rights by granting limited voting rights on the local level to foreigners in some of the Länder has failed due to the decision of the Federal Constitutional Court declaring such an attempt to be unconstitutional.[7] The Federal Constitutional Court stated that the concept of democracy as laid down in the Basic Law does not permit a disassociation of political rights of the concept of nationality. Nationality therefore is the legal prerequisite for the acquisition of political rights legitimising the exercise of all power in the Federal Republic of Germany. The Federal Constitutional Court, however, stated that the only possible approach to solving the gap between the permanent population and democratic participation lies in changing the nationality law, for example, by facilitating the acquisition of German nationality to foreigners who are living permanently in Germany and thereby have become subject to Germany sovereignty in a manner comparable to German nationals.[8]

Basic principles of German law on nationality and citizenship

The core of the German Citizenship legislation is the 'Reichs- u. Staatsangehörigkeitsgesetz' of 1913. Although is has been amended repeatedly, particularly by laws in 1955 and 1956 aimed at introducing equal treatment of men and women and in 1990 and 1993 due to a facilitation of the naturalisation of immigrants, its basic principles remain effective. German citizenship is basically acquired by descent, by legitimisation, by adoption or by naturalisation. According to article 4, a child acquires German citizenship by descent from a German mother or a German father. In the absence of a marriage, descent by a German father requires a formal procedure to determine fatherhood. Acquisition by naturalisation for foreigners living in Germany requires certain minimum requirements, such as the absence of criminal prosecution, the possibility of making a living and adequate accommodation. If these minimum requirements are fulfilled, the authorities have a wide discretion whether to grant naturalisation. Administrative discretion is determined by binding administrative guidelines, which are enacted by the Federal Ministry of the Interior in accordance with the interior ministers of the Länder.[9] According to the Administrative Guidelines, the applicant must present sufficient evidence of having been a legal resident in Germany for at least 10 years. In addition, an attachment to Germany is required as well as a certain knowledge of the German language. A candidate for naturalisation must also not be opposed to the ideas inherent in the Basic Law of the Federal Republic of Germany. The requirement to give up a former nationality is not a binding legal requirement but is laid down in the Administrative Guidelines as a reflection of the general requirement of proof of attachment to the German living conditions and its legal and social order. Therefore, dual nationality has always been considered as being inconsistent with the concept of loyalty and attachment to Germany.

Based on the concept that naturalisation has to be considered an exception rather than a regular procedure terminating a process of immigration,[10] discretionary naturalisations based on article 8 of the Nationality Act of 1913 have remained a rather exceptional measure even for the substantial number of migrant workers who had been recruited in the early 1970s and who were originally thought of as temporary workers who would eventually return to their home countries. Only about 12 000–17 000 persons were naturalised each year from

1974 until 1989 in spite of an increasing number of persons having their permanent residence in Germany.

Spouses of German citizens had always been in a privileged position under the law of 1913. Originally a foreign woman marrying a German national acquired German citizenship automatically while foreign husbands had a possibility of being naturalised. With the equal treatment legislation of 1969, spouses of German nationals acquired a right of naturalisation provided that they were renouncing their previous nationality and that they fulfilled certain requirements of integration into the German living conditions.

In the context of a general debate about Germany's immigration policy and its factual change into an immigration country, the pressure increased in the late 1980s for a reform of the German citizenship legislation. There were numerous proposals ranging from simplifying the naturalisation process and increasing the acceptance of multiple nationality to introducing a *jus soli* 'principle' for third-generation foreigners born in Germany.[11] The Bundestag therefore decided in 1990 substantially to facilitate the acquisition of German citizenship for young foreigners of ages 16–23, provided that these renounced their previous citizenship, had lived permanently and lawfully in Germany for eight years, had attended a school in Germany for at least six years and had not been prosecuted for a criminal offence. In addition, the acquisition of German citizenship for the first generation of recruited migrant workers was also facilitated substantially by giving a right to acquisition of German citizenship, provided that certain requirements were met:

- renouncement of previous nationality;
- absence of criminal conviction;
- ability to earn a living.

By a further amendment in December 1993, these rules were changed by establishing an individual right entitling every foreigner fulfilling certain requirements to demand naturalisation.[12] Although these provisions of the Aliens Act granting an entitlement to German citizenship still provided for a renouncement of the previous nationality, a number of exceptions were made which led in fact to a steadily increasing number of naturalisations with dual nationality. Exceptions were granted for instance if a foreigner could not renounce his previous nationality or only under particularly difficult conditions, particularly if the original home country required military service before giving up nationality.

The recent figures show a substantial increase of naturalisations based on these provisions.[13] The general number of naturalisations in 1995 increased to 313 606, compared to 34 913 in 1985.[14] However, it must be taken into account that this figure includes a substantial number of naturalisations of foreigners who can be considered 'Germans' who acquire German citizenship very easily on the basis of a special provision giving them a constitutional right to obtain German citizenship as a refugee or expellee of German ethnic origin or as their spouse or descendant, provided that they had been admitted to the territory of the German Reich within the frontiers of 31 December 1937. Nevertheless, in 1990, naturalisations based upon the provisions of the Aliens Act for the immigrant population increased at a rate of about 35 per cent, and in 1994 even at a rate of 54 per cent, in 1995 at a rate of 23 per cent and in 1996, by 20 per cent compared to the preceding year.[15] With 1.18 per cent of the total foreign population, the rate of naturalisations in 1996 was still relatively small compared to other western European states, although it had quadrupled since 1986. The share of women was substantially higher with 1.37 per cent than the share of men with 1.03 per cent.

Of a total of 82 913 naturalisations based primarily upon the provisions of the Aliens Act (§§ 85, 86), 39 111 (47.2%) were Turkish nationals, 4,010 (4.8%) were Moroccans, 3,119 (3.8%) were Vietnamese, 1,989 (2.4%) were nationals from the Federal Republic of Yugoslavia, 1,942 (2.3%) from Poland, 1,789 (2.2%) Croatians, 1,677 (2.0%) Tunisians, 1,547 (1.9%) from Romania, 1,454 (1.9%) Afghans, 1,382 (1.7%) Eritreans, 1,362 (1.6%) from Sri Lanka, 1,176 (1.4%) Palestinians, 1,134 (1.4%) from Lebanon, and 1,118 (1.3%) Italians.

There are very different naturalisation rates for the different nationalities. The Tunisians with 6.60 per cent, the Moroccans with 4.78 per cent and the Vietnamese with 3.55 per cent have a relatively high naturalisation rate. Afghans (2.19%), Turks (1.86%) and Hungarians (1.29%) are in a middle group. Very low rates of naturalisation were registered with Croatians (0.87%), Iranians (0.81%), Yugoslavs (0.28%), Italians (0.18%) and Greeks (0.10%). One of the reasons for these differences is obviously that EU citizens do not have a substantial interest in acquiring German citizenship as a result of Union citizenship. Another reason for lower quota may be that certain states do not easily release their citizens from their original nationality. This implies usually a very difficult process for acquisition of German nationality while maintaining a previous nationality.

Statistics also show that there is a substantial number of dual nationals living in Germany which has steadily increased as a result of manifold exceptions made under the new provisions of the Alien Act.

Of a total of 79 442 naturalisations (excluding Hamburg) in 1997 based upon the provisions of the Alien Act, 17 423 (21.3%) have been granted under acceptance of dual nationality. Dual nationality has particularly been accepted in the case of Iranians (90.1%), Greeks (87.2%), Moroccans (89%), Eritreans (88.5%), Lebanese (83.3%), Afghans (82.7%), Tunisians (82.3%), Syrians (76.0%), Bosnians (74.8%) and Yugoslavians (63%). Frequently, dual nationality is accepted in such cases in which a release of the original nationality is dependent upon conditions which are difficult to fulfil. In spite of a substantial facilitation of Turkish laws on property, military service and heritage, dual nationality has been granted in the case of Turks in 8.45 per cent of all cases. These figures, however, only partly reflect the reality of dual nationality for two reasons. One of the reasons is that the official statistics on acceptance of dual nationality are also registering those naturalisations in which dual nationality has only been accepted temporarily, which means that naturalisation has been granted under the condition that the person deposit a formal application for renouncement of a previous citizenship. On the other hand, the true number of dual nationals in the case of the Turkish population may be even higher, since in many cases the Turkish citizenship was only formally renounced and with the co-operation of the Turkish authorities readily reacquired after naturalisation. This was made possible by a provision in the German nationality law which provided for a loss of German citizenship as a result of the acquisition of a foreign nationality only if the German national had a permanent residence abroad, wherefore, Turks living in Germany would not lose their German citizenship if they reacquired their Turkish nationality immediately after formally renouncing their Turkish nationality. It was an open secret that Turkish authorities encouraged the re-acquisition of Turkish nationality, since the Turkish concept of nationality was very much based on the idea that persons of Turkish origin should remain attached to the Turkish state by the Turkish citizenship. It seems that only recently this practice has been changed under pressure from the German authorities to prevent an 'abuse' of German legislation. There were, however, estimates that a high percentage of Turkish nationals who have been naturalised were in fact dual nationals. Therefore, the debate about dual nationality as the major obstacle for a reform of the German citizenship law may at least partly be considered as obsolete and missing reality.

Proposals for reform

A quasi nationality for immigrant children

According to a coalition agreement between the Christian Democratic Party and the Liberal Party of 1994, it was envisaged to introduce a special nationality for children (*Kinderstaatsangehörigkeit*[16]) of the third generation which were born in Germany. In order to be eligible for this special nationality, which was intended to insure equal treatment between German nationals (German identity card), at least one of the child's parents would have to be born in Germany and both would have to reside lawfully in Germany during the 10 years preceding the child's birth. Additionally, both parents would have to be entitled to an unlimited residence permit. The 'quasi nationality' for children would require an application by parents before the child's twelfth birthday. With the child's eighteenth birthday, it would acquire full German nationality unless its previous nationality was not given up. It is very doubtful whether the proposal is practicable and whether a 'quasi nationality' would be acceptable in international relations and what effect such a limited nationality may have for instance with regard to the application of international treaties relating to visa and travel documents.[17]

Acquisition of German nationality by *jus soli*

Based on a proposal of the Bundesrat, the upper house of Parliament,[18] German nationality would be acquired automatically by a child whose foreign parents were born in Germany and who, at the time of the child's birth, surrender of a residence permit. Children whose parents surrender an unlimited residence permit and have been living in Germany for five years are to be given a right to naturalisation. In both cases, the acquisition of German citizenship would be independent of the renouncement of a previous nationality.

The proposals of the Social Democratic Party and the Green Party are going in the same direction. The Social Democratic Party has suggested to supplement the principle whereby German nationality is acquired by descent by the principle of territoriality (*jus soli*). Children of foreign parents therefore ought to automatically acquire German citizenship as a result of birth on German territory, provided that at least one parent has been born in Germany and has obtained its permanent residence in Germany. Dual nationality is not to be prevented in such cases. Additionally, for permanent residents, individual rights to the acquisition of German nationality are to be created independently of a renouncement of their previous nationality. The draft suggests a facilitation of naturalisation for the following groups of citizens:

- foreigners with a permanent residence permit after eight years of residence;
- foreigners belonging to the so-called 'second generation' of aliens who have grown up in Germany;
- spouses of Germans after three years of lawful residence, provided that they have been married for at least two years.

Additionally, the proposal provides for a facilitation of discretionary naturalisation, which should be enabled after a residence of five years and only be dependent upon the capacity to earn a living, absence of a criminal conviction for a serious offence and absence of a reason for expulsion for endangering public safety or violent behaviour.[19]

A 'compromise' has been worked out by the Liberal Party, which provides for the acquisition of a full nationality by birth on German territory if both parents apply and at least one of the parents does have a right of residence in Germany. The proposal of the Liberal Party suggests a loss of dual nationality by obliging the naturalised person to opt for one nationality once that person has reached the age of 21. If the previous (dual) nationality is not given up, the German nationality would be lost.[20]

The proposal of the Green Party[21] would go even further in the direction of an automatic acquisition of German citizenship on the basis of *jus soli*. The Green Party suggested that children of foreign parents were to acquire German citizenship automatically by birth on German territory if one parent is living in Germany with a permanent residence permit. Neither the application of a parent, nor the renouncement of a previous citizenship would be required for the acquisition German citizenship.

None of these proposals have received the necessary majority in the German Bundestag.[22] Although a number of deputies from the Christian Democratic Party and the Liberal Party were in favour of some of the proposals submitted by the draft law in the Bundesrat, no majority was achieved since the time and the circumstances of submitting the draft law were clearly primarily directed towards splitting the coalition between the Christian Democratic Party and the Liberal Party.

Pros and cons

Although there is a consensus on the need to integrate second and third generation foreigners by facilitating the acquisition of German citizenship, opinion is deeply divided on the issue as to whether this should be achieved by introducing elements of *jus soli* and/or accepting dual nationality. Difficulties arise with regard to constitutional law as well as international treaties, such asthe Council of Europe Convention on the reduction of dual nationality of 1963.

Objections on the grounds of constitutional law are particularly voiced against the proposal of a temporary dual nationality which is to be terminated automatically by reaching the age limit of 18. Article 16 (1) provides that nobody may be deprived of their German citizenship. Loss of citizenship may only occur pursuant to the law, and against the will of those affected only if they do not thereby become stateless. This provision, which is basically a reaction against the Nazi legislation depriving Jews of their German citizenship, may be an obstacle to the technique of granting German citizenship which will be withdrawn if the dual national does not give up its previous nationality at the age of 18. Whether an automatic loss of German citizenship as a result of maintaining the nationality of another state amounts to 'deprivation' in the sense of the Basic Law, is very much disputed.[23] Be that as it may, a number of practical problems will have to be solved in implementing a technique of temporary dual nationality. It will be necessary to introduce exceptions to the obligation to give up another nationality based on those exceptions that are already admissible under existing legislation. This means that in every individual case an examination will have to take place as to whether a second or third generation foreigner is entitled to maintain dual nationality. A number of protracted and difficult legal proceedings can be easily foreseen.

A major debate has been focused upon the issue of dual nationality. It has been argued that dual nationality is opposed to the concept of integration and a certain loyalty towards the state. In addition, problems relating to diplomatic protection and the application of international treaties may arise in cases of dual nationality. Finally, increased acceptance of dual nationality may result in unjustified privileges compared to individuals with only one nationality.[24] The principle of avoidance of dual nationality has repeatedly been confirmed by the Constitutional Court arguing that dual nationality may lead to loyalty conflicts and uncertainty concerning diplomatic protection. The court is frequently quoted for a doctrine laid down in its jurisprudence:

> It is accurate to say that dual or multiple nationality is regarded, both domestically and internationally, as an evil that should be avoided or eliminated if possible in the interest of states as well as in the interest of the affected citizen: most international conventions in the field of nationality concern this subject or at least attempt to ameliorate the difficulties that arise out of the possession of several nationalities.... States seek to achieve exclusivity of their respective nationalities in order to set clear boundaries for their sovereignty over persons...; they want to be secure in the duty of loyalty of their citizens – which extends if necessary as far as risking one's life – and do not want to see it endangered by possible conflicts with a loyalty owed to a foreign state. Accordingly, the duty of military service provides the principal reason for avoiding dual nationality. Conflicts between the two countries of nationality can also arise from such inconsistent duties and from competitive assertions of diplomatic protection, agencies and courts of third states face the problem of deciding which of the two nationalities they should give priority.[25]

It seems doubtful, however, whether the traditional arguments voiced against dual nationality do indeed outweigh the need to integrate second and third generation foreigners into the political system of the Federal Republic. As a more practical argument one may point to the steadily increasing numbers of dual nationals who are in fact living in Germany and so far have not created substantial problems in the application of international treaties or in the exercise of diplomatic protection. There is no precise account of the exact number of dual nationals. Originally dual nationality had to be registered. This was given up some years ago. Therefore nobody knows exactly the number of dual nationals in Germany. One can assume, however, that with the heavily increasing numbers of mixed marriages the number of dual nationals has grown substantially, particularly since children as a rule obtain by law the nationality of those parents.

As to the argument of loyalty, one has to be aware that the concept of the German State has undergone substantial changes with the immigration of a large foreign population and the process of European integration. Germany, having become a de facto immigration country, cannot ignore that part of its population consists of migrant workers and their children. The basis of German nationality cannot, therefore, be seen any longer in the attachment to the idea of a nation with identical cultural identities and backgrounds, primarily transferred by descent. One may note, however, that the common observation that

German nationality law is based upon blood is an incorrect interpretation of existing legislation. That German nationality is in fact not exclusively based on 'blood' can easily be shown by the naturalisation provisions which I mentioned earlier.

A different concept of German nationhood does not, however, necessarily mean that elements of *jus soli* should be introduced or that requirements of integration into the German society should be abandoned. There is a legitimate concern that foreigners joining the 'Club' fulfill those requirements, which are necessary to achieve an integration into the social, political and economic order. Therefore it may reasonably be asked to prove knowledge of the German language and absence of criminal convictions in order to acquire German citizenship. Under these conditions, however, dual nationality does not appear as a serious obstacle to naturalisation.

Still, dual or multiple nationality may raise the problem of transferring nationality to descendants who may have no or almost no tie to Germany. With the reform of German Citizenship Law, the issue of loss of German citizenship by taking permanent residence abroad will have to be solved. There should be an automatic loss of German citizenship for dual nationals if permanent residence is established abroad. That will, however, create constitutional problems in relation to the provision of article 16 (1) on deprivation of German citizenship.

The debate concerning the introduction of *jus soli* elements is even more controversial. Proponents of the introduction of *jus soli* argue that problems relating to unequal treatment and growing discrimination may only be solved by an automatic acquisition of German nationality for third generation foreigners born on German territory. On the other hand, it may be argued that acquisition of German citizenship on the basis of *jus soli* has always been strange to the German nation concept, which has never considered itself as a country of immigration. The fact that Germany has become a de facto country of immigration does not necessarily argue in favour of changing its basic rules as to who should be admitted to German citizenship. From a practical point of view, the disadvantage of *jus soli* acquisition of German citizenship is that it excludes any examination whether there is a sufficient prospect of integration. One may object that the requirement of being born in Germany in connection with residence rights of parents should be sufficient to indicate integration. Recent experience, however, shows that this assumption is not always true. An increasing number of foreigners are deliberately rejecting any attempt to be integrated in German society. It is likely that children under these circumstances will not be integrated easily.

Recent developments and the new law dated 15 July 1999

A renewal of the discussion was provoked when the coalition agreement of the Social Democrats and Buendnis 90/Die Gruenen of 20 October 1998 was presented to the public. According to the intentions of the coalition, German citizenship should be conferred at birth to children born on German territory if one foreign parent was already born on German territory or if he or she entered Germany before the age of fourteen, furthermore providing that, in both cases, he or she currently is in the possession of a residence permit (*Aufenthaltserlaubnis*). Other amendments intended by the coalition were a facilitation of the naturalisation process when applying on the grounds of an entitlement to German citizenship. It was proposed that naturalisation be allowed if the foreigner was able to sustain himself and his dependants, if there were no convictions for criminal offences and, finally, if no grounds for expulsion or deportation had arisen; the residence requirement was to be reduced from 15 to 8 years. Other proposed amendments related to a right to naturalisation for minor children and a reduction of the residence requirement to three years for spouses of German nationals. Double or multiple nationality[26] was to be accepted in all those cases.

Those intentions, however, have not been fully realised, although the first draft presented by the Ministry of the Interior provided for a broad acceptance of double and multiple nationality and the introduction of the *jus soli* principle.[27] Due to changing majorities in Parliament, a new proposal was submitted by the Social Democrats, Buendnis 90/Die Gruenen and the Liberal Party (FDP) comprising not only the introduction of the *jus soli* principle, but also the insertion of the 'optional model'. Both chambers went on to adopt this draft with minor changes[28] in May 1999.[29] The new law on the reform of the German citizenship law of 15 July 1999[30] will enter into force on 1 January 2000. In addition, administrative guidelines for its application are to be adopted.

One of the major changes is the introduction of the *jus soli* principle in article 4 of the German Nationality Law, meaning that a child of foreign parents acquires German citizenship under the condition that one parent has legally had his habitual residence in Germany for eight years and that he or she is in the possession of a residence permit, an '*Aufenthaltsberechtigung*' or an unlimited '*Aufenthaltserlaubnis*' for three years; the model of the double *jus soli* in force in some other European states therefore has not been introduced. Foreign children legally residing in Germany are entitled to naturalisation upon their eighth birthday if the above-mentioned conditions were fulfilled at the time of birth (§ 40b StAngG). Due to the fact that children usually acquire the nationality of their parents by descent, the introduction of the *jus soli* principle will entail at least double if not multiple nationalities for foreign children born in Germany. Therefore, § 29 StAngG introduces the highly disputed optional model and the duty to decide on reaching the age of 18 which nationality to keep and which to renounce. If the young adult declares that he intends to keep his foreign nationality or if he does not declare anything on reaching 18, he will suffer the loss of his German citizenship. If, on the other hand, he declares an intention to keep his German citizenship, the young adult is obliged to prove the loss or renouncement of the foreign nationality (§ 29 (2) (2) StAngG) unless German authorities have formally approved that he may keep his foreign nationality. According to article 29 (4) StAnG, this permission to retain the former nationality (*Beibehaltungsgenehmigung*) is to be issued if renunciation of the foreign nationality is either impossible or unreasonable or if – in the case of naturalisation – multiple nationality would be accepted according to article 87 AuslG.

Besides the introduction of the *jus soli* principle, the naturalisation process has been facilitated. The foreigner now is entitled to naturalisation after a residence of eight instead of fifteen years on condition that he declares himself bound to the free and democratic order of the constitution (*'freiheitliche und demokratische Grundordnung'*), that he is in the possession of a residence permit (*'Aufenthaltserlaubnis'* or *'Aufenthaltsberechtigung'*), that he is capable of earning a living without any recourse to public assistance or unemployment benefits (except in those cases in which the dependence on those benefits is not attributable to the applicant's fault or negligence), that there is no criminal conviction and, finally, that loss or renunciation of the previous nationality take place. Double nationality is accepted in more cases, e.g., if the applicants are elderly persons and double nationality is the only obstacle to naturalisation, if the dismissal of the previous nationality is related to disproportionate difficulties, and if a denial of the application for naturalisation would constitute a particular hardship (§ 87 (1) no. 4 AuslG); moreover, double nationality is accepted in cases in which the renuncation of the previous nationality entails – in addition to the loss of civil rights – economic or financial disadvantages (no. 5), or, in the case of EU-citizens, provided that reciprocity exists (§ 87 (2) AuslG). According to the new § 86 AuslG, naturalisation is not permissible if the foreigner does not demonstrate sufficient knowledge of the German language, or if there is actual evidence that the applicant pursues or supports activities contrary to the constitution.

Due to the fact that the acquisition of German citizenship has been facilitated, some amendments relate to the loss of German citizenship and the limitation of acquisition by descent. On the one hand, acquisition of German citizenship abroad is excluded if the German parent who has his habitual residence abroad was born abroad after 31 December 1999, except in those cases in which statelessness would be the consequence. Despite this provision, the acquisition of German citizenship remains possible if both parents are in the possession of German citizenship or if the one parent who has German citizenship notifies the competent diplomatic representation at the time of birth. According to the amended § 25 StAngG, the loss of German citizenship, which did not occur automatically at naturalisation if the person continued to have a vital interest in Germany, now should also apply in those cases in which the applicant continues to live in Germany when acquiring another nationality.

After years of discussion, new provisions concerning the German citizenship law finally have been adopted. Nevertheless, some issues concerning legal aspects are still under discussion.[31] Other aspects relate to the implementation of the new provisions, especially the handling of the duty to opt for or against the German nationality at the age of eighteen and the fact that, besides some practical problems, this might be the starting point for a broad acceptance of double and multiple nationality in those cases.[32] Thus, in the future, further reforms, particularly relating to double nationality, the acquisition of German citizenship when returning to the country of origin, or the assertion of minority rights, have to be discussed. It should be noted, however, that changes in citizenship law might influence the integration of foreigners, but that they are not by themselves a means of integration. The main objective should be the active participation of the foreign part of the population in Germany in actual political life.

Notes

1 See *Beauftragte der Bundesregierung für Ausländerfragen, Daten und Fakten zur Ausländersituation*, 18th edn, June 1999, p. 7 (Government Commissioner for Issues Concerning Foreign Nationals in Germany).

2 See *Daten und Fakten*, at fn. 1, at p. 9; for the facts see also *Bericht der Beauftragten der Bundesregierung für Ausländerfragen über die Lage der Ausländer in der Bundesrepublik Deutschland*, June 1999, p. 19 *et seq*; *Migration und Integration in Zahlen, ein Handbuch*, November 1997.

3 See for instance Münz and Ulrich, *Das zukünftige Wachstum der ausländischen Bevölkerung in Deutschland, demographische Prognosen bis 2030*, Berlin, November 1997.
4 Münz and Ulrich, at p. 57.
5 Münz and Ulrich, at p. 557.
6 See e.g. the statement of the Federal Government in Official Records of the Bundestag, *Bundestagsdrucksache* 10/2071.
7 See Decisions of the Federal Constitutional Court Vols 83, 37, 51.
8 *ibid.*, Vols 83, 51
9 *Einbürgerungsrichtlinien vom 1.7.77*, see Hailbronner and Renner, *Staatsangehörigkeitsrecht*, 2nd edn 1998, p. 863 et seq.
10 No. 2.3. of the Guidlines: 'The Federal Republic of Germany is not an immigration country; it does not seek to increase the number of German citizens through naturalisation.'; correspondingly Federal Administrative Court, BVerwG, Buchholz 130 § 8 RustAG No. 10, 14, 16.
11 On the topic of the reform debate see: Apel, *Zeitschrift für Ausländerrecht* 1992, 99; Blumenwitz, *Zeitschrift für Auländerrecht* 1993, 151; Hobe, *Juristenzeitung* 1994, 191; Jessurun d'Oliveira, *Zeitschrift für Auländerrecht* 1990, 114; John, *Zeitschrift für Ausländerrecht* 1991, 85; Löwer, *Zeitschrift für Ausländerrecht* 1993, 156; Lübbe-Wolff, *Juristische Ausbildung* 1996, 57; v. Mangoldt, *Das Standesamt* 1994, 33; Marx, *Zeitschrift für Ausländerrecht* 1997, 67; Meireis, *Das Standesamt*, 1994, 241; v. Münch, *Neue Juristische Wochenschrift* 1994, 1199; Predeick, *Deutsches Verwaltungsblatt* 1991, 623; Renner, *Zeitschrift für Familienrecht* 1994, 865; Schrötter and Möhlig, *Zeitschrift für Rechtspolitik* 1995, 374.
12 See also Hailbronner, *Ausländerrecht, Kommentar*, March 1999 article T 5, at number 1 ff.
13 See Table 11.3 of this book (p. 231).
14 In 1997, however, the number decreased to 278 662 naturalisations.
15 See *Daten und Fakten zur Ausländersituation*, June 1999, at p. 11; in 1997, however, the number of naturalisations decreased by about 4 per cent.
16 *Neue Juristische Wochenschrift* 1995, XVII, XVIII; as to the coalition agreement see Eylmann, *Zeitschrift für Rechtspolitik* 1995, 161, 163; Leutheuser-Schnarrenberger, *Zeitschrift für Rechtspolitik* 1995, 81, 85.

On the issue of the '*Kinderstaatszugehörigkeit*' refer also to Ziemske, *Zeitschrift für Rechtspolitik* 1995, 380, and the parliament's *Plenarprotocol* 13/18, p. 1217
17 Among others, refer to *efms* (*Europäisches Forum für Migrationsstudien*), *Staatsangehörigkeit und Einbürgerung*, p. 11, 19; Lübbe-Wolff, *Juristische Ausbildung* 1996, 57, 69; Ziemske, *Zeitschrift für Rechtspolitik* 1995, 380, 381.
18 *Bundestagsdrucksache* 13/8157.
19 See *Bundestagsdrucksache* 13/259.
20 On the optional model see the report by the German Parliament's '*Wissenschaftliche Dienste*' from June 11, 1996, WF III-113/96.
21 *Bundestagsdrucksache* 13/3657 – *Mindestkriterien für eine Reform des Staatsangehörigkeitsrechts* and *Bundestagsdrucksache* 13/7677 *für eine sofortige Reform des Staatsangehörigkeitsrechts*
22 See *Bundestagsdrucksache* 13/130 of 4 March 1998
23 Cf. Lübbe-Wolff, *Juristische Ausbildung* 1996, 57, 59; Ziemske, *Die deutsche Staatsangehörigkeit nach dem Grundgesetz*, 1995, 273; Decision of the Federal

Constitutional Court of 22 June 1990, *Neue Juristische Wochenschrift* 1990, 2193; Kokott, in Sachs (ed.), *Grundgesetz, Kommentar*, Article 16, No. 11; Pieroth, in Jarrass and Pieroth, *Grundgesetz, Kommentar*, 3rd edn, Article 16, No. 3.

24 Dealing with this issue: Blumenwitz, *Zeitschrift für Ausländerrecht* 1993, 151; Löwer, *Zeitschrift für Ausländerrecht* 1993, 156, 158; v. Mangoldt, *Juristenzeitung* 1993, 965; Marx, *Zeitschrift für Ausländerrecht* 1997, 67, 73; Badura, v. Mangoldt and Löwer in the minutes to the experts' hearing in the inner commitee of the German Parliament (*'Protokoll der Sachverständigenanhörung im Innenausschuß des Deutschen Bundestages'*) of 27 Sept. 1993, 12th term, Protokoll No. 75, pp. 256, 43 and 164 respectively; an overview is offered by the *'Wissenschaftliche Dienste des Deutschen Bundestages'* in a report from 11 June 1996, WF II/113/96, p. 14.

25 *Antwort der Bundesregierung auf eine Kleine Anfrage der Abgeordneten Ulla Jelpke und der Gruppe PDS/Linke Liste*, BT-Drs. 12/2035 (1992).

26 Cf. as to a discussion of double and multiple nationality: Hailbronner, *Zeitschrift für Ausländerrecht und Ausländerpolitik* 1999, p. 51 et seq.

27 Cf. *Zeitschrift für Ausländerrecht und Ausländerpolitik* 1999, pp. 50, 95, and Barwig *et al.* (eds), *Neue Regierung – neue Ausländerpolitik?*, Baden-Baden, 1999.

28 *Bundestagsdrucksache* 14/867.

29 Plenary protocol 14/40, p. 3415 *et seq.*; *Bundesratsdrucksache* 296/99. Cf. as to the consultation of the Committee on the Interior (*Innenausschuss*) protocol no. 12 dated 13 March 1999.

30 *Bundesgesetzblatt I*, p. 1618. Cf. as to the amendments: Hailbronner, *Neue Zeitschrift für Verwaltungsrecht* (forthcoming); Huber and Butzke, *Neue Juristische Wochenschrift* 1999, p. 2769 *et seq.*

31 Cf. as to the notion of 'nationality' and constitutional aspects: Hailbronner, *Neue Zeitschrift für Verwaltungsrecht* (forthcoming) discussing expecially the views of Scholz and Uhle, *Neue Juristische Wochenschrift* 1999, p. 1510, at 1511; Ziemske, *Die deutsche Staatsangehörigkeit nach dem Grundgesetz*, 1995, p. 221, at p. 230 *et seq.*; cf. as to the optional model and the prohibition of any deprivation of citizenship in Article 16 (1) of the Constitution as well as the principle of equal treatment in Article 3 (1) of the Constitution: Hailbronner, *Neue Zeitschrift für Verwaltungsrecht* (forthcoming).

32 Cf. to these political aspects: Hailbronner, *Neue Zeitschrift für Verwaltungsrecht* (forthcoming).

6

Patterns of Privilege: Citizenship Rights in Britain*

Zig Layton-Henry

Citizenship and nationality

In the English non-Republican tradition citizenship concerns the various privileges, duties and obligations that define one's place as a fully participant member of society. These privileges include voting rights, the ability to stand for election, eligibility for appointment to public office and entitlements to social welfare benefits and public housing. Obligations include the duty of allegiance to the Crown, perhaps better defined as loyalty to the state, though some would still dispute this,[1] obeying the laws, paying taxes and performing military service, especially in times of national emergency. In the Common Law tradition the notion of citizens' rights is absent. Dummett and Nicol argue that the *Calvin* case in 1606 reduced allegiance to passive obedience and asserted that this obedience was due both from subjects and resident aliens. Thus no rights arose from subject status but permanent obligations did.[2] The view that voting rights are a civic privilege which could be removed by Parliament can be seen in the Labour Government's Green Paper of 1977 where they are openly listed under civic privileges.[3] Even such an influential constitutional document as the Declaration of Rights, 1688, which limited the powers of the Monarch and established the supremacy of Parliament, was a Parliamentary Statute and was not entrenched, for example, in a written constitution. It could therefore be amended by Parliament. While it seems inconceivable that Parliament would dare to remove such civic privileges as voting rights, major constitutional changes, such as establishing a devolved parliament in Scotland or changing the electoral systems for national and European elections, only need a simple majority in Parliament. The use of referenda to legitimate major constitutional changes is purely a matter of Parliamentary discretion.

Nationality refers to one's international identity in belonging to a specific state. This status is shown on one's passport. Dual nationality indicates that one belongs to two states and if, for example, one was in difficulty abroad, one would have a choice as to which country from which to seek diplomatic assistance. However, if present in one of these states, then the other would have no jurisdiction as every state has sole jurisdiction over its citizens in its own territory. States have historically been opposed to dual nationality as they prefer the nation-state ideal whereby the nation and the state are identical and every citizen belongs to one nation and one state. In other words states demand the absolute loyalty of all their citizens. Citizenship is thus largely a domestic matter which involves rights and duties under domestic law within a given state. Nationality is more an international matter referring to a person's position in international situations.[4]

British subject status

Historically in Britain the key concept is neither citizenship nor nationality but British subject status. The concept of British citizenship is very recent and was only created by the Nationality Act 1981 in which the British government attempted to end the disjuncture that had occurred between the imperial ideal of 'civis Britannicus sum', which allowed British subjects throughout the world the right to enter and reside in Britain with full civic, social and political rights; and the restrictions imposed on the entry and settlement of Commonwealth and Colonial British subjects by the post-war immigration laws.

Under the English Common Law people born on the King's territory, or, as it is often put more grandly, in the Crown's dominions,[5] were English subjects who owed allegiance to the King. After 1603 and the Union of the Crowns of England and Scotland, the King had both English and Scottish subjects which the Calvin case decided owed him their personal allegiance.[6] After the Act of Union in 1707 when England and Scotland became united under one Parliament, we can begin to talk of British subjects. As Britain acquired an Empire in the eighteenth and nineteenth centuries, the Crown's dominions extended to all the territories in the British Empire and also to British ships. The number of British subjects thus rose dramatically.

Acquisition of British subject status

The acquisition of British subject status was predominantly by *jus soli*, that is by birth within the Crown's dominions. The only exceptions to this were the children of foreign ambassadors and children born to members of invading armed forces. An element of *jus sanguinis* also existed so that children of British ambassadors born abroad and children of the Monarch, wherever they were born, owed allegiance to the Crown and so were British subjects. A statute of 1350 – De Natis Ultra Mare – stated that children born outside the King's allegiance 'whose fathers and mothers at the time of their birth be and shall be at the faith and lineage of the King and shall enjoy the same benefits and advantages as those born within the Sovereign's allegiance'. This statute thus allowed *jus sanguinis* to the first generation of British subjects born abroad. This was confirmed by a statute of 1708 – An Act for Naturalising Foreign Protestants – which stated that 'the children of all natural born subjects born out of the lineage of Her Majesty, her heirs and successors, shall be deemed...to be natural born subjects of this Kingdom to all intents, constructions and purposes'.[7] An Act of 1730 specified that it was the father who had to be a natural born subject and that British subject status could be transmitted to only one generation born abroad. This was extended to two generations in 1772.[8]

Before 1708 the acquisition of British subject status by naturalisation required an Act of Parliament and so was very rare. In 1708, to encourage Protestant immigration to add to the wealth and population of the country, an Act for Naturalising Foreign Protestants was passed. The Act required the taking of an oath of allegiance and receiving the sacrament. It was very successful and a substantial amount of immigration took place. This made the Act unpopular and it was repealed after only three years in 1711. The taking of the sacrament was required even under the Act of Parliament procedure, and this barred Catholics and Jews from naturalising. This requirement was repealed in 1826. In 1844 a Naturalisation Act was passed giving the Secretary of State power to naturalise applicants wishing to settle in Britain. They had to take an oath of allegiance and pay an appropriate fee. Wives of natural born subjects or naturalised persons were considered to be naturalised also. They thus gained British subject status automatically. Women married to aliens kept their British subject status under the 1844 Act but lost it under a new Naturalisation Act of 1870. The aim of the 1870 Act was to minimize the incidence of dual nationality and to ensure that wives and minors took the nationality of their husbands and fathers. The Act laid down a five years residence qualification and did not require renunciation of one's existing nationality.[9]

A major cause of the acquisition or loss of British subject status has been changes in the political status of territories. People living in territories conquered and annexed by Britain became British subjects and territories given up or transferred to others were no longer part of the King's dominions and people born in these territories would not be British subjects. The independence of the United States caused problems because at that time British subject status could not be given up by British born subjects. The Bancroft Convention in 1870 confirmed that Britain would recognise existing and future American naturalisations and this was extended to other states by the Naturalisation Act of 1870. The people in states that were British Protectorates were British Protected Persons (BPPs) and not British subjects, although in practice they were often treated in the same way. However BPPs did not have British subject status and so could not pass it on to their children. Independence granted to British colonies in the post-war period has resulted in the loss of British subject status to people in territories like Burma which refused to join the Commonwealth.

The common code

By the end of the nineteenth century British nationality law was very confused. The self-governing Dominions had their own immigration controls and naturalisation procedures. It was felt that it would be sensible to have a common nationality code throughout the Empire and this was agreed at the Imperial Conference of 1907. However, the self-governing Dominions wished to continue to exercise local jurisdiction. This is clear in the statement by the Colonial Secretary, Winston Churchill, to the conference when he said 'Imperial nationality should be worldwide and uniform, each Dominion being free to grant local nationality in such terms as its legislature should think fit.'[10] On the one hand consistency required that nationality provisions and procedures for naturalisation should be uniform throughout the Empire but practical politics dictated that each self-governing Dominion should be free to frame its own nationality legislation. This contradictory position did not deter the conference and a Bill was drawn up and passed as the British Nationality and Status of Aliens Act 1914.

This Act retained *jus soli* as the basis of British subject status throughout the Empire with the exceptions of children of diplomats and enemy aliens. The acquisition of British subject status by descent was restricted to one generation though this was amended in 1922 to allow British subjects by descent to register their children, born abroad, at a British Consulate. No generation limit was specified.[11] The privileges of British subject status could be exercised in the United Kingdom but were subject to local legislation in each Dominion or Colony. The main advantage accruing to all British subjects was the unrestricted right of entry to the United Kingdom but Britain was the only part of the Empire that allowed such a right. The attempt to encourage a common citizenship code was thus unsuccessful and in practice the Dominions became more and more assertive of their independence. A crisis arose in 1921 when Ireland gained her independence and the Irish Free State was established. Ireland reluctantly remained a member of the Commonwealth so Irish citizens remained British subjects. However, Irish representatives stopped attending Commonwealth meetings in 1937 and Ireland adopted a position of neutrality in World War II. Ireland became a Republic in 1949 and formally left the Commonwealth. The British Government responded by passing the Ireland Act (1949) which gave Irish citizens a unique status. They were treated as if they were Commonwealth citizens and not as aliens so they continued to enjoy all political, civic and social privileges if resident in Britain. People born in Ireland before 1 January 1949 could make a declaration to the Home Office that they had not ceased to be a British subject and so were entitled to a British passport. As both Britain and Ireland allow dual nationality, there are no disadvantages from holding the two passports and many Irish people have found it convenient to do so.[12]

In 1931 the Statute of Westminster recognised the independence of the Dominions by legislating that the British parliament should not pass legislation for a Dominion except at their request and with the consent of its government. Dominions were also able to repeal or amend British legislation affecting their jurisdiction. In 1937 all pretence of a common citizenship code was dropped and the Imperial (Commonwealth) conference confirmed that:

> a Dominion government was free to decide who was a member of its community either by legislative definition of its nationals or citizens, or otherwise, decide to regard as belonging to it for the purpose of civil and political rights, immigration, deportation, diplomatic representation or in the exercise of extraterritorial jurisdiction.[13]

The British Nationality Act 1948

The onset of the Second World War delayed any changes in British subject status but immediately afterwards the Canadian Government decided to introduce its own citizenship legislation. The Canadian Citizenship Act 1946 made Canadian citizenship the primary allegiance of Canadians and reduced British subject status to a secondary role. Moreover to accede to the sensitivities of French Canadians the new

Act stated that the term Commonwealth citizen would be an alternative name for British subject.[14]

The British Government realised that the Canadian Citizenship Act would be quickly followed by similar legislation in other Commonwealth countries, especially those like India and Pakistan, which were about to gain their independence, and which would wish to assert this by passing their own citizenship laws. The British Government decided to recognise this new reality and, after consultations with Commonwealth countries, proposed to restrict British nationality to recognise two types of British subject: firstly citizens of the UK and Colonies; and secondly citizens of independent Commonwealth countries. The British Government had no intention of relinquishing responsibility for its Colonies and changing their citizenship, nor did it wish to remove British subject status from citizens of independent Commonwealth countries. British subject status, although it would become much less important for Commonwealth citizens, was still seen as contributing to the unity of the Commonwealth and to Britain's leading role.

The British Nationality Act 1948, reaffirmed citizenship acquisition through *jus soli*, that is birth on the territory of the UK and Colonies and birth outside the territory to a citizen father and also through naturalisation at the discretion of the Home Secretary. It introduced a simplified procedure of registration, after 12 months' residence, for citizens of Commonwealth countries who wished to become citizens of the UK and Colonies. Presumably, because of the large number of marriages by British women to foreign nationals during the war, it changed the law by which British women lost their citizenship on marriage to an alien, and allowed those who had lost their citizenship in this way to have it restored, The Act recognised that independent Commonwealth countries would wish to give priority to their own individual citizenships, but it tried to maintain an element of the Common Code through the affirmation of the status of British subject (or Commonwealth citizen) which would continue for both citizens of the UK and colonies and citizens of independent Commonwealth countries.[15] It did not define British citizenship or nationality in a restrictive way. A wide variety of peoples were subsumed under the heading of citizens of the UK and Colonies, and all these, as well as citizens of independent Commonwealth countries, had the right of access to, and settlement in, the UK. British subjects, resident in Commonwealth countries, who did not acquire the citizenship of that country, would become citizens of the UK and Colonies. No-one would be left stateless as a result of these changes.

The impact of post-war immigration

The British Nationality Act 1948 confirmed the right of access of British subjects to the UK and this was supported by both the major parties. In the debate on the Nationality Act, Sir David Maxwell Fyfe, the Conservative spokesman on home affairs, said 'We are proud that we impose no colour bar restrictions making it difficult for them when they come here we must maintain our great metropolitan tradition of hospitality to everyone from every part of our Empire'.[16] Given the colour bars that operated in the services during the war, this was an ironic statement, but the following year a Conservative policy document gave a similar message stating that 'there must be freedom of movement amongst its members within the British Empire and Commonwealth. New opportunities will present themselves not only in the countries overseas but in the Mother Country, and must be open to all citizens.'[17]

As is well known this position could not be sustained once post-war immigration to Britain from the colonies in the West Indies and West Africa and from the Indian subcontinent took place. Between 1953 and 1962 net immigration from the West Indies was 272 000 and from the New Commonwealth as a whole was 485 000. This rather modest level of immigration resulted in a sustained political campaign in favour of controls and these were introduced by the Conservatives in 1962 and were tightened by Labour in 1965.[18] In the late 1960s a migration of Asians from Kenya to Britain raised the issue of citizenship as these people had not taken Kenyan citizenship when Kenya became independent in 1963, and retained their British nationality. They were not subject to controls under the 1962 Commonwealth Immigrants Act as their passports had been issued by the British government. The second Commonwealth Immigrants Act (1968) was passed to make them subject to controls. The Act specified that any citizen of the UK and Colonies, who held a passport issued by the UK government, would be subject to immigration control, unless they, or at least one parent or grandparent, had been born, adopted or naturalised in the UK or registered as a citizen of the UK and Colonies.

This restriction of entry to the UK of British subjects with British passports and no other citizenship made a nonsense of the earlier expansive notion of citizenship expressed in the imperial ideal of 'civis Britannicus sum'. It was a betrayal of imperial obligations and was even more embarrassing to the Labour government as the legislation was clearly designed to restrict the entry of non-whites into Britain. It was clear that Britain had to develop a new modern concept of citizenship designed to reflect its role as a post imperial power. The Labour party began the process, while in opposition, with a Green Paper in 1972 called *Citizenship, Immigration and Integration*,[19] and when it returned to government it produced another in 1977 called *British Nationality Law: Discussion of Possible Changes*.[20] This argued that a new scheme of citizenship should reflect the strength of connection that various groups of people had with the UK It proposed two categories of citizen: namely British Citizens and British Overseas Citizens. This latter group was to consist mainly of people connected with existing dependencies and those who had retained their British citizenship when the colonies or dependencies in which they lived became independent.[21]

The British Nationality Act 1981

The defeat of the Labour govemment in 1979 meant that it was the Conservatives who finally reformed British Nationality Law. A White Paper was published in July 1980 and the Bill itself, in January 1981. The Bill set out three major categories of citizenship: British Citizenship; Citizenship of the British Dependent Territories; and British Overseas Citizenship. British citizens would be those citizens of the UK and Colonies who had a close personal connection with the UK, either because their parents or grandparents had been born, adopted, naturalised or registered as citizens of the UK, or through permanent settlement in the UK. This caused consternation among expatriate Britons all over the world and also to Britons working or serving abroad, many of whom had not themselves been born in Britain as their parents had been engaged in imperial service or work overseas. The government was forced to amend the Bill so that citizens by naturalisation or registration would be allowed to transmit citizenship to children born abroad in the same way as British born citizens. The Bill also proposed that children born in Britain of certain categories of foreign parents, or whose parents were of uncertain status – because of illegal immigration or through overstaying their period of residence, for example – would not automatically be entitled to citizenship. This was a move away from absolute *jus soli* but the Bill was amended so that any child born in the UK, who did not acquire British citizenship at birth would acquire it after 10 years continuous residence, irrespective of the status of the parents.

Citizenship of the British Dependent Territories would be acquired by those citizens of the UK and Colonies who had that citizenship by reason of their own or their parents' or grandparents' birth, naturalisation or registration in an existing dependency or associated state. British

Overseas Citizenship was essentially a residual category with virtually no rights. It was intended for those citizens of the UK and Colonies who did not qualify for either of the first two categories and related mainly to holders of dual citizenship in Malaysia and to the East African Asians entitled to come to Britain under the quotas established in the Commonwealth Immigrants Act 1968. British Overseas Citizens would not be able to pass on this citizenship nor would they have any right of abode in any British territory.

The position of dependent territories caused considerable concern, and there was much lobbying on behalf of specific dependencies. As a result of this, citizens of Gibraltar were given special access to British Citizenship under the 1981 Act. This was extended to the Falkland Islanders in 1983 after the war with Argentina. Hong Kong was by far the most important Dependency and the British Government was under pressure to make special arrangements for British subjects in Hong Kong. The British Nationality (Hong Kong) Act 1990 was passed allowing 50 000 heads of household in key occupations to register as British citizens. The scheme ran from 1990 to 1 July 1997 when sovereignty passed to China and 50 000 principals and 86 400 dependants were registered. Two further British Nationality Acts were passed in 1996 and 1997, the first allowing Hong Kong war wives and widows to register as British citizens and the second allowing registration for the Colony's non-Chinese ethnic minorities who would have become stateless on 1 July 1997.[22] In 1998 the inhabitants of Montserrat were given rights of access and abode in the UK after much of the Island was devastated by a volcanic eruption. In February 1999 it was confirmed that the remaining citizens of the British Dependent Territories would be given full British citizenship. This was only expected to affect about 125 000 people resident in such colonies as Bermuda, the Cayman Islands and St. Helena.[23] The status of British Overseas Citizenship is currently being challenged before the European Court of Justice to see whether its holders should have the right of free movement across the European Union. If this case is successful it may reopen the question about the viability of this category of a citizenship without rights and which, in any event, cannot be passed on.

Acquisition of citizenship

Under the Nationality Act 1981 all citizens of Commonwealth countries as well as Irish British subjects and aliens have to naturalise rather than register to acquire British citizenship. Applicants must be 18 years old and of full capacity. The requirements are five years residence (three if married to a British spouse), good character, a basic knowledge of the

Table 6.1 Naturalisation applications and refusals 1987–98

	Grants	*Refusals*	*Processed*	*% Refused*
1987	64 876	5 693	70 569	8.1
1988	64 584	5 272	69 856	7.6
1989	117 129	8 801	125 930	7.0
1990	57 271	9 149	66 420	13.8
1991	58 642	8 985	67 627	13.2
1992	42 243	9 253	51 496	18.0
1993	45 793	8 041	53 834	14.9
1994	44 033	5 855	49 888	11.7
1995	40 516	5 032	45 548	11.0
1996	43 069	4 770	47 839	10.0
1997	37 010	4 747	41 757	11.3
1998	53 934	3 750	57 684	6.5

Source: Home Office Statistical Bulletin: *Persons Granted British Citizenship, United Kingdom*, 1998, Issue 6/99, 20 April 1999.

English, Welsh or Scottish Gaelic language and the intention to have the principal home in the UK. Granting a certificate of naturalisation is at the discretion of the Home Secretary. British Protected Persons and people holding another form of British nationality, such as British Overseas Citizenship, can register. Refusals of applications are unusual and in recent years accounted for less than 12 per cent of total applications, as can be seen in Table 6.1. The process is subject to a fee and to bureaucratic delays due to staff shortages. The British Nationality Act 1981 caused considerable insecurity among ethnic minorities in the UK and a huge rise in applications to register or naturalise as British citizens. Applications are now running at the rate of 50 000 per year.

Loss of citizenship

British citizenship can be renounced by making a declaration of renunciation. Citizenship can also be lost by deprivation in respect of those who have registered or naturalised if the acquisition was fraudulent, for treason, or for the commitment of a serious crime within five years of naturalisation and which led to a prison sentence of over twelve months (unless the loss would result in statelessness). There have been no deprivations since the 1960s. British Dependent Territories citizenship will be lost if the territory becomes independent.

The rights of aliens

the meaning of alien for Britain

Anyone who was not a subject of the King and who therefore did not owe him allegiance was an alien. In the middle ages aliens seem to have had many of the same rights as subjects. They were able to hold office under the Crown, could engage in trade and were free to travel in and out of the country as they wished. The early common law barred aliens from the Courts but, to encourage their involvement in trade and therefore increase his tax revenues, Edward I allowed aliens to sue for debt and for double damages for their wrongs. Alien merchants were allowed to be tried by juries half of whose members were aliens. These privileges did not protect aliens from arbitrary actions by the King as the expulsion of the Jews in 1290 shows.[24] One source of anti-foreigner resentment among the aristocracy was the gifts showered on foreign favourites by various English monarchs and, in order to limit the patronage of the Hanovarian Kings, the Act of Settlement 1701 barred aliens from sitting in the Privy Council or Parliament, or from enjoying any office or place of trust, either civil or military, or to receive any gifts of land, tenements or hereditaments from the Crown. Earlier in 1698 Parliament had prohibited aliens from voting in Parliamentary elections.[25]

The rights of aliens have always been seriously undermined in times of war and national emergencies when xenophobia is at its highest and the national interest can be used to justify anti-alien legislation and actions. The danger is that controls established during emergencies then continue long after the emergency has passed. During the wars with Revolutionary France, the British government was terrified that revolutionary ideals and fervour would spread to England and these concerns led to the Aliens Act 1793. This gave the government the power to register aliens, restrict their movements within Britain and to deport them. Ships captains had to provide customs officers with the details of all aliens on their ships and their landing could be forbidden. At the end of the war these powers were allowed to lapse. A tolerant and relaxed period followed for the rest of the nineteenth century.[26]

In the early twentieth century a number of historical events combined to stimulate a series of measures introduced to control aliens and restrict their rights. The Aliens Act 1905 was passed to introduce a measure of control over Jewish immigration from Russia and eastern Europe, which had begun in the 1880s as a result of Tsarist pogroms. The Act created an Aliens inspectorate with powers to exclude 'undesirable aliens' who were defined as criminals, those unable to support themselves, the mentally ill, and those who might become a charge on the rates. Only ships carrying twenty or more immigrants were covered by this legislation and there were rights of appeal both for those excluded and the carriers. It had little effect on immigration but was important as the first significant measure attempting to control immigration.[27]

Anti-alien hysteria grew considerably in Britain with the approach of World War I and the rise of revolutionary movements in Russia. The day after war was declared an Aliens Restriction Act 1914 was passed giving sweeping powers to the Home Secretary who through Orders in Council could ban the entry of aliens, limit their movement and restrict their stay. Aliens, for the first time, had to register with the police and internment was introduced for enemy aliens such as Germans, Austro-Hungarians and Turks. Passports were introduced to ensure the effectiveness of the controls and work permits were also introduced.

After the war most of the controls were kept and the Aliens Restriction (Amendment) Act was passed in 1919. These powers were renewed annually by the Expiring Laws Continuance Act. The impact of the Bolshevik resolution in Russia was such that all aliens were regarded as potential subversives who might encourage Bolshevism and Communism to take root in Britain. The Aliens Restriction (Amendment) Act therefore included heavy penalties for aliens spreading sedition or disaffection among either the armed forces or the civilian population and also for promoting industrial unrest.

After World War II the focus of popular attention in the British media and from politicians has been on immigration from the New Commonwealth. Alien immigration, as such, has hardly been a matter of political controversy at all in contrast to Jewish immigration at the turn of the century and before the Second World War. The European Volunteer Workers scheme, which was established immediately after the war, and under which 200 000 people were recruited from Europe, was hardly noticed due to the severe labour shortage. The settlement of the Polish armed forces and their families in Britain in 1947 and the acceptance of Hungarian refugees in 1956 was similarly facilitated by low levels of unemployment. More surprisingly, the entry and settlement of the Chileans in 1972 and the Vietnamese in 1981 caused little comment in the press or on public opinion. In contrast, the entry of East African Asians from Kenya in 1967, Uganda in 1972 and Malawi in 1976, all of whom were British passport holders, caused uproar in the press and a storm of popular protest.

The Contemporary rights of aliens

Just as there are a confusing number of categories of British citizens with different rights, so there are numerous categories under which aliens can enter the UK. Two groups of non-citizens are not classified as aliens. These are Irish citizens and citizens of independent Commonwealth countries. Any of these people resident in Britain have access to full civic, political and social rights. In addition 'patrials', that is Commonwealth citizens descended from a British grandparent, are free from immigration controls and have the right of entry and settlement in the UK. This is also the case for anybody who has a British father. They will not qualify for voting rights unless they are Irish citizens or Commonwealth citizens.

Aliens who are nationals of a European Union country have freedom of movement within the EU and have the right of residence and the right to bring their spouses and other members of their family with them, providing they are working in the UK or are not working but able to support themselves. They have access to social welfare benefits and can vote in local and European elections but not in parliamentary elections.

Residential rights

All foreigners are subject to immigration control and there are specific regulations covering visitors, students, spouses and fiancées, au pairs, working holidaymakers, ministers of religion, doctors and dentists and investors. Visitors must stay less than six months and be able to support themselves without working or recourse to public funds. Visitors do not have to register with the police. Students qualify to enter the UK if they are accepted for a course of study at an independent fee paying school or a publicly funded institute of further education on a recognised course. They must be financially independent and leave at the end of the course. Ministers of religion are admitted if they intend to work as a minister and can maintain themselves. They can apply for permanent residence after four years. Doctors and dentists can enter the UK to undertake postgraduate training. If they wish to work they need a work permit and pass an English language test. EU doctors can, of course, work in the UK but will need to pass the language test. Working holidaymakers are young people aged 17–27 inclusive who are Commonwealth citizens taking extended holidays before returning to settle in their own country. They can stay up to two years. They are restricted to casual or part-time work.

Investors are people who wish to make the UK their main home, have £1 million of their own money and wish to invest £750 000 in the UK. They will be given permission to stay for twelve months and can then ask for an extension. After four years they can apply for permanent residence.

Social and economic rights

If non-citizens are permanent residents then they are entitled to social benefits and pensions. Temporary visitors are specifically excluded from seeking income support, housing and homelessness benefit, family credit, child benefit or disability allowances. Overstayers and illegal entrants are also excluded from such benefits but their children can be registered in the schools. Foreign ex-servicemen are not guaranteed war-related compensation. The introduction of a national curriculum in Britain has reduced the scope for multi-cultural education, though schools in areas of immigrant settlement do support cultural activities. There is little pressure in the UK for mother tongue education except in some parts of Wales. This may be partly because of the usefulness of English as an international language.

There are no limitations on property rights for aliens or on the right to self-employment, providing this is not a condition of entry. A number of government posts are closed to aliens such as national political offices, senior posts in the civil service and armed forces. Public offices often require an oath of allegiance to the Queen and, are thus reserved for British and Commonwealth citizens.

Work permits are required for people who enter to work from places outside of the European Economic Area. They are not required for permanent residents, patrials, people with a British father, refugees with a UN passport and wives of registered overseas students or EEA citizens who are working in the UK. Others must have relevant skills, competence in English, usually be working full time and with permission to work. There must be no suitable UK or EEA worker available to do the work. After four years a worker can apply for the removal of the time limit on his or her stay. If this is granted he or she is free of conditions on their employment and they achieve permanent resident status.

Concern about illegal immigration and also about visitors and asylum seekers breaking the conditions of their entry caused the government to include sanctions against employers in the Asylum and Immigration Act 1996. This Act made it a criminal offence for employers to employ someone who does not have permission to be in, or to work in, the UK. Employers can defend themselves from prosecution by keeping a copy of the document they have checked to determine the employment status of new employees recruited after 27 January 1997 when the Act came into force. The maximum penalty is a fine of £5,000.[28]

Political rights

As has been explained, a large number of non-citizens do have national voting rights in Britain. These include Commonwealth citizens and Irish citizens. European Union citizens can vote in local and European elections. Those who can vote for particular elections are also able to stand for those political offices. In theory there are no limitations on the rights of aliens to organise, express their views and engage in political activities. However, the Home Secretary has the power to deport non-citizens on grounds of 'the public good'. This means that aliens are under pressure to limit their political activities especially if their actions damage the relations between Britain and other countries. Extreme political action, for example against their home government could result in deportation. Some governments have been concerned that the British government should control the activities of their citizens in Britain. The Indian government, for example, has been furious about the activities of the supporters in Britain of a free Kashmir and also about Sikh residents in Britain who support an independent Khalistan. Aliens engaged in criminal activities can be deported. In time of 'national emergencies' people defined as enemy aliens can lose their rights so that during the Gulf War, for example, the British government interned over 90 people defined as a threat to national security. This caused considerable concern as many of those interned were long established permanent residents without a record of political activity and the arrests seemed to have more to do with portraying the British government as 'patriotic' rather than protecting national security. No other country engaged in the Gulf War interned so many people.

In recent years in Britain the most controversial area of immigration and alien rights has concerned refugees and asylum seekers. During the 1980s asylum applications to Britain were very modest. They rose from 1,563 in 1979 to 5,700 in 1988. However, applications rose strongly thereafter to 45 000 in 1991.[29] The government reacted by imposing mandatory visas on countries from where asylum seekers came such as Haiti, Turkey and Somalia and doubling the fines under the Carrier's Liability Act (1987) from £1,000 for an undocumented passenger to £2,000. In 1993 the Conservative government introduced an Asylum and Immigration Appeals Bill which introduced fingerprinting to reduce social security fraud. It reduced the obligations on local authorities to provide permanent accommodation and removed some rights of appeal. Concern about absconding has caused many asylum seekers to be held in detention centres and the government has seen this as a useful means of showing that Britain is not a soft touch for 'bogus' asylum seekers.

The Labour government has been just as anxious as its predecessor to be seen to be tough on asylum seekers and has been concerned at an epidemic of stories in the press about the entry of gypsies from central European countries and illegal immigrants from Kosovo often smuggled in by lorry. The government has reacted by extending carrier's liability to Eurostar and Road Hauliers. In July 1998 it published a White Paper entitled *Fairer, Faster and Firmer: A Modern Approach to Immigration*[30] and has introduced a Bill which, for example, provides for social benefits for asylum seekers to be paid for in kind (food vouchers and accommodation), rather than cash, and to allow for the dispersal of refugees across the country to reduce the concentration in London and some of the main receiving ports such as Dover. To aid integration the qualifying period for settlement has been reduced to four years and those recognised as genuine refugees will have the right to immediate settlement.[31] The general attitude of the British government to refugees is very discouraging.

Conclusions: citizen rights for aliens

In many countries there has been a fierce debate over the rights of resident aliens and the need to take more vigorous action to include them in society and the political system. Concern has been expressed at the low rates of naturalisation, sometimes caused by high barriers imposed by states which demand a high degree of assimilation before allowing the acquisition of their citizenship.[32] In Britain this debate has been much less evident. This is because most post-war immigrants to Britain have come either from Ireland or from Commonwealth countries and so have been treated as British subjects with full civic, political and social rights. Immigrants who came to Britain from non-Commonwealth countries such as Poland, Hungary, Chile and Vietnam did not have citizenship rights but were able to naturalise after five years' residence. Many of these immigrants were refugees and their naturalisation rates were high, as is often the case for refugees.

Nationals of Member States of the European Union have a privileged status in Member States other than their own. This privileged status now extends to some political rights granted under the Maastricht Treaty, so European Union nationals can now vote in local elections and elections to the European Parliament in any Member State where they reside. They cannot be discriminated against in the labour market and are also protected by reciprocal agreements.

There is thus no strong demand in Britain for the extension of citizenship rights, such as voting rights to non-citizens. Many non-citizens have voting rights already and the largest groups of non-citizens in Britain without such rights are groups like the Americans and Japanese who are well educated, in highly paid positions and who see themselves as temporary residents and not settlers. They are able to exert political influence through their contacts and embassies.

The fiercest debates in Britain with regard to alien rights are not over extending formal political rights to permanent residents but over other forms of discrimination. Certain groups of non-citizens are subject to arbitrary and harsh treatment and certain groups of citizens are subject to discrimination.[33]

The non-citizens who are most harshly treated are asylum seekers and refugees. The government has made it very clear that it does not wish Britain to be seen as a 'soft touch' for asylum seekers so it has gone to great lengths to discourage them. A battery of measures have been introduced such as the imposition of visas, the Carriers Liability Act, the reduction of benefit, restrictions on the right to work, and imprisoning asylum seekers in detention centres while their cases are investigated.[34] New Legislation introduced by the government will streamline the rights of appeal and make provision for benefits to be provided in kind, such as in the form of accommodation and food vouchers and not in cash. Asylum seekers do not have the right to work while their cases are being investigated. The government's policy of holding some asylum applicants in detention centres has been fiercely attacked by the Chief Inspector of Prisons.[35] It is deeply resented by asylum seekers who feel they have not committed any crime and should therefore not be imprisoned.

Non-citizens with permanent residence have a much more secure status and are generally free from arbitrary treatment. They can, of course, be legally discriminated against in the labour market unless they are a national of a state belonging to the European Economic Area. However, the commission of a serious crime[36] can lead to a recommendation by a court to the Home Secretary for deportation. Also, in times of national emergency, if a person is defined by the Home Secretary as an enemy alien and a threat to national security, they can be detained. In some areas the Home Secretary thus has extensive powers over aliens' rights and may not have to give reasons for his actions. Naturalisation, for example, is entirely at the discretion of the Home Secretary and he does not normally have to give any reasons for the refusal to grant citizenship. However in December 1997 Mr Fayad, the owner of Harrods, obtained a court ruling that he should be told the reason why he was refused citizenship.[37] Recently the Home Secretary has promised to reduce waiting lists for applications for British citizenship to give a more welcoming signal to prospective citizens.[38] This action is overdue as the Immigration and Nationality Department is notorious for bureaucratic inefficiency and delays.

The concern that the extension of citizen rights, especially voting rights, to non-citizens will have a detrimental effect on the political system, have not been borne out in the British case. The extension of voting rights to citizens of independent Commonwealth countries, the Irish and British Protected persons has not led to new parties and styles of politics at the local or national levels. In general these voters have worked through existing structures and when new parties have been formed it has often been due to frustration caused by feelings or exclusion by the major parties.[39] Fears of 'ethnic entryism'[40] have been overdrawn and the fact that the Irish and Commonwealth citizens have had voting rights has forced politicians to pay some attention to their needs and concerns. It has removed one considerable barrier to inequality, discrimination, and arbitrary treatment.

Notes

* The research for this chapter was funded by a grant from the Economic and Social Research Council, no. L214252021. The author acknowledges the support of the ESRC.

1 The oath that is taken, for example, on assuming public office or service in the armed forces, is an oath of allegiance to the Queen. The toast to the Queen on formal occasions is known as the 'loyal toast'.
2 A. Dummett and A. Nicol, *Subjects, Citizens, Aliens and Others: Nationality and Immigration Law* (London: Weidenfeld & Nicolson, 1990).
3 British Nationality Law: Discussion of Possible Changes, Cmnd 6795, 1977, para. 66.
4 L. Fransman, *British Nationality Law* (London: Butterworths, 1998) pp. 3–5.
5 The Crown's dominions were the Crown's territories under British Rule, but the Dominions were the self-governing territories which later became known as the Old Commonwealth. These included Australia, Canada, Ireland (until 1949), Newfoundland until 1949, New Zealand and South Africa (until 1961). Southern Rhodesia was granted responsible self-government in 1923, but not full Dominion status.

6 A. Dummett and A. Nicol, *op. cit*, pp. 60–2.
7 L. Fransman, *op. cit*, p. 155
8 *ibid.*, p. 256.
9 *ibid.*, pp. 160–2.
10 Dummett and Nicol, *op. cit*, p. 125.
11 *ibid.*, p. 130.
12 *ibid.*, p. 129.
13 *ibid.*, p. 130.
14 *ibid.*, p. 134.
15 Southern Rhodesia, which was neither an independent Commonwealth country nor a colony, was also allowed to define its own citizenship.
16 *Parliamentary Debates*, Commons (Hansard), vol. 453, col. 405, 7 July 1948.
17 *The Right Road for Britain*, Conservative Central Office, 1949.
18 Z. Layton-Henry, *The Politics of Immigration* (Oxford: Blackwell, 1992).
19 Labour Party, *Citizenship, Immigration and Integration: A Policy for the 1970s*, 1972. Enoch Powell also called for reform of the citizenship laws in his Eastbourne speech, 1972.
20 Home Office, *British Nationality Law: Discussion of Possible Changes*, Cmnd 6795, HMSO, 1977.
21 *ibid.*
22 L. Fransman, *op. cit*, p. 271. Some three million people in Hong Kong ceased to be citizens of the British Dependent Territories when Hong Kong returned to China. They then became Chinese citizens and British Nationals (Overseas).
23 *The Independent*, 19 February 1999.
24 A. Dummett and A. Nicol, *op. cit*, pp. 29–31.
25 *ibid.*, p. 73.
26 *ibid.*, p. 83.
27 Z. Layton-Henry, *op. cit.*, p. 7.
28 Home Office, *Asylum and Immigration Act, 1996, Prevention of illegal working: Guidance for Employers*, Immigration and Nationality Directorate, December 1996.
29 Home Office Statistical Bulletin, Asylum Statistics, UK, 1984–97, Home Office.
30 Home Office, *Fairer, Faster and Firmer: A Modern Approach to Immigration and Asylum*, Cmnd 4018, HMSO, 27 July 1988.
31 *ibid.*
32 G. de Rham, 'The Acquisition of Citizenship' in Z. Layton-Henry (ed.), *The Political Rights of Migrant Workers in Western Europe* (London: Sage, 1990).
33 There is huge and constant debate in the UK about discrimination against women, ethnic minorities, gays and lesbians, and the disabled. The literature on this is vast; see for example T. Modood *et al.*, *Ethnic Minorities in Britain: Diversity and Disadvantage* (London: Policy Studies Institute, 1997).
34 *The Guardian*, 9 April 1998; *The Times*, 9 April 1998; *The Daily Telegraph*, 21 October 1998; *The Times*, 21 October 1998.
35 *The Times*, 16 March 1998; *The Independent*, 17 April 1998; *The Observer*, 12 November 1998.
36 A crime that can lead to a sentence of imprisonment of twelve months or more.
37 *Daily Telegraph*, 7 May 1999.

38 *Parliamentary Debates*, Commons (Hansard), Immigration and Asylum, cols 35–38, 27 July 1998.
39 J. Eade, *The Politics of Community* (Aldershot: Avebury, 1989).
40 S. Fielding and A. Geddes, 'The British Labour Party and "ethnic entryism", participation, integration and the party context', *Journal of Ethnic and Migration Studies*, vol. 24, no. 1, January 1998.

7
The Rights and Obligations of Immigrant Citizens and Non-Citizens in Australia[1]

Stephen Castles and Gianni Zappalà

The history of modern Australia goes back only to 1788, when the first British colonists arrived. In 1901 Australia became a self-governing entity through Federation and the adoption of a Constitution. However, this did not mean full independence, since Australia remained a dominion within the British Empire. Nor did Federation create the Australian citizen, since the Constitution did not mention citizenship and Australians were to remain British subjects until 1949. Even then, despite the introduction of its own citizenship, Australia continued to lack some of the trappings of nationhood: for instance a foreign monarch is still head of state (though this seems likely to change soon). Unlike most modern countries, therefore, it is impossible to state precisely when the Australian nation-state was born.

Similar contradictions are to be found in the development of the Australian people. The Aboriginal and Torres Strait Islander peoples (referred to below as Indigenous Australians) were decimated, dispossessed and marginalised by white settlement:[2] their number fell from an estimated 500 000 in 1788 to just 67 000 in 1901. In the nineteenth century immigration became an issue of class conflict, with employers wanting cheap 'coolie labour', and unions demanding immigration control and wages 'fit for white men'. Chinese and other non-European immigrants encountered considerable racism. By the time of Federation, the White Australia Policy was considered vital for national survival.[3] Up to the Second World War, Australia continued to develop its identity as a white society based on British culture and heritage. Yet after 1945, Australia embarked on a mass immigration policy, designed to strengthen the nation demographically and economically. Against the intentions of its architects, this immigration programme was to transform Australia into one of the most culturally diverse countries in the world.[4]

Table 7.1 shows how Australia's population has changed in the last half-century. The aim was to bring in mainly British immigrants, but the source areas became increasingly diversified: Eastern and Northern Europe in the late 1940s, Southern Europe in the 1950s and 1960s, and then – with the collapse of the White Australia Policy – Asia in the 1980s and 1990s. Table 7.2 shows how Australia's immigrant population has changed since 1971. While the UK- and Ireland-born have remained

Table 7.1 Australian population, 1947–96

Census year	*Overseas-born*	*Total population*	*O/S-born as percentage of total*
1947	744 187	7 579 385	9.8
1954	1 286 466	8 986 530	14.3
1961	1 778 780	10 508 186	16.9
1971	2 579 318	12 755 638	20.2
1976	2 718 318	13 548 448	20.1
1981	3 003 834	14 576 330	20.6
1986	3 247 301	15 602 163	20.8
1991	3 689 128	16 407 045	22.5
1996	3 908 213	17 892 418	21.8

Source: Australian Censuses

Table 7.2 Australia: immigrant population by birthplace (thousands)

Country of birth	*1971*	*1981*	*1991*	*1996*
Europe	2 197	2 233	2 300	2 217
UK & Ireland	1 088	1 133	1 175	1 124
Italy	290	276	255	238
Former Yugoslavia	130	149	161	n.a.
Greece	160	147	136	127
Germany	111	111	115	110
Other Europe	418	418	457	618
Asia (incl. Middle East)	167	372	822	1 007
New Zealand	81	177	276	291
Africa	62	90	132	147
America	56	96	147	151
Other and not stated	18	36	75	95
Total	2 581	3 005	3 751	3 908

Source: Australian Censuses

fairly constant, some of the older European immigrant groups have declined (Italy, Greece), while 'other Europe' has grown. The big increases, however, are in Asia-born and New Zealand-born immigrants.

Today, 22 per cent of the Australian population are overseas-born, and a further 20 per cent are children of immigrants. Settlers have come from over 100 countries; Australians can have any skin colour, speak a vast range of languages, adhere to any of the worlds' religions, and follow a great variety of cultural practices.

The term 'alien' is not very useful for analysing the situation of Australia's overseas-born population. Alien was used in official documents up to the 1980s. Today, the usual term is 'non-citizen'. Debates on citizenship mainly relate to the situation of 'permanent settlers', who are popularly referred to as 'immigrants'. These are expected to become citizens and usually do. Naturalisation is easy to obtain after only two years in the country. Australia also has temporary immigrants – people who enter for periods of some months or years for work, business or education purposes. However, this does not usually lead to settlement.

It is useful to separate between English-speaking background (ESB)[5] and non-English-speaking background (NESB) immigrants. About 2.5 million members of the Australian population in 1996 were immigrants from NESB countries. If we add the second generation, about 4.8 million people, or a quarter of the Australian population were of NESB origin. Yet Australia has no large minorities: apart from the Italians (1.4 per cent of total population), no first-generation NESB group makes up more than 1 per cent of Australia's population. Up to the 1960s, ethnic difference was dealt with through policies of assimilation, designed to create a mono-cultural identity based on Anglo-Australian traditions. This policy failed to create an homogeneous population, and was replaced from 1972 by a model of multiculturalism, which combined recognition of cultural difference with government intervention to prevent social marginalisation of minorities.

Australian citizenship should be understood in the context of the country's development as part of the British Empire and then the Commonwealth. The Constitution adopted at the time of Federation in 1901 had very little to say about issues such as who was a citizen of Australia, and what were their rights. One reason for this was that the framers of the Constitution associated the term 'citizen' with republicanism, and the status of 'British subject' was seen as more appropriate. Indigenous people and non-European immigrants from British colonies (e.g. India, parts of China, the New Hebrides) were British subjects, but Australia's founding fathers did not want to give them equal rights.

Leaving the definition of rights to parliamentary statutes made it easier to discriminate against 'inferior races'. That is why Australia has no document stating the rights of citizens, like the US Bill of Rights or the French Declaration of the Rights of Man.[6]

Citizenship and nationality

After the Second World War, there was a move to greater autonomy on the part of British dominions such as Australia, and the Nationality and Citizenship Act 1948 was introduced. It was thus not until 26 January 1949 that 'Australian citizens' came into being, although this was in addition to the general status of British subject that they still held. Despite the 1948 Act, citizenship continued to be seen in terms of British culture and identity, rather than in terms of rights and responsibilities. This led to positive discrimination in favour of British immigrants and obstacles against non-British immigrants.[7]

Although Australia's formal rules of citizenship were based on the principle of *jus soli*, behind these rules lay an ethno-blood notion of the 'national family' which made Australia similar to countries whose citizenship laws were based on *jus sanguinis*.[8] This conception of citizenship was problematic for a nation which was embarking on mass immigration. Initially it was expected that 9 out of every 10 immigrants would be British. But as immigrants increasingly came from non-British origins, they had to show that they belonged to the British 'national family'. Australia became one of the most multi-ethnic states in the world, and imposing a notion of belonging to a pre-existing British nation became increasingly tenuous. This began to receive serious recognition from 1972 with the emergence of the policy of multiculturalism. Several important changes have been made over the years to the laws and concepts governing citizenship. Australia is shifting away from a culturally-bound notion of citizenship towards a civic one permitting equality of rights for all Australians irrespective of their origins. One symbol of this was the change in name from the Nationality and Citizenship Act to the Australian Citizenship Act in 1973.

Acquisition of citizenship

Jus soli: Acquisition of citizenship by birth is dealt with in section 10 of the Australian Citizenship Act. In general, a person born in Australia on or after 20 August 1986 will be an Australian citizen if: a) one of their parents was at the time of their birth an Australian citizen or permanent resident; or b) they have been ordinarily resident in Australia for a ten year period from the time of their birth. Children born on Australian soil of illegal immigrants are therefore not Australian citizens. However, the law does allow children born in Australia on or after 20 August 1986 to become Australian citizens on their 10th birthday if they did not become citizens at birth and have been resident in Australia for the 10 years since their birth. In general, people born in Australia between 26 January 1949 and 19 August 1986 are Australian citizens, while those born prior to 26 January 1949 (i.e. those who were British subjects) are also Australian citizens.

Jus sanguinus: Section 10B of the Act provides that people born outside Australia are Australian citizens where the following conditions are satisfied: their name is registered at an Australian consulate within 18 years of their birth, and at least one of their parents was at the time of their birth an Australian citizen who had acquired that citizenship other than by descent; or at least one of their parents was at the time of their birth an Australian citizen who had acquired that citizenship by descent and before registration was present in Australia for a period/s amounting to not less than two years.

Acquisition of Australian citizenship by naturalisation or grant is contained in section 13 of the Citizenship Act which gives the Minister for Immigration discretion to grant citizenship to people who satisfy all of the following at the time they apply for citizenship: i) they are permanent residents; ii) they have reached the age of 18; iii) they understand the nature of the application; iv) they have been present in Australia as a permanent resident for a period (or periods) amounting in total to not less than one year during a period of two years immediately preceding the date that the application was lodged; v) they have been present as a permanent resident in Australia for not less than two years during a period of five years immediately preceding the date that the application was lodged; vi) they are of good character; vii) they possess a basic knowledge of English; and viii) they have an adequate knowledge of the responsibilities and privileges of Australian citizenship. Finally, the Act also states that if granted citizenship, the person/s would be likely to reside in Australia or maintain a close and continuing association with Australia.

The Nationality and Citizenship Act 1948, stated the conditions which had to be met in order for 'aliens' to become Australian citizens. It is not coincidental that the first Act which created an 'Australian citizenship' came into being at the same time that Australia embarked on its massive post-war migration programme. The intention was that these 'aliens' would be turned into 'New Australian' citizens and assimilate to the existing cultural norms. It was the Department of Immigration, therefore, that was responsible for administering citizenship and naturalisation matters. Although immigrants were encouraged to become Australian citizens, many did not do so, which caused several government inquiries and campaigns to encourage citizenship take-up amongst immigrants. In order to increase citizenship rates various amendments were made to the 1948 Act. However, despite evidence that the requirement of renunciation of an immigrants' former nationality was a key factor in low citizenship take-up rates, in 1966, the government incorporated the renunciation into the Oath of Allegiance to the Queen. It was also in 1966 that the restriction of age, invalid and widow's pensions to British subjects only was removed. In 1967, in the context of Australia's involvement in the Vietnam War, conscription for aliens was introduced, giving them a major responsibility of citizenship whether they wanted to become naturalised or not.

Throughout the 1960s, only just over half of all eligible aliens had applied for citizenship. It had become obvious that low naturalisation rates had less to do with administrative complexity (although the gradual easing and simplifying of the rules did help) than with the failure of assimilationist policy. Changes to the Act after this period began to alter the terms of citizenship in more significant ways. After 1964, the heading of the Australian passport was changed from 'British Subject' to 'Australian', although the words 'British passport' still appeared under the Australian coat of arms. In 1969, the initial five-year waiting period for naturalisation was reduced to three but only for aliens who could read and write English.

It was not until 1973, however, that really substantial changes to the 1948 Act began. The privileged status of British immigrants was abolished, with both British and other immigrants required to reside in Australia for three years before they could apply for citizenship. British immigrants were now also required to take the oath or affirm their allegiance to become citizens of Australia, although it was only from 1984 that British immigrants who now came to Australia no longer had automatic voting rights. Further changes to the Act were made in 1984, 1986 and 1994. These included a further reduction in the residence requirement from three to two years, and replacing the allegiance to the British Monarch with allegiance to Australia and its people. Naturalisation procedures in Australia are now some of the most liberal in the world.[9]

Loss of citizenship

The laws governing the loss and resumption of Australian citizenship are also contained in the Australian Citizenship Act 1948.[10] There are five main ways in which Australian citizenship may be lost:

1. The *acquisition of another nationality or citizenship*. Section 17 of the Act states that a person shall cease to be an Australian citizen where they are 18 years of age or over and undertake any act or thing whose dominant purpose and effect is to acquire the nationality or citizenship of a foreign country.
2. The *renunciation* of Australian citizenship (s. 18). In this case a person shall cease to be an Australian citizen where they are 18 years of age or over and a national or citizen of a foreign country, or were born or normally resident in a foreign country and under that law are not entitled to acquire the citizenship of that country because they are an Australian citizen, and lodge with the Minister a declaration renouncing their Australian citizenship.
3. A person may lose their Australian citizenship where they are a citizen of a foreign country and *serve in the armed forces* of that country if it is at war with Australia (s. 19).
4. Citizenship may be lost through *Ministerial deprivation* (s. 21). This discretion normally relates to persons who make false or misleading statements when applying for citizenship or those who are convicted of an offence under an Australian or foreign law which is punishable by death, life imprisonment or imprisonment for 12 months or more, prior to the grant of citizenship.
5. Where a parent of a child under 18 years of age ceases to be an Australian citizen because they have acquired another citizenship, renounced their Australian citizenship or served in the armed forces of an enemy country, and their child is recognised by the law of that respective country as a citizen of that country then their child also ceases to be an Australian citizen from that time (s. 23). Where the Minister exercises his or her discretion of deprivation of citizenship under section 21, the Minister may also direct that all or any of the children of that person under 18 years of age also cease to be Australian citizens.

In 1995, the Minister for Immigration announced new policy guidelines to facilitate the resumption of Australian citizenship which had been lost on the acquisition of another citizenship. In order to resume

Australian citizenship, people must show the following: a) that they did not know they would lose their Australian citizenship or that they would have suffered significant hardship or detriment had they not acquired the other citizenship; b) that they have lived in Australia for a total of at least two years during their lifetime and either indicate that they will continue to reside in Australia, or if now a resident overseas, that they will reside in Australia within three years; and c) that they have maintained a close and continuing association with Australia. The broader guidelines were a recognition that many Australian citizens continue to have links with their countries of origin for economic or cultural reasons and that dual citizenship (which in some ways this policy allows retrospectively) is beneficial. Furthermore, people who have lost their Australian citizenship can apply to be granted Australian citizenship after 12 months from when they lost it, if they have been present in Australia as a permanent resident for 12 months out of the two years immediately before lodging their application for citizenship.

Distinctions between nationality and citizenship

Until the 1970s, nationality and citizenship were generally seen as being virtually identical. This was reflected in the title of the Nationality and Citizenship Act 1948 itself, which placed the two side by side. Being Australian meant having Anglo-Australian cultural characteristics, which in turn were linked to British heritage. Aliens could only become Australian citizens if they were willing and able to shed their own cultural characteristics, and take on the dominant ones through a process of assimilation. However, not all groups were considered 'assimilable' the White Australia Policy excluded non-Europeans until the late 1960s, and doubts were cast on the assimilability of even some European groups (such as Southern Italians).

From the 1970s, a distinction was made between nationality and citizenship, as symbolised in the renaming of the law as the Australian Citizenship Act 1948. According to multicultural policy, Australia was seen as a nation made up of many ethnic groups, with their own cultures and identity. The new civic identity was meant to be based on shared citizenship rather than shared nationality. However, this view has not secured universal acceptance. The election of a Liberal-National Party Coalition Government in 1996 gave rise to new debates on these issues, with the Government showing considerable ambivalence on multiculturalism. The rise of a new anti-immigrant movement, Pauline Hanson's One Nation Party has received the support of up to 10–15 per cent of the electorate for nostalgic concepts of homogeneous national identity. Thus it appears that the delinking of nationality and citizenship in Australia is neither final nor complete.

Stateless persons

There are no significant groups of stateless persons in Australia, and statelessness is not an issue. This is because it is very easy for permanent residents to acquire Australian citizenship.

Dual citizenship

In general, immigrants who apply for Australian citizenship can legally become dual citizens, by retaining their former citizenship after naturalisation. By contrast, Australians who apply for and are granted citizenship of another country (for instance while living abroad) are not permitted to retain Australian citizenship. Dual citizenship has been an issue of increasing debate and discussion in Australia over the last decade. It has been estimated that in 1986 there were three million dual citizens in Australia[11] with the number now probably being closer to five million. The majority of these dual citizens fall within one of the following four categories:

1 People not born in Australia who have applied for Australian citizenship yet have retained their previous citizenship if the citizenship laws of their respective country of origin allows them to do so.
2 People who were born in Australia who are recognised as citizens by descent by their parents' country of birth.
3 People born overseas of Australian parents who are therefore Australian citizens by descent but who may also acquire the citizenship of their country of birth if that country allows citizenship by *jus soli* rules.
4 Australian citizens who have applied for the citizenship of another country without informing the relevant authorities of their action.

It is only people in this last group who risk losing their Australian citizenship under section 17 of the Australian Citizenship Act 1948. Australian citizenship law is inconsistent in its treatment of dual citizenship. This was recognised in the 1994 report of the Parliamentary Joint Standing Committee on Migration[12] (JSCM) which argued that section 17 of the Australian Citizenship Act discriminates against Australian citizens by birth compared with those who become citizens by naturalisation. While the former, in most cases, are not allowed to acquire another citizenship, the latter may, in some cases, retain their previous citizenship. The JSCM recommended that former Australian citizens who had lost their citizenship under section 17 should have the right to apply for its resumption. The JSCM Report was significant in that it represented one of the first official views to explicitly support dual citizenship.

In recent years, the main controversy about dual citizenship has concerned the right of dual citizens to hold political office. Section 44(i) of the Constitution provides for the disqualification of a person from being chosen or of sitting as a Senator or House of Representatives member if he or she is: '. . . under any acknowledgment of allegiance, obedience, or adherence to a foreign power, or is a subject or a citizen or entitled to the rights or privileges of a subject or a citizen of a foreign power'. This means that candidates for parliamentary office cannot be eligible for or hold, dual citizenship. On 25 November 1992, for instance, the High Court found in the *Sykes v. Cleary* case that two candidates in a House of Representatives by-election were ineligible due to section 44(i). Up to 40 sitting Members of Parliament were thought likely to be affected by this decision because they held or had the right to dual citizenship.[13]

The requirement for renunciation of all other allegiances was removed from the Citizenship Act in 1986, although it still required an oath of 'true allegiance'. The question therefore becomes whether 'true allegiance' is satisfied in cases where there is dual citizenship. The oath of allegiance was replaced in 1994 by a new Pledge of Commitment in which mention of previous allegiances is virtually absent. Several reports have dealt with the issue of dual citizenship since the late 1970s, most recommending that section 44(i) be deleted from the Constitution and that disqualification provisions be placed solely in the relevant Acts of Parliament. The most recent review was undertaken by the House of Representatives Standing Committee on Legal and Constitutional Affairs in 1997. The Committee recommended that section 44(i) prohibiting dual citizens from parliamentary positions be deleted and replaced with the requirement that candidates and members of the Federal Parliament should be Australian citizens. This would enable an Australian citizen who may also hold another citizenship to stand for parliament.[14] However, it is unlikely that the present government will move to relax restrictions on dual citizenship as this would be contrary to its views on national identity and commitment to Australia.

Factors affecting the naturalisation rate

Changes in Australian citizenship law have had the desired effect of increasing citizenship take-up rates from their relatively low levels in the pre-1973 period. In 1996, there were 15.89 million Australian citizens living in Australia and an estimated additional 1 million people who would be entitled to become citizens if they so wished. In 1996–97, the number of people granted citizenship was 108 266, with the major countries of former citizenship in that year being (in rank order): Britain, China, New Zealand, Former Yugoslavia, Vietnam and the Philippines.[15] At present the highest rates of naturalisation of immigrants in Australia for at least ten years (over 95%) are shown by people from Greece, Lebanon, Poland, Vietnam and the Philippines. The lowest rates (below 50%) are found among people from the United Kingdom and New Zealand.

Several factors are involved in differing citizenship rates. The low rate of British-born immigrants is mainly due to the fact that pre-1984 entrants still enjoy all rights of citizenship, including the right to vote, without naturalisation. For other groups, length of residence is an important factor: the longer people have been in Australia, the more likely they are to become citizens. Type of migration is also significant: refugees are more likely to take up citizenship as soon as they are eligible, in order not to become or remain stateless. Government action also plays a part: to secure the high level of 'commitment to Australia' regarded as necessary, citizenship campaigns or 'Years of Citizenship' have been periodically organised (for instance in 1989 and 1994). These have led to increased rates of naturalisation, although usually only for a short period.

Rights of entry and residence

Restrictions on freedom of entry for foreigners

All foreigners who wish to enter Australia have to apply for visas in advance. The only exception is citizens of New Zealand, as the Trans-Tasman Agreement lays down reciprocal rights of free entry for Australians and New Zealanders. The procedure for obtaining tourist and short-stay business visas was recently simplified, so that in most cases these can now be obtained through travel agents when purchasing tickets. Long-term temporary immigrants (persons coming for a limited period for work or study) and permanent settlers have to apply for visas through Australian High Commissions, Consulates or Immigration Offices in their country of origin. Permanent settlers enter Australia primarily through one of the two official programmes for visaed permanent entry: the Migration Program, and the Humanitarian Program. Admission is based on economic, social and humanitarian criteria. Numbers in all permanent entry categories are strictly limited, with the Government deciding on an annual basis. Due to Australia's geographical position, immigration control is fairly easy to enforce, and there are few illegal entrants. Total entry levels in the 1990s have averaged around 80 000 per year, with a downward trend recently due to the current Government's more restrictive policies.[16]

Types of residence status

Immigration rules cover all foreign persons who enter Australia, except New Zealanders. There are three types of entrant:

1. Permanent settlers (or permanent immigrants), who express an intention to make Australia their home, and who are admitted without any time restriction (85 800 entrants in 1996–97).
2. Long-term temporary immigrants, who are admitted for a limited period of some months or some years for work or study purposes (95 100 in 1996–97).
3. Short-term temporary immigrants, mainly tourists and business visitors, who stay for a few weeks or months (4.2 million in 1996–97).

Requirements for permanent residence status

People wishing to become permanent settlers must apply for this status before entering Australia. Persons in Australia as temporary immigrants who wish to seek a change in status to permanent settler are generally asked to return to their country of origin and apply from there. However, some exceptions are made, especially for persons applying for refugee status. Several thousand Chinese students were allowed to change status to refugee (and eventually permanent resident) after the suppression of the Democracy Movement in 1989.

Far more people apply for admission than can be admitted under the annual quotas, and selection processes are quite rigorous. Applicants must meet health standards, be of good character, and meet skill or other requirements for particular visa types. The Migration Program provides entry for 'Family stream' and 'Skill stream' immigrants under various visa categories, together with a small number of other persons under the 'Special Eligibility stream'. Skilled and business migrants are selected on the basis of a Points Test, which takes account of qualifications, work experience, age, and proficiency in English and other languages. Permanent settlers have a right to bring in their spouse and dependent children. More distant relatives are admitted on a range of economic and social criteria, which have recently been tightened up to prevent admission of persons likely to need social or medical services.

The Humanitarian Program has three components. Consistent with the United Nations definition, Refugee immigrants include persons outside their own countries seeking protection from persecution. Special Humanitarian entrants seek relief from forms of discrimination amounting to a substantial violation of human rights, while the Special Assistance Category permits entry to other overseas persons in particularly vulnerable situations who have close family or community links with Australia.[17]

Re-entry rules

Permanent settlers who have not become Australian citizens and long-term temporary immigrants who go overseas must apply for re-entry visas before leaving. These are granted as a matter of course, as long as the original entry visa is still valid.

Discrimination according to country of origin

In the past, Australian immigration policy discriminated on the base of race and national origins. Under the Immigration Restriction Act of 1901 (the White Australia Policy) non-Europeans were generally not admitted at all, while certain Europeans were seen as less desirable than others. The White Australia Policy was watered down in the 1960s and finally abolished in 1972. Since then Australia's immigration policy has been non-discriminatory in that persons from any country can apply to come, whatever their ethnic origin, sex, colour or religion. Selection is made, however, on economic, social and humanitarian criteria, which may lead to covert forms of discrimination against certain groups, especially from less-developed countries, who cannot easily meet the requirement. The only explicit discrimination is the positive one in favour of New Zealanders.

Alien registration process

There is no alien registration process in Australia. Immigrants are expected to give their planned address in Australia when applying for visas, but little is done to check on this, or to monitor changes. Population registers and identity cards have been rejected by Australians on grounds of civil liberties, although all adult citizens are listed on electoral registers. Foreign residents can be traced through a variety of data bases connected with employment, social security and taxation. Temporary immigrants who stay longer than permitted or who work without permission generally find it hard to do so for long without detection due to the need for documents of these kinds.

Social rights

It is difficult to differentiate clearly between the rights of citizens and non-citizens in Australia, because the rights of citizens themselves are not always clearly and consistently defined. This problem arises because (as noted above) the Constitution does not specify the rights of Australian citizens. Rights of citizens and non-citizens are laid down in legislation at both the Federal and state levels. Such important matters as the right to vote, access to public service employment and eligibility for jury service are not consistently regulated throughout Australia. In addition, many significant issues are laid down in common law through court decisions.[18] Despite these ambiguities, it appears that in most legal areas the differences between the rights of citizens and of lawful permanent residents are quite small. Once accepted for entry as permanent settlers, immigrants enjoy a range of substantive citizenship rights that may be denied in many other countries of immigration. Non-citizen residents in Australia may therefore be considered to have highly developed rights of quasi-citizenship, or of what Hammar in the European context has called 'denizenship'.[19] This applies to social, economic and political rights.

Retirement pensions

Permanent residents have the same entitlements as Australian citizens to government retirement pensions, as well as to participation in occupational and private superannuation schemes. Some immigrants also have entitlements from their previous country of residence; the extent to which these are paid in Australia depends on the law of the country concerned. In general, Australian pension rights are portable if immigrants leave for their countries of origin or elsewhere.

Social security system

In general, permanent settlers have access to all employment-related, social security and medical benefits. However, the long-standing principle of equal treatment with regard to welfare rights has been undermined in recent years for recent arrivals. In January 1993, the Australian Labor Party (ALP) Government decided to deny unemployment and sickness benefits to immigrants for the first six months after arrival. Fees were introduced for English-language courses for adult migrants, although some categories such as refugees were exempted. People sponsoring their relatives as immigrants had to give a two year 'assurance of support' (i.e. promise to support their relatives if these were unemployed or in need). Since 1996, the Liberal-National Party Government has made further changes. Fees for visas and compulsory English language courses for new immigrants have been sharply increased. The waiting period for most welfare benefits has been increased to two years for new entrants. In addition the Office of Multicultural Affairs, which had had an important role in monitoring services for immigrants, was abolished.

Limitations for temporary residents

Temporary immigrants do not have access to medical and social benefits. Such entrants are advised to take out private insurance, and this is a requirement for students. There are exceptions for people from countries which have reciprocal agreements with Australia, especially on medical care (e.g. the UK). Emergency medical treatment is normally provided for all who need it, but temporary immigrants are likely to be asked to pay the costs later.

Limitations for irregular residents

Irregular residents are not entitled to medical and social benefits, although emergency treatment is provided in case of need. However, making use of medical or other services is likely to lead to detection and subsequent deportation.

Situation of former military personnel

There is no parallel situation in Australia to the Japanese use of people of colonised countries as soldiers. However, the Defence Act 1903 does not exclude non-citizens from voluntarily joining the armed forces. Nor have they been excluded from conscription at times of war. Resident non-citizens were conscripted during the Second World War and the Vietnam War, and this practice was upheld by a High Court decision in 1945. Although there is no compulsory military service in Australia at present, the legal basis for it still exists. All persons who have resided in Australia over six months and who are aged from 18 to 60 are liable for service, unless exempted on grounds of physical or mental disability. Immigrants from hostile countries (Germany and Italy) were not conscripted during the World Wars, but many were interned for lengthy periods. The practice of conscripting non-citizens is questionable on the grounds that they were forced to defend a nation-state in which they had no right of political representation. Indeed non-citizens in the armed forces had no clear right of re-entry to Australia following overseas service.[20]

Multicultural education

Securing a good education for their children was one of the main aspirations of post-war immigrants. But the assimilation policies of the 1950s and 1960s meant that immigrant children were put into normal classrooms without any special help in learning English or adapting to the new environment. Linguistic and cultural maintenance was discouraged. Serious problems arose in overcrowded inner-city schools, where teachers found it hard to cope with large numbers of children from diverse backgrounds. The result was frequent failure at school, leading to the fear that immigrant children would inherit their parents' disadvantaged class position.[21]

Education played an important part in the multicultural policies that emerged from the 1970s. The Federal Government introduced a Child Migrant Education Program (CMEP) in 1971, to provide intensive English courses for newly-arrived children. By 1975–76, there were 1,407 schools and 90 810 children participating. The program was subsequently renamed the English as a Second Language (ESL) Program and transferred to the states. All immigrant children whose first language is not English still have a right to special tuition. At the same time, immigrant parents often want their children to retain the language and culture of their country of origin. In the 1950s and 1960s, parents, churches and cultural associations set up ethnic schools, which taught after normal school hours or at the weekend. Since the mid-1970s, such schools have received official support and funding.[22]

At the same time, multicultural education was introduced into the curriculum of mainstream schools to foster understanding, tolerance and respect for other cultures. A further aim was to raise the self-esteem of migrant children. Multicultural education was at first a Federal Government programme for the whole country. However, in 1986 Federal funding was cut for both multicultural education and ESL teaching. Both were now left to the authorities of the states. This meant unevenness in programmes between different states, and a reduction in the priority given to multicultural education.[23] Nonetheless, all states do claim that helping children to respect other cultures and to understand Australia's multicultural society is an important part of the curriculum.

Economic rights

Property rights

Non-citizen permanent residents have full rights with regard to owning land or other property.

Self-employment

Non-citizen permanent residents have full rights to self-employment and to establishing businesses in Australia. Businesses owned by immigrants play a major and dynamic role in the Australian economy.[24] The only restriction concerns the need for formal qualifications, registration or membership of professional bodies in order to carry out certain occupations or professions. The conditions here are the same for citizens and non-citizens, but there is evidence of discrimination in recognising the qualifications of overseas-trained personnel.[25]

Public employment at the federal and state levels

The Public Service Act 1922 does not permit non-citizens to take up permanent positions in the Commonwealth Public Service. Non-citizens may be employed on a probationary basis, provided they undertake to apply for Australian citizenship. However, state rules are inconsistent: in Victoria for instance resident non-citizens can become permanent public servants.[26] This limitation of the right to work is significant, since the public service includes not only central administration, but also policing and the judiciary. On the other hand, the importance of the exclusion is tempered by the ease and rapidity with which immigrants can become citizens.

Local authority employment

There appear to be no general rules on employment of non-citizens by local authorities. In general, there do not appear to be any formal barriers in this area.

Distinctions between different national origin groups

No distinctions are made on the basis of national origin. In this area, New Zealanders have the same situation as other permanently resident non-citizens. However, pre-1984 British immigrants who have not naturalised do enjoy the same situation as Australian citizens.

Political rights

Federal and state electoral rights

As already noted, the Constitution does not regulate the right to vote in Australia. Rather it is set out in laws of the Commonwealth and the states. These create not only a right of citizens to vote, but also an obligation. Those who do not vote in Federal and state elections are liable to be fined. However, some citizens are excluded from the right to vote: persons of unsound mind and prisoners. 'Therefore, Parliament has the power to decide which citizens have the right to vote'.[27] Resident non-citizens do not have the right to vote or to stand for public office in Federal and state elections.

The main anomaly with regard to voting rights is that pre-1984 British immigrants still have the right to vote at all levels without being naturalised. The exact size of this group is unknown, but estimates of the number of non-Australian British citizens on the electoral rolls vary from 200 000 to 1 million. This has long been an issue of contention, especially with ethnic communities, as they see it as a continued discrimination in favour of British non-citizens.

Local electoral rights

Non-citizens may have the right to vote in local government elections in the states of Victoria, South Australia, Western Australia and Tasmania, where persons holding rateable land in the area can be enrolled as voters, irrespective of citizenship.[27]

Voter participation

In general, nearly all eligible people, whatever their origins, vote in Federal and state elections, since this is compulsory under Australian law. Participation in local elections is only compulsory in some states. However, no data is available on the participation of immigrants in those local government areas where it is not compulsory.

Representation of immigrants

The representation of immigrants in the political system has slowly improved since the early 1970s. This has particularly been the case at local and state levels. For instance, the Victorian State Parliament now has a Vietnamese–Australian and a Cambodian–Australian member. Indeed, in 1996, it was the most multi-ethnic Parliament in Australia, with almost 14 per cent of its Upper House from NESB and 11 per cent of its Lower House from NESB.[28] This reflects both major parties' attempts in that state to woo and incorporate ethnic constituents.

Despite the growing number of local and state level politicians of NESB, immigrants still remain under-represented in relation to their share in the population, especially at the Federal level. Between 1947 and 1989, for instance, only eight people born in NESCs had entered the national Parliament.[29] In 1991 only 6.7 per cent of legislators and government appointed officials at the three levels of government were of first or second-generation NESB, compared with their share in the population of about 25 per cent.[30] The participation rate of indigenous Australians in government was 0.6 per cent, compared with a 1.6 per cent share in the population. NESB people were also under-represented in the Public Service and particularly in the Senior Executive Service, although the situation showed some improvement since 1989. Participation by NESB and indigenous people was low in many other important areas, such as judges, magistrates, mediators and police officers. As examination of membership of government consultative bodies showed that NESB and indigenous people were well represented on bodies concerned with social and cultural issues, but significantly under-represented in other councils, such as those concerned with economic decision making.

The numbers of Federal politicians from NESB has continued to be low in the 1990s, with the Labor Party (traditionally favoured by many immigrant voters) only having one Member of Parliament born in a NESC prior to the October 1998 Federal election. The low numbers of ethnic representatives continues despite evidence which suggests that they may be more responsive to ethnic constituents and their needs.[31]

Eligibility to stand for office

The conditions of eligibility to stand for office at various levels are generally the same as those for voting. The only exception concerns the right of dual citizens to stand for Parliament (see above).

Restrictions to political freedoms for non-citizens

In general, all non-citizens in Australia (including permanent temporary entrants and even illegal entrants) enjoy a range of civil and political rights guaranteed to everyone by law. Although, these rights do not add up to a principle of legal equality for aliens,[32] it is quite possible for permanent residents to live a full life in Australia without ever feeling the need to become naturalised. In principle Australia's ratification of the International Covenant on Civil and Political Rights (ICCPR) should give equal civil and political rights to resident non-citizens in all areas but the right to vote and stand for public office, and the right to employment in the public service.

However, the right to free speech is more complex. It is not directly protected by the Constitution (either for citizens or non-citizens). The Aliens Power of the Constitution (s. 51(xix)) gives Parliament power to enact discriminatory laws concerning aliens. There is no Australian equivalent to the 14th Amendment to the US Bill of Rights which provides equal protection to all aliens, even those illegally present in the USA. Rather, equal protection in basic civil rights areas such as the right to due legal process is the result of both statutes and common law decisions. Common law does appear to recognise the general principle of equality before the law, but a recent High Court decision on the right to free communication on political matters (one aspect of freedom of speech) failed to confirm the existence of that right for aliens in Australia. The High Court Justices linked free speech to the right to participate in representative government, which is not available to aliens.[33,34]

Conclusion

Australia, like other European settler colonies that have become mass immigration countries, has evolved from an assimilationist to a pluralist model of incorporation. It could be argued that this is the only way to create an inclusive national community when large parts of the population no longer share the ethnic origins of the founding group. However, substantial variations can be found between pluralist countries, for instance with regard to the role of the state in managing ethnocultural difference: Australian multiculturalism has involved a far more active role of the state in social and cultural policy that is to be found in the USA, where the tendency has been to rely on equal legal rights and to leave social and cultural matters to private initiative. Australia has developed complex ways of defining citizenship and managing ethnocultural difference.

The failure of the Constitution to define citizenship rights has left such matters to the laws of the Commonwealth and the states, as well as to common law. This has resulted in considerable inconsistency. The background to this is the fact that Australia did not become fully independent in 1901, and Australians remained British subjects. Moreover, the Constitutional vacuum with regard to citizenship rights was designed to legitimate racial discrimination against Indigenous people and non-European immigrants. It was not until the 1960s, in response to growing non-British immigration and the pressure from international public opinion, that Australia's racist definition of belonging was officially changed.

Since the 1970s, great efforts have been made to redefine the meaning of citizenship in a more inclusive way. Important legal measures include the Racial Discrimination Act 1975; measures to enfranchise indigenous people and to recognise their land rights; and changes in citizenship law to encourage easy naturalisation, permit dual citizenship and remove the privileges of British settlers. Yet, as we have seen, both as a legal framework and as societal membership, Australian citizenship remains contradictory and incomplete in many respects. Moreover, current trends appear retrogressive. Many of the reform impulses of the late 1980s and early 1990s have been abandoned – often tacitly rather than overtly. The situation is marked by oscillation between conservative models based on nostalgia for a bygone age of British hegemony, and neo-liberal models based on the perceived needs of Australian business as part of globalised capital. There is no clear direction for Australian citizenship at present, and this can only heighten the insecurity of immigrants, Indigenous people and other minorities.

Notes

1 This contribution is partly based on work done by the authors as part of a project entitled Intercultural Relations, Identity and Citizenship with funding from the Volkswagen Foundation (Hannover) and the Australian Research Council. It is also partly based on work done for the Comparative Citizenship Project of the Carnegie Endowment for International Peace. Research assistance was provided by Colleen Mitchell, who also prepared the tables in this chapter.
2 H. Reynolds, *Frontier* (Sydney: Allen and Unwin, 1987).
3 H. McQueen, *A New Britannia* (Ringwood Victoria: Penguin, 1970).
4 S. Castles, M. Kalantzis, B. Cope and M. Morrissey, *Mistaken Identity: Multiculturalism and the Demise of Nationalism in Australia* (Sydney: Pluto Press, 1992).
5 English-speaking background countries are generally listed as the UK, USA, New Zealand, Canada and the Republic of South Africa.
6 B. Galligan and J. Chesterman, 'Aborigines, citizenship and the Australian Constitution: did the Constitution exclude Aboriginal People from citizenship', *Public Law Review* (1997) vol. 8, no. 1, pp. 45–61.
7 A.-M. Jordens, *Redefining Australians: Immigration, Citizenship and National Identity* (Sydney: Hale and Iremonger Pty Limited, 1995).
8 A. Davidson, *From Subject to Citizen: Australian Citizenship in the Twentieth Century* (Cambridge: Cambridge University Press, 1997).
9 Davidson, pp. 119–20.
10 I. Ireland and C. Field, *Loss of Australian Citizenship*, (1995) Research Note 19, Canberra, Parliamentary Research Service, Department of the Parliamentary Library.
11 Davidson, p. 139.
12 Joint Standing Committee on Migration 1994, *Australians All-Enhancing Australian Citizenship*, Canberra, AGPS.
13 S. O'Brien, *Dual Citizenship, Foreign Allegiance and s. 44 (i) of the Australian Constitution*, (1992) Background Papers (Law and Government Group) Canberra, Parliamentary Research Service, Department of the Parliamentary Library.

14 House of Representatives Standing Committee on Legal and Constitutional Affairs 1997, *Committee Report on Aspects of Section 44 of the Constitution* Canberra, AGPS.
15 DIMA 1998, *Australian Citizenship*, Fact Sheet 66, Canberra, Department of Immigration and Multicultural Affairs.
16 S. Castles, W. Foster, R. Iredale and G. Withers, *Immigration and Australia: Myths and Realities* (Sydney: Allen & Unwin, 1998).
17 Castles, *et al.*, 1998.
18 K. Rubinstein, 'Citizenship in Australia: unscrambling its meaning', *Melbourne University Law Review* (1995) 20, 2.
19 T. Hammar, *Democracy and the Nation-State: Aliens Denizens and Citizens in a World of International Migration* (Aldershot: Avebury, 1990).
20 Rubinstein.
21 J. Martin, *The Migrant Presence* (Sydney, George Allen and Unwin, 1978).
22 M. Kalantzis, B. Cope, G. Noble and S. Poynting, *Cultures of Schooling* (London: Falmer Press, 1990).
23 D. Cahill, *Immigration and Schooling in the 90s* (Canberra: BIMPR, 1996).
24 J. Collins, K. Gibson, C. Alcorso, S. Castles and D. Tait, *A Shop Full of Dreams: Ethnic Small Business in Australia* (Sydney: Pluto Press, 1995).
25 R. Iredale and I. Nivison-Smith, *Immigrants' Experiences of Qualifications Recognition and Employment: Results form the Prototype Longitudinal Survey of Immigrants to Australia (LSIA)* (Canberra: AGPS, 1995).
26 Rubinstein.
27 Rubinstein.
28 C. Mitchell, G. Zappalà and S. Castles, *Post 1947 migration to Australia and modes of socio-political mobilisation* (1998) Working Paper Number 4, Wollongong, Institute of Social Change and Critical Inquiry, University of Wollongong.
29 J. Jupp, B. York and A. McRobbie, *The Political Participation of Ethnic Minorities in Australia* (Canberra: AGPS, 1989).
30 NMAC (National Multicultural Advisory Council) *Multicultural Australia, The Next Steps: Towards and Beyond 2000* (Two Volumes) (Canberra: AGPS, 1995).
31 G. Zappalà, 'The influence of the ethnic composition of Australian Federal electorates on the parliamentary responsiveness of MPs to their ethnic subconstituencies', *Australian Journal of Political Science* (1998) vol. 33, no. 2, pp. 187–209.
32 B. Wells, 'Aliens: the outsiders in the Constitution', *University of Queensland Law Journal* (1996) 19, 1, pp. 45–74.
33 Rubinstein.
34 Wells, pp. 45–74.

8

Aliens and Citizens in New Zealand[1]

Paul Spoonley

Introduction: aliens in New Zealand

1 Colonial period with British settlement (1800–1907)
2 Fully independent but remaining British subjects (1907–49)
3 Labour migration with significant non-white (Pacific Island) migrant flows (1949–90)
4 Immigration policy reformed and new conceptions of citizenship (1990–)

New Zealand has always had something of a problem with national identity, and therefore with who constitutes a citizen of a nation, and who is an alien, by virtue of its historical status as a colonial outpost for absorbing British settlers.[2] The contemporary nation-state evolved from the signing of the Treaty of Waitangi in 1840 between some Maori and representatives of the European settlers and the colonising power, Britain. But the process of actually establishing the **nation**-state has been compromised by the process of settlement and its role as an outpost of Britain, the presence of a significant indigenous population, Maori, and the ambiguities that arose from membership of a dependent state. For much of the country's history, nationality was defined by being a British colony. It is only in the second half of the twentieth century that new understandings, new policies and new constructions of nationality and citizenship have evolved, at times dramatically.

British settlement began in earnest in the first half of the eighteenth century, and the signing of the Treaty of Waitangi provided the grounds for increasing numbers of British settlers. At the time of signing, only 10 per cent of the local population were Europeans, but by 1860 there was parity in population size between European settler and indigenous

Maori. The vast majority of those new settlers were British, and it remained this way until major changes to immigration policy in 1986. In the 1921 census, 99.35 per cent claimed British nationality, emphasising the fact that even though many had been born in New Zealand, the pre-eminent legal, and social, identity was defined by having the same rights and legal status as British citizens. In this climate, aliens were defined by their non-Britishness, the degree to which they differed from the characteristics which were seen as quintessentially British, as well as the prejudices held towards particular racial groups.

The definition of the 'other' was initially legally encoded in the British Registration of Aliens Act 1836 which required every alien to produce a passport and to declare their nationality.[3] Aliens could become British subjects by undergoing a process of naturalisation as prescribed by an ordinance dating from 1844. Subsequently, the New Zealand Aliens Act 1866 further established the opportunity for some aliens to register as residents and to become British citizens. The same act 'liberalised the circumstances under which aliens could hold property'.[4] Those who did go through the process of naturalisation had their names recorded and published.

What emerges was a definition of who belonged, and who did not, by virtue of New Zealand's connections with Britain.

> The contrast in experience between British and non-British immigrant, between the kin and foreigner or alien, as all foreigners were officially known until 1977, was marked. Britons could enter the country as they wished, the foreigner had to be admitted or permitted... Thus in policy as in attitude, New Zealand in this respect was not a new country embracing people from all over the world... it was a British country and other people did not belong or could stay only on sufferance.[5]

The issue of who did not belong, of who was an alien, became particularly significant at certain points in New Zealand' history. Nineteenth-century racial beliefs about the inferiority of Asians combined with the arrival of Chinese goldminers in the 1860s led to public concern, a Parliamentary Commission of Enquiry in 1871, some vigorous and racist political opposition, and legislation and policies to exclude and control Asians. Legislation such as the 1881 Chinese Immigration Restriction Act sought to discourage and penalise Chinese immigration, while once in New Zealand, their status as 'race aliens' was confirmed by their exclusion from the state-provided old age benefits (introduced in 1898), the right to enter Chinese homes without a warrant under the

1901 Opium Prohibition Act, and the 1908 Immigration Restriction Act which deprived Chinese of any right to naturalisation and therefore New Zealand citizenship until 1951, despite the fact that they first arrived in 1866. They were defined as unacceptable residents and immigrants, a status that was made very clear by a series of acts (27 in all) in the late nineteenth and early twentieth centuries.

The second significant series of events which led to questions about who was a New Zealander and who constituted an alien were the world wars. During the First World War, the opportunity for non-British immigrants to become naturalised was suspended, and the war regulations sought to identify anybody who might be a potential enemy resident in New Zealand. The Registration of Aliens Act 1917 required that anybody who was not British subjects by virtue of birth or because of naturalisation had to be registered, and by July 1918, 6,150 people were on the register.[6] The Revocation of Naturalisation Act 1917 gave authorities the right to take away the status of British/New Zealand citizen if they were deemed to be a threat to public order and security. Much the same happened during the Second World War, and in both cases, those who were seen as 'enemy aliens' were imprisoned, often for the duration of the war.

At the end of the Second World War, along with other British 'dominions' (colonies) such as Canada and Australia, a new form of nationality was established that reflected citizenship of a particular country. As of 1 January 1949, all British subjects born in New Zealand, naturalised in New Zealand or who had been residents of New Zealand for one year, became New Zealand citizens.[7] Now immigrants had to register, including British immigrants although few of the latter group did in any number.[8]

The first significant wave of non-British migrants was Dutch who arrived in the 1950s under a scheme jointly promoted by both Dutch and New Zealand governments. These migrants did not excite a lot of hostility, but very different conditions prevailed in the 1960s and 1970s when large numbers of Pacific Island migrants from Samoa, Tonga, the Cook Islands, Niue and Tokelau arrived in New Zealand to provide labour in the expanding urban, manufacturing sector. With an economic downturn in the early 1970s, these migrants were seen as responsible for a deteriorating employment situation (they were taking the jobs of 'New Zealanders'), law and order issues and the deterioration of certain areas of major cities. The notion of 'overstayer', someone who stays on in New Zealand after they are legally required to have left became an excuse for authorities such as the police and immigration to harass these newly resident communities. The question of their right to be in New Zealand,

and what rights they might have whilst they are in the country, became a political and legal issue. The Privy Council in Britain ruled that a Western Samoan, Falema'i Lesa, who was facing prosecution under the Immigration Act 1964, was under previous legislation a natural-born British subject and therefore a New Zealand citizen.[9] This had the effect of establishing that two-thirds of the population of Western Samoa, some 100 000 people, were New Zealand citizens. This led to concern in New Zealand and the Citizenship (Western Samoa) Act 1982 was introduced to control migration and the status of those Samoans in New Zealand. It was based on a Treaty of Friendship between the New Zealand and Western Samoan governments and specified the access of Samoans to New Zealand citizenship. The Act qualifies the provisions of the Citizenship Act 1977. It was an important point in a period of New Zealand history which was often marked by explicit, public racism.

The most recent issue to provoke questions of membership and who might be an alien was the departure from immigration policies which privileged European migrants in general, and British migrants in particular. The entry of Britain into what was then called the EEC, and the loss of favoured access to the British market for New Zealand exporters began a process of reconsidering New Zealand's geo-political links. By the 1980s, a reforming Labour Government had begun to focus on links with Asia. Part of this included a new immigration policy from 1986 which reduced the previous racially exclusionary policies and sought to attract migrants who had skills or capital that would enhance New Zealand's economic performance. The effect were new migrant flows. In the mid-1980s, two-thirds of migrants came from Europe and North America. By 1995, 60 per cent of those approved for residence were Asians – a major reversal. The Immigration Act 1987 removed 'race', culture and national origins as criteria for immigrant selection, but then a subsequent moral panic about the numbers of Asian migrants saw the introduction of English language requirements (since softened in January 1998) that were seen as racist because they targeted Asians.

The notion of 'aliens' is not now used in either public or private discourses, although there are residual perceptions and prejudices that have the effect of treating some as though they were aliens, or in the language of earlier in the century, 'race aliens', those who represent a racial, political or economic threat.[10] But the administrative processes and the public policies are now largely free of such exclusionary notions and the process of deciding who should be allowed to come to New Zealand, their status once they get here and how they can gain the status and benefits of nationality are straightforward. This is not to say that nationality, and citizenship, are unproblematic. At the same time that immigration policies have been altered to reflect New Zealand's new geo-political interests, domestic politics have been dominated by the rediscovery and, to some extent, the restoration of the rights of the indigenous people, Maori. This has had a significant impact on discussions about what being a citizen of New Zealand means, especially given the fact that Maori have citizenship rights which are specified in the Treaty of Waitangi and which are different to the citizenship rights of other New Zealanders.

Citizenship and nationality

Acquisition/loss of citizenship

Citizenship was defined for most of New Zealand's colonial history, from 1840 through to 1948, as identical to British citizenship and nationality.[11] As with other Dominions such as Canada and Australia, a new citizenship act was passed in 1948 (British Nationality and New Zealand Citizenship Act 1948) which conferred on all British subjects born in New Zealand, those naturalised in New Zealand or who had been resident in New Zealand for one year, the status of New Zealand citizenship from the 1 January 1949. It established for the first time the legal status of New Zealand citizenship and therefore nationality. A further act was passed in (Citizenship Act 1977) although, as McKinnon notes, 'there was in practice little distinction made in rights and obligations between citizens and those who were usually called permanent residents, that is, those with rights to live in New Zealand but without citizenship'. The areas in which this distinction were important included returning to New Zealand but even here, acquiring a returning residents visa allowed people in this category to return to the country as required.[12]

Citizenship is guaranteed to people born in New Zealand (*jus soli*), including to those born to residents who are not planning to live in the country indefinitely, and to those from the Cook Islands, Niue and Tokelau. It is also guaranteed to children under the age of 21 years who are born to New Zealand citizens living overseas (*jus sanguinis*) although such children must come and live in New Zealand to retain this entitlement. A child that is adopted by a New Zealand citizen under the Adoption Act 1955 acquires New Zealand citizenship. Citizenship is also open to any permanent resident after three years of approval of such residence, subject to meeting the requirements for naturalisation under New Zealand's citizenship laws (*jus domicilii*). The requirements of citizenship include: three years' residence; holding a residence permit; being of 'good character'; understanding the 'responsibilities and privileges attaching to New Zealand citizenship'; and being over 18 years of age. The Minister of Internal Affairs may also require an oath of allegiance although this does not require the renunciation of the citizenship of other countries.[13]

A person can lose their New Zealand citizenship or be deported under two circumstances. The first is if they have acted in any way that is 'contrary to the interests of New Zealand'. This includes anyone threatening national security, suspected terrorists and criminal offenders who are resident in New Zealand. The second is they have obtained their citizenship fraudulently.[14]

Distinction between nationality and citizenship

There are few distinctions made in daily usage between nationality and citizenship although there are important qualifiers to this.[15] For most purposes, citizenship would be the preferred usage as it indicates a set of rights and responsibilities. However, the rise of indigenous issues and politics has tended to divorce the concepts to some degree (see below). The irony is that while there is little to distinguish the terms, in practice, access to the services and rights of citizenship are available to all those who are legally resident in New Zealand, irrespective of whether they are New Zealand nationals. Residency confers the advantages of citizenship without requiring residents to be New Zealand nationals.

New concepts of citizenship

The concept of citizenship has undergone two major changes during the twentieth century. The first occurred after the Second World War and the establishment of a New Zealand specific citizenship as opposed to being part of a generic British citizenship. The more recent and radically challenging debate has been about the separate rights of Maori citizenship. New Zealanders, whether Maori (indigenous people) or Pakeha (descendent from European settlers), are New Zealanders in the sense of nationality. However, debates concerning the Treaty of Waitangi have confirmed that there are two sorts of citizenship: one that specifies the rights of New Zealanders as individual subjects with all the rights and protection afforded to individuals; the other is the right, exclusive to Maori, which recognises their membership of *iwi* (tribes) and *hapu* (sub-tribes or extended familial groups) and the fact that have been guaranteed possession of traditional resources, including land, and that the protection of their culture. This has resulted in the significant transfer of resources such as land, control over fisheries and the promotion of language. The distinctions that have emerged in the late 1980s and 1990s, means that what constitutes citizenship is evolving although the implications for nationality are not at all clear. Maori spokespeople have tended to declare their interest in continuing to be New Zealanders and to be active in the affairs of the state of New Zealand but exercising a form of citizenship which differs from that of non-Maori.

Stateless persons

As with Australia, there are no significant groups of stateless people as it is normally relatively easy to gain residency and thereafter New Zealand citizenship. There is no definition of 'statelessness' or 'stateless persons' in the Citizenship Act 1977 and New Zealand is not party to the Convention relating to the Status of Stateless Persons. The Minister of Internal Affairs does have the power to grant citizenship to stateless persons.[16] The one exception is that of asylum seekers, some of whom can be considered stateless. As many as 5,000 asylum seekers have arrived in six years in the mid-1990s, with 2,670 in 1997, a four-fold increase since 1992. Of these, 1,204 claims for residency have been approved with 523 still being considered or under appeal.[17] At least, some of these either claim statelessness or are under threat from the governments in their country of origin.

Dual citizenship

New Zealanders can have multiple citizenship and they are not required to renounce their New Zealand citizenship or nationality when becoming a citizen of another country, unless that is a condition imposed by the other country concerned. Dual nationality is a relatively normal and standard option for New Zealanders, as long as they fulfil the conditions required to be a citizen of the other country and if they see any advantage. It has been possible to gain British or Irish nationality, notably a passport, and to claim other nationalities at the same time as a New Zealand passport and nationality. Given the significant proportion of the New Zealand population that fulfil the conditions of Irish or British nationality, this has been seen as an option with certain advantages, especially given the possibility of access to the European Community offered by a British or Irish passport.

In addition to the possibility of dual nationality, New Zealand also has a special relationship with Australia which is covered by the unique bilateral agreement known as the Trans-Tasman Travel Arrangement (TTTA). This was not reflected in Australian law until 1994 but was part of the exercise of ministerial discretion. Since 1994, the conditions of the agreement have been expressed in law, and the effect is to give New Zealand and Australian citizens the right to reside and work in each others country without applying for visas. This represents a form of dual nationality to the extent that the citizens of either country are treated as if they are citizens in common, with few restrictions on travel, work or the access to services in the other country.

Factors affecting the naturalisation rate

New Zealand's Citizenship Act 1977 made it more difficult to re-enter New Zealand after having travelled overseas. This encouraged those who had few reasons to undergo the naturalisation process to consider taking out citizenship. In particular, British migrants began to increasingly consider taking out New Zealand citizenship. However, the fact that permanent residence conveys nearly all of the advantages of citizenship without requiring New Zealand nationality has meant that there are few pressures to naturalise. If anything, it is often a symbolic gesture involving a public ceremony and a personal commitment to the new country of residence. The rate has not changed significantly in recent decades, with the possible exception of the campaign against 'overstayers' which saw pressure on certain Pacific Island groups to establish their right to be in New Zealand. But even here, the right to permanent residence still conveyed many of the advantages of citizenship without actually requiring New Zealand nationality. Currently, about 18 000 people gain New Zealand citizenship annually.[18]

Residential rights

Restriction on freedom of entry for foreigners

The status and therefore entry of non-citizens to New Zealand falls into two categories. There are permanent residents who must apply for entry prior to arriving, and must declare their intention of staying either long-term (typically more than one year) or migrating permanently. To be considered in these categories, the migrants must meet some of the immigration priorities or categories set by the government and administered by the New Zealand Immigration Service. Since 1986, and the changes to immigration policy, the numbers in these categories have been adjusted by the government and NZIS using a points system whereby potential migrants obtain points according to certain criteria that meet the social and economic needs of New Zealand.

The second category are visitors. Procedures concerning the arrival of short term visitors have been relaxed in recent years, and 80 per cent of New Zealand's short term arrivals enter New Zealand on visa waivers which covers the citizens of 30 other countries. All that they require is a valid passport. The bulk of these short term visitors are tourists.

Types of residence status

The status of arrivals and what they can expect is determined by the category of entry. In relation to short term arrivals, most arrive under the visa waiver option and they are entitled to live in New Zealand on a temporary basis. If they wish to work, then they must obtain a permit to do so. This applies to those who enter as visitors, for educational purposes or for short-term contract employment. This can be done prior to arrival (work visa) or after arrival (work permit). The major consideration is whether there is available work for the applicant. In seasonal horticultural employment, or certain sorts of manual labour in manufacturing, it is relatively easy to obtain permission to work. There are also bi-lateral working holiday schemes that permit young people from Japan, the UK, the USA, Malaysia and Canada to enter and work in New Zealand for up to 12 months.[19]

Requirement for permanent residence status

In terms of permanent residents, they must apply and be considered under four main categories. The first of these is the General Skills category which grants approval if the applicant meets certain criteria (age, ability to settle in New Zealand), especially their employability and work experience. It reflects the government's aim of accepting those who have skills that will benefit New Zealand's economy. The second is the Business Investor category which also considers such factors as age and settlement issues, but the main criteria here is the availability of capital to invest in New Zealand (a minimum of $NZ750 000). The third category is Family which provides for New Zealand residents to be joined by members of their family. More than half are partners (married or de facto) of the New Zealand resident, including same sex partners (as long as they have lived in a stable relationship for four years prior to entry), and another third are parents of New Zealand residents. A Humanitarian category allows for the entry of people whose circumstances are resulting in serious physical or emotional harm to themselves or a New Zealand relative, and that the granting of New Zealand residence is the best option. By 1996, more than half of all approvals fell into the two 'social' (Family, Humanitarian) categories compared to less than a third in 1993.

In addition to the above, there are two quotas. The first applies to Samoans, and up to 1,100 are granted New Zealand residence each year. The second quota is 750 for refugees who have been nominated by the UNHCR and are normally in refugee camps after having to flee their homeland. There are also a growing number of asylum seekers who appeal for residence after having arrived in the country. The numbers in this category increased significantly in the 1990s (as noted at p. 164 above), with 5,000 applying between 1992 and 1997, of which, 1,204 were approved for residence while another 523 are still being considered or under appeal. Once they have been approved for residence, as with other long term and permanent residence approvals, they have all the rights of New Zealand citizens.

In the case of permanent and long term migrants, the right to reside in New Zealand is established prior to arrival. Once in New Zealand, if they have been approved for permanent residence, there are very few distinctions between a New Zealand citizen and a permanent resident. Any immigrant with permanent residence status who has lived in New Zealand for a minimum of three years can apply to become a citizen although there is no pressure placed on residents to become citizens, and citizenship is not a requirement to access social services or state-funded benefits.

Re-entry rules

While there is no differentiation between citizen and permanent resident in terms of accessing resources and services in New Zealand, the main issue for those who retain a passport from another country is the issue of re-entry to New Zealand. Those without a New Zealand passport need to apply for a returning resident's visa. They are easy to obtain, especially for those who have tax status in New Zealand, and it allows multiple re-entry for the life of the visa. However, a New Zealand passport which is available once citizenship has been granted, does not require anything further in order to re-enter New Zealand and as long as a current New Zealand passport is held, the length of time outside the country is irrelevant.

Alien registration process

The aliens register which was used during the mid-part of the century when there was concern about foreign nationals who might pose a threat to New Zealand security does not exist any longer. Contemporary data bases which provide information about residents for such purposes as taxation, border control or benefits are sufficient to locate people in most cases. The only possible exception are the lists of 'overstayers', those who have stayed on in New Zealand after they should have left. At certain points in the 1970s and 1980s, these lists became an important issue for the New Zealand government as they sought to identify and reduce the number of overstayers, notably Pacific Islanders. Research by the Race Relations Office in 1986 established that Pacific Islanders constituted about one-third of overstayers but were 86 per cent of those who were being prosecuted at the time.[20] The rest of the overstayers, mostly from North America and Europe were not targeted by the authorities in the same way indicating considerable racial discrimination. In order to resolve the status of those who were overstayers, the government offered an amnesty on two occasions with some able to gain permanent residence while others were given the opportunity to leave without any criminal proceedings or a police record.

Social rights

Limitation for permanent residents

The right to permanent residence also conveys full rights to benefits, including government-funded retirement income. A distinction between citizen and non-citizen, at least those non-citizens with permanent residence, does not exist for benefit purposes.

The same is true for any social benefits. Permanent residents, even if they are not New Zealand citizens, have access to state-provided health care and education, compensation for industrial accidents and illnesses, unemployment benefits and various training packages for unemployed and welfare benefits. Immigrants enjoy the same rights as any New Zealand citizen, and this is specified in legislation such as the ace Relations Act (introduced in 1971 and subsequently amended), the Human Rights Act and the New Zealand Bill of Rights Act (1990).

In the 1990s, a number of reciprocal agreements have been signed with other countries to provide for residents of one country to be paid benefits if they now live in the other country concerned. The social security agreements have been signed with the United Kingdom (1990), the Netherlands (1990), Ireland (1993), Greece (1994), Australia (1994), Denmark (1997) and Canada (1997). Benefits such as the retirement pension, invalids benefits, war veterans pensions or widows benefit are paid to those from these countries living in New Zealand, or vice versa. In some cases, the numbers are significant. There are 32 000 British pensioners living in New Zealand, and 20 000 have applied for a special option for the payment of pensions.[21]

Limitations for temporary residents and irregular residents

Temporary visitors are covered while in New Zealand for personal injury under New Zealand's comprehensive accident compensation legislation which is based on providing for those who have been injured on a no-fault basis. The terms of this legislation are currently being changed in certain regards, but for the moment, temporary visitors to New Zealand are covered.

The same facility applies to those who are classed as overstayers, although there has been a growing issue for health care providers in recent years as they have moved to a user-pays basis for certain illnesses and treatments. Some have come to New Zealand because of the specialist or hospital care that is available but are legally resident elsewhere. Because they have not had an accident (and therefore fall outside the accident compensation legislation and provisions), their health care is either not funded by the New Zealand government (they are not permanent residents) or because they are seeking treatment which would be paid for by the individual anyway. In some cases, these visitors and their treatment is paid for by their own governments or communities because the only option is available via New Zealand health care providers. But there are also growing debts that have been incurred by short-term visitors seeking medical treatment in New Zealand. Some health care organisations, especially in Auckland, regularly complain about these debts and their difficulty in obtaining payment.

Multicultural education

The issues faced by speakers of LOTEMs (languages other than English and Maori) has been of increasing concern, particularly with the arrival of significantly greater numbers of non-English speaking migrants since the Second World War. It is increasingly accepted that language maintenance helps migrants adapt as well as being a source of individual and community pride. However, there are no national policies for dealing with any aspect of immigrant language and culture with the exception of some Pacific Island communities.[22] There is a statement about immigration policy which talks about social cohesion[23] but still no reference to immigrant community languages. Schools that have significant numbers of non-English speaking students receive additional support but this is in order to help improve the English language and other skills of these students. Some support is available to Pacific Island communities and the teaching of Pacific Island languages and culture but this is modest. If language is going to be maintained, then it is held to be the responsibility of the community concerned. There is one important initiative which provides a model for language retention. There was concern during the 1970s at the rapid loss of Maori and the possibility that very few would speak it in the future. *Kohanga reo* (language nests) were established in the early 1980s. They provided immersion care and education for pre-schoolers (under five years of age) in Maori, and were minimally funded by the government but relied extensively on community support and funding. Within a decade, there were more than 800 *kohanga reo* around New Zealand, and the results were impressive in terms of improving community participation and individual esteem and skills. The flow-on effects included a demand for primary, then secondary and finally university education using Maori as the language of instruction. Other communities have subsequently adopted the pre-school aspect of these developments so, for example, that the Samoan community has a number of *a'oga amata* which repeat the Maori experience and structures. However, these are very much community initiatives even if they are seen in a positive light by the government and educational authorities.

Economic rights

Property rights

There are no restrictions on the property rights of anyone who has permanent residence in New Zealand, especially if they New Zealand residents for tax purposes:

> Every person who is not a New Zealand citizen is entitled to take, acquire, hold, and dispose of real or personal property in the same manner in all respects as if that person were a New Zealand citizen.[24]

The only other restriction relates to individuals and companies who are normally resident overseas, and here, the government has a commission – the Overseas Investment Commission – which receives and considers such applications. The commission has been criticised in the 1990s for the fact that it has turned down very few request from overseas organisations or individuals and that it is not performing its role as a watchdog for New Zealand's interests. The effect is to confirm that property rights for non-citizens, whether New Zealand residents or not, are much the same and there are few if any barriers to owning New Zealand property.

Self-employment

Current immigration policy encourages immigrants to establish businesses, including self-employment, especially those immigrants who have been accepted under the Business Investor category. It has not been easy to be successfully self-employed for immigrants[25] but there are no restrictions. However, once these businesses have been established, they must meet all the requirements such as the code of employment and such issues as statutory minimum wages, equal pay for men and women and special leave (e.g. parental leave), requirements which do not always accord with immigrants and their cultural or social beliefs and practices.

The government also has a programme to encourage the participation of Pacific Islanders in business, especially in terms of self-employment. The Ministry of Pacific Island Affairs supports the Pacific Island Business Development Trust which sponsors the entry of Pacific Islanders into business enterprises.

Public employment

There are only two jobs that require a person to be a citizen of New Zealand. One is a Member of Parliament while the other is as an employee of the New Zealand Security Intelligence Service. In the latter case, the reason is one of national security. In the case of parliamentarians, the issue is one of national interest and loyalty. All other occupations are open to permanent residents.

There are no occupations or jobs at local government level which are closed to non-citizens who have the right to permanently reside in New Zealand. Indeed, there have been a number of local authority councillors elected who have not had New Zealand citizenship.

There are no statistics kept of non-citizens employed in government posts, because there are so few restrictions and no legal distinction.

Permanent residence conveys all of the rights of citizenship without formally requiring an immigrant to become a citizen. Australian citizens, due to the Trans-Tasman Travel Arrangement, have the right to reside, work and access social services as New Zealand citizens and those with a permanent right to reside.

Political rights

State electoral rights

The right to vote in national elections is based upon certain criteria (the person must be over 18 years of age, have lived continuously in New

Zealand for one year and one month in the electorate in which they are voting and must be a citizen or permanent resident). Again, there is no distinction between residents, as long as they have the right to permanent residence. This is partly a legacy of the fact that British citizenship was synonymous with New Zealand citizenship, at least until 1977. British residents had all the rights of a New Zealand citizen, and approved residents gained the same rights, including political participation in the voting process. It is a reflection of a political history in a small democracy which has a strong tradition of participation and enfranchisement. Subsequently, liberal and human rights-based political movements have ensured that both the provisions remain generous and inclusive, and that new notions of what it means to be a citizen have emerged, especially in relation to the citizenship rights of Maori.

Local electoral rights

Immigrants who are permanent residents are also entitled to vote in local authority elections in those electoral districts in which they live. Parliamentary electors are automatically qualified as local authority electors and can vote for candidates in the local authority area in which they reside. If they own property and pay rates (property taxes) in another area, they are also entitled to vote in that are as well. However, the same provision for parliamentary candidates applies. Candidates for local authorities must be New Zealand citizens, either by birth or naturalisation, according to the Local Government Act (1974).

Voter participation and representations of aliens

There is no research to indicate whether immigrants participate in voting at the same rates as New Zealand citizens, Rates are typically very high in New Zealand but everyone, citizen or otherwise, is encouraged to vote. New Zealand citizens are required by law to register and appear on the electoral rolls but they are not required by law to vote.

New Zealand had a Westminster political system up until 1996 when a Mixed Member Proportional system was introduced. It provided for proportional representation, as well as an increase in the number of parliamentarians. There is also a separate Maori roll (Maori can choose to register on either the Maori or general rolls) that provides for election to five Maori seats in parliament. These seats were established in 1867 by legislation, and four Maori seats elected by voters on a separate Maori electoral roll have been elected since then, with a further seat being added in the mid-1990s. The effect was to dramatically alter the number of minority groups representatives in Parliament. Out of 120 seats, 15 were occupied by Maori, 3 by Pacific Islanders and 1 by an Asian Member of Parliament. This roughly accords with the proportion of the population from each of these groups. This resulted from the first MMP election in 1966, and another scheduled for 1999. A number of the minority ethnic MPs were elected from the lists that each party constructs (there are 55 list seats) as opposed to representatives from specific electorates (65 seats). Parties have increasingly sought to appeal to ethnic communities, and it was noticeable that a number of new immigrants stood as candidates. There was even an 'ethnic party' which sought to encourage representation on behalf of new immigrants and drew attention to the issues that were important to them. It failed to get any representatives elected, but it indicates the growing significance of such issues in the national political arena.

Eligibility to stand for office

The right to vote is extended to all permanent residents in New Zealand, whether they are citizens or not, while becoming a Member of Parliament requires that the person be a New Zealand citizen. The latter requires citizenship as a statement of loyalty and commitment.

Restrictions on political freedom for aliens

The political rights of immigrants are identical to those of New Zealand citizens and are enshrined in the New Zealand Bill of Rights Act 1990 which defines and guarantees rights such as the freedom of assembly, speech, the right to protection against discrimination, rights of access to lawyers and a fair trial. Furthermore, the Human Rights Act 1993 makes it illegal for any individual to discriminate against others on the grounds of political opinion, national origins, race or ethnicity. The rights of all permanent residents are the same and these are affirmed in New Zealand's legislation.

Conclusion

New Zealand's political and legal environment was dominated for most of the nineteenth and twentieth centuries by its links to Britain, with the result that being a British and New Zealand citizen were much the same, at least until 1977. This excluded migrants or citizens of other countries, most notably migrants from China and India who faced major barriers to entry and racism once they were resident in New Zealand. Like Australia, New Zealand adopted a 'whites only' policy although in the New Zealand case, it was effectively a 'British only' policy. Also like Australia, even though New Zealand became an independent country in 1970, in reality New Zealanders remained British citizens for legal purposes until 1977.

The 1970s saw the disruption of this link, and since, New Zealand has re-aligned itself in economic and political terms and broken many (but not all) of its economic and political ties with Britain. Domestic changes have also encouraged a growing interest in New Zealand nationality and citizenship and what it might entail. Maori ethnic assertiveness has helped redefine what citizenship entails, and an historic agreement, the Treaty of Waitangi, now dominates the constitutional landscape. Other contributions to an evolving and more inclusive notion of citizenship include human rights legislation and a New Zealand Bill of Rights Act. New Zealand is rapidly moving towards defining membership of both a national and specific rights-bearing ethnic group in terms of bicultural and multicultural initiatives and legislation. The aliens of the early twentieth century – Chinese and Indian migrants – have now become encompassed in the more liberal and inclusive policies concerning immigration and settlement. This is not to say that there is not political opposition, but the barriers to entry and residence have gone as New Zealand moves towards a citizenship which is differentiated by ethnicity but as a means of specifying and enhancing the rights of an indigenous and eventually migrant ethnic populations.

Notes

1 This chapter draws upon an earlier paper, R. Bedford, J. Goodwin, E. Ho, J. Lidgard, C. Macpherson and P. Spoonley, 'Regulating International Migration: A New Zealand Perspective' *International Migration: Conference Proceedings and the Regulations of International Migration in New Zealand,* (Auckland: Asia-Pacific Migration Research Network, 1998). The research associated with this publication is funded by the Foundation for Research, Science and Technology.

2 A. Fleras and P. Spoonley, *Recalling Aotearoa. Indigenous and Ethnic Politics in New Zealand* (Auckland: Oxford University Press, 1999); M. McKinnon, *Immigrants and Citizens. New Zealanders and Asian Immigration in Historical Context,* (Wellington: Institute of Policy Studies, 1996).

3 M. McKinnon, *op. cit.*, p. 13.

4 *ibid.*, p. 13.

5 *ibid.*, p. 12.

6 *ibid.*, p. 17.

7 *ibid.*, p. 36.

8 See *ibid.*, pp. 36–37.

9 B. Macdonald, 'The Lesa Case, and the Citizenship (Western Samoa) Act 1982', in A.D. Trlin and P. Spoonley (eds), *New Zealand and International Migration. A Digest and Bibliography, Number 1*, (Palmerston North: Massey University, 1986), p. 73.
10 R. Haines ('Citizenship and Nationality', *The Laws of New Zealand* (Auckland: Butterworths, 1994), p. 31 comments that: 'New Zealand legislation contains no generally applicable definition of "alien"'. However, for the purposes of the Citizenship Act 1977, an alien is a person who does not have the status of a New Zealand citizen, a Commonwealth citizen (British subject), a British protected person, or an Irish citizen.
11 Citizenship is the accepted usage although '"[n]ationality" and "citizenship" are used ... as equivalent terms, as New Zealand law makes no distinction between a "citizen" of New Zealand and a "national" of New Zealand'. *ibid.*, p. 6.
12 M. McKinnon, *op. cit.*, p. 44.
13 See R. Haines, *op. cit.*, p. 13.
14 *ibid.*, p. 34.
15 See footnote 11.
16 R. Haines, *op. cit.*, p. 33.
17 See Fleras and Spoonley, *op. cit.*
18 For further details, see the *New Zealand Official Yearbook 1998* (Wellington, Government Publications, 1998, p. 124).
19 Bedford *et. al.*, *op. cit.*, p. 10.
20 P. Spoonley, *Racism and Ethnicity*, Second edn (Auckland: Oxford University Press, 1993), p. 14.
21 New Zealand Official Yearbook, 1998, pp. 148–9.
22 M. Roberts, 'Immigrants and Language in New Zealand', in A.D. Trlin and P. Spoonley (eds), *New Zealand and International Migration. A Digest and Bibliography, Number 3*, (Palmerston North: Massey University, 1997), p. 85.
23 *ibid.*, p. 87.
24 R. Haines, *op. cit.*, p. 32.
25 R. Bedford *et. al.*, *op. cit.*, p. 11.

9

Citizenship Rights and Non-citizens: a Canadian Perspective

Donald Galloway

Introduction

A chronology of Canadian law relating to citizenship

The Dominion of Canada came into being in 1867, when the United Kingdom Parliament united pre-existing colonies by enacting the British North America Act 1867,[1] since renamed as the Constitution Act 1867.[2] This statute divides legislative authority over specified subject matters between the Parliament of Canada and the provincial legislatures. Section 91(25) grants to Parliament authority over 'Naturalization and Aliens', while section 95 grants concurrent authority over immigration to both the federal and provincial legislatures. However, this latter section also provides that provincial law on immigration will be operative only as long as it is not repugnant to federal law. Over the years, the test of how to determine repugnancy has changed and is, to this day, somewhat controversial.

The Constitution Act 1867 did not create a fully sovereign state. The Colonial Laws Validity Act,[3] enacted by the United Kingdom Parliament in 1865 continued to operate. It rendered void any colonial law that was repugnant to a United Kingdom statute which was intended to apply to that colony (known as an 'imperial statute'). One such statute was the Naturalization Act 1870,[4] section 4 of which defined a natural-born British subject as a 'person born within the dominions of Her Majesty'. In effect, this merely continued the English common law which, at an early date, had embraced the principle of *jus soli*.

The Colonial Laws Validity Act was in effect until 1931. As a result, until that date, the Parliament of Canada did not have the full power to define the membership of Canadian society by identifying a Canadian citizenry. Individuals who may have considered themselves as

Canadians by birth or by parentage had to be content with their legal status as British subject. While section 91(25) of the Constitution Act 1867 did allow for naturalisation, people were naturalised as British subjects.

Nevertheless, the Parliament of Canada did struggle against the fetters of imperial power. In the Immigration Act 1910,[5] it employed the term 'Canadian citizen' to refer to one group of persons who had a right to enter Canada. Likewise, the Canadian Nationals Act[6] of 1921 created the status of Canadian National for the sole purpose of dealing with a requirement imposed by the International Court of Justice that countries be able to nominate only their own nationals for membership of that court. Without this concept, Canada could not gain representation.

In 1931, the Statute of Westminster granted to Canada the authority to amend and repeal imperial statutes. Only in 1946, did Parliament make use of this power by defining its members as citizens. It enacted the Canadian Citizenship Act[7] which came into effect in the following year. This statute was the first to identify exhaustively the qualifications for citizenship as well as the means by which it could be lost. It was superseded in 1977 by the Citizenship Act[8] which continues to apply today. However, currently, a bill is being considered by Parliament which, if enacted, will become the Citizenship of Canada Act. It will alter the provisions of the current law in significant ways as outlined below. It is expected that it will take effect in 1999.

In 1982, the Canadian Constitution was fully repatriated from the United Kingdom and the Canadian Charter of Rights and Freedoms[9] was entrenched as one of its parts. The Charter specifies and guarantees substantive rights that individuals hold against the various levels of government. A number of these rights are vested only in citizens. Thus, section 3 recognises that every citizen has the right to vote in federal and provincial elections and to be qualified for membership in the relevant legislature.[10] Section 6(1) of the Charter recognises that every citizen has the right to enter, remain in and leave Canada.[11] And section 23(1) of the Charter vests in citizens who meet certain qualifications the right to have their children educated in one of the two official languages.[12]

However, it should be noted that the Charter does not explicitly define citizenship. One anomalous feature of Canadian law is that while the Constitution grants rights to citizens, the qualifications for citizenship are found in a federal statute. This raises the question whether there are implied constitutional standards that could be imposed on Parliament when it defines the qualifications for citizenship. Is it constitutionally permissible to exclude classes of individuals from the status, or to include others? The reference to citizenship in the Charter raises the possibility that the Constitution embraces a moral conception of citizenship that should be regarded as being more fundamental than the positive law conception found in the Citizenship Act. Peter Hogg, a noted constitutional lawyer, rejects this possibility and suggests that the term 'citizen' found in the Charter should be regarded as having a flexible definition, with the legislature being the proper body to make decisions about its content.[13] However, this interpretation seems counterintuitive. If Parliament could redefine those who are the beneficiaries of Charter rights, one would think that, analogously, it could also redefine 'Government', the body which is subject to Charter obligations, and thereby immunise itself from its application. The issue is yet to be settled.

A chronology of Canadian law relating to alienage

I turn now to consider the legal status of aliens. Many early battles in Canada over the rights of aliens were fought in British Columbia, where the provincial legislature attempted to pass racist statutes which aimed to discriminate against Asians. Between 1878 and 1908, it attempted repeatedly to control the access of Asians to the province by enacting explicit prohibitions on their entry, by imposing entrance requirements which could not be met, or by imposing discriminatory burdens on those who had been admitted previously by, for example, disqualifying them from working in particular sectors and from participating in political decision-making.[14] In doing so, it cited section 95 of the Constitution Act 1867 as the source of both its authority to exclude immigrants and its authority to use racial criteria in doing so. It also cited other heads of power found in section 92 of the Constitution Act 1867 to justify restrictions on Asians who were already in the province.[15] Many of these statutes were found to be unconstitutional, on the ground that they infringed on federal powers, but some were upheld.

Although the British Columbian anti-Asian policy initially met strong resistance from the federal government and also failed to meet judicially imposed criteria of legality, the province was eventually able to persuade the federal legislature to enact very restrictive legislation regulating Chinese immigration which continued to be in effect until 1947.

Race was not the only factor that was taken into account in determining who was welcome as an immigrant. In early legislation, one finds vague prohibitions against the mentally and physically infirm and against those likely to become a public charge and those involved in crimes of moral turpitude.

Slowly, these rules relating to aliens began to change in two significant ways. First, the grounds of exclusion became more precise and less value-laden. This can be explained by the fact that the Canadian government had become more attuned to principles which underlie the doctrine of the Rule of Law. The Immigration Act 1976[16] which is the primary source of current law, attempts to specify precisely grounds of exclusion and removal, although, particularly in relation to grounds of health, it still relies on indefinite generalities.

Secondly, racial criteria disappeared from both immigration laws and laws of general application in Canada. The establishment of the United Nations, the adoption of the Univeral Declaration of Human Rights and the Canadian Government's perception of its diplomatic role within the international community promoted a gradual shift towards the adoption of classifications that were not based on race.

The entrenchment of the Canadian Charter of Rights and Freedoms was a significant event for those who did not hold the status of citizenship. First, section 6 specifically grants mobility rights within Canada to permanent residents. Also, and more significantly, the Charter contains provisions which apply to every individual, including section 15(1), which states:

> Every individual is equal before and under the law and has the right to equal protection and equal benefit of the law without discrimination and, in particular, without discrimination based on race, national or ethnic origin, colour, religion, sex, age or mental or physical disability.[17]

This section, like other sections granting substantive rights is qualified by section 1, which stipulates that the guaranteed rights are subject 'to such reasonable limits prescribed by law as can be demonstrably justified in a free and democratic society.'[18] While this qualifying section allows governments to adopt legislation that restricts the identified rights, courts have imposed heavy demands on a government attempting to do so, because the rights identified in the Charter are regarded as essential elements of human dignity or the moral status of an individual. Specifically, not only must the government's objectives be pressing and substantial, but the measures taken to achieve these objectives must be proportional to the objectives and must be tailored to have minimal impairment on individual rights.[19] As noted below, one of the most significant Supreme Court of Canada decisions concerning the application of section 15 and section 1 of the Charter relates to an attempt to discriminate between citizens and permanent residents.

Citizenship and nationality

Acquiring and losing citizenship

As noted above, the Citizenship Act is the primary source of citizenship law, although it may soon be superseded by the proposed Citizenship of Canada Act. The current law recognises three principal ways by which one may gain the status of citizenship.[20] First, a person who is born in Canada, is automatically a Canadian citizen,[21] unless he or she is the child of a foreign diplomat.[22]

Second, a strand of *jus sanguinis* is also recognised in the Citizenship Act, in that a person automatically becomes a citizen by being born to a Canadian citizen outside Canada.[23] However, a qualification is attached: if the parent had also gained citizenship through this provision, the child will lose the status unless, before the age of twenty-eight, he or she applies to retain the status, and registers as a citizen and either resides in Canada for at least a year before applying or establishes a substantial connection with Canada.[24] The proposed legislation establishes that these rules apply only to two generations: the third generation born outside Canada will not have a claim to citizenship.

Currently, the rules relating to gaining citizenship through parental descent do not apply to children adopted by a citizen outside Canada. Such children must be sponsored as immigrants if they are to gain status in Canada. Should the sponsorship be permitted, the child will be admitted to Canada as a permanent resident and may later seek naturalisation.[25] Similarly, the rules do not apply to the children of permanent residents who are born outside Canada. In the proposed legislation, children adopted outside Canada may obtain citizenship automatically.

The third principal method of gaining citizenship is outlined in section 5(1) of the Citizenship Act which sets out the qualifications which must be met by a person seeking to gain citizenship by naturalisation. It provides that:

> The Minister shall grant citizenship to any person who
> (a) makes application for citizenship;
> (b) is eighteen years of age or over;
> (c) has been lawfully admitted to Canada for permanent residence, has not ceased to be a permanent resident pursuant to section 24 of

the Immigration Act, and has, within the four years immediately preceding the date of the application, accumulated at least three years of residence in Canada . . . ;

(d) has an adequate knowledge of one of the official languages of Canada;

(e) has an adequate knowledge of Canada and of the responsibilities and privileges of citizenship; and

(f) is not under a deportation order. . . .

Section 3(1) of the Citizenship Act also stipulates that a person who meets these requirements is a citizen only when he or she takes the oath of citizenship, a requirement which can be waived only in the case of a minor or a person with a mental disability. Moreover, section 24 of the Immigration Act, to which reference is made, provides that a person ceases to be a permanent resident when he leaves Canada or remains outside Canada with the intention of abandoning Canada as his place of permanent residence, and that a person who has been outside the country for six months in a one-year period shall be deemed to have abandoned Canada unless he proves that he did not have that intent.[26] The Citizenship Regulations flesh out these statutory requirements. For example, they provide that knowledge of Canada and of the responsibilities and rights of citizens is to be tested by questions relating to such matters as the election process, social and cultural history, political history or physical and political geography.[27]

The reference to three years of accumulated residence in section 5(1) of the Citizenship Act has created interpretive difficulties. Some judges have regarded it as requiring actual physical presence in Canada, while others have thought it to require something lesser, like maintaining a principal residence. Under the proposed legislation physical presence in Canada for three years out of five is required.

The Citizenship Act and the Citizenship Regulations also provide for loss and renunciation of citizenship. Section 10 of the Act provides that where the Governor in Council (i.e. the Federal Cabinet) is satisfied that a person has obtained citizenship 'by false representation, or fraud or by knowingly concealing circumstances' the person ceases to be a citizen. Moreover, where a person has gained permanent resident status through such means he or she is deemed to have obtained citizenship also by such means. These provisions have been used by the Federal Government in recent years with mixed results against individuals who have concealed alleged war crimes when applying for permanent resident status. To find such individuals guilty of the offences would require proof beyond a reasonable doubt. To strip them of their citizenship and therefore qualify them for deportation requires only proof on the balance of probabilities.

A person may renounce Canadian citizenship where he or she has assumed or is about to assume citizenship of another country.[28]

Citizenship and nationality

Canadian law refers to the status of citizenship and, unlike some other jurisdictions, such as Mexico, does not draw a distinction between citizenship and nationality. However, colloquially, the terms 'citizenship' and 'nation' are used in a variety of diverse contexts. For example, non-governmental organisations which promote concerns relating to democracy refer to themselves as citizenship groups; citizenship is commonly promoted as the virtue of participating in civil society. Each of these usages has ensured that the lexicon of citizenship is complex and varied.

Changes in the concept of citizenship

Two important changes are worth noting. First, during the period when the Canadian Constitution did not explicitly guarantee political rights and freedoms, influential jurists in the Supreme Court of Canada relied on the concept of citizenship as a device to prevent provinces from enacting laws that violated fundamental rights. Most prominent among these was Mr. Justice Ivan Rand, who asserted that being a citizen meant being able to exercise basic human rights and freedoms in all parts of the country. In essence, he argued that the federal legislature's authority over citizenship included authority over those rights that define the meaning of citizenship. At different moments, Mr. Justice Rand identified the right to free speech and the right of mobility as constituent elements of the status rather than incidental benefits. Consequently, any attempt to curtail these would be an attack on the status of citizenship and would therefore be beyond the powers of the provinces.[29] Thus, Mr. Justice Rand found in the concept of citizenship a device which promised to achieve two goals simultaneously – protecting fundamental human rights and maintaining a powerful central government. While the Canadian Charter of Rights and Freedoms has since disconnected the link between citizenship and the enjoyment of human rights, the connection between citizenship and a strong central government endures.

A second important change is gradually revealing itself. In a treaty recently negotiated between the Federal Government, the Province of British Columbia and the Nisga'a Nation,[30] an aboriginal people in

British Columbia, individuals who are determined to belong to the Nisga'a are called Nisga'a citizens. The treaty, which is yet to be ratified by the Federal Government, defines the Nisga'a Nation as 'the collectivity of those aboriginal people who share the language, culture and laws of the Nisga'a Indians of the Nass Area and their descendants.' More importantly, it defines 'Nisga'a citizen' as 'a citizen of the Nisga'a nation as determined by Nisga'a law.' The treaty allows the Nisga's to adopt their own constitution, establish institutions of self-government and define their own citizenry. This treaty may serve as a blueprint for future negotiations between the governments and First Nations.

Statelessness and dual nationality

Statelessness is not an issue of great concern in Canada, although the law relating to renunciation of citizenship clearly aims to prevent individuals from becoming stateless.

Currently, Canadians who take citizenship of another state do not lose their Canadian citizenship, nor are persons who naturalise in Canada required to renounce their prior citizenship. The issue of whether it is defensible to permit a person to hold more than one citizenship is not infrequently raised in public debate. For example in 1994, the Parliamentary Standing Committee on Citizenship and Immigration issued a report that included three recommendations regarding dual nationality: that the government consider the possibility of stripping of their citizenship those Canadian citizens who voluntarily acquire a second citizenship; that those who hold dual citizenship by virtue of events beyond their control, while living in Canada, accord primacy to their Canadian citizenship; and that those becoming naturalised be required to declare that they will accord primacy to their Canadian citizenship over all other citizenships.[31]

Specifically, the report states,

> [T]he Committee finds persuasive the arguments of most of our witnesses who expressed concerns about the current practice of allowing dual citizenship. They questioned how it is possible to swear loyalty and allegiance to more than one country, and believe the practice diminishes the value of our citizenship. It may also aid and abet those who view Canadian citizenship primarily as a convenient commodity, useful to enhance their international trading ability, or as an 'insurance policy' which they may wish to use in the future, while in the meantime residing elsewhere. Among the advantages of such a 'policy' would be the guaranteed right to retire

> to Canada and have access to whatever benefits are then available to residents – health care in particular – without having contributed in taxes to the country.[32]

The Committee's recommendations may contain a hidden subtext. They were published shortly before a referendum was held in Quebec to determine if it should remain a part of Canada, at a time when federalists were anxious to convince undecided voters that the consequences of an affirmative vote would be extreme. Also, the recommendations leave open a number of basic questions, most notably, that of determining how one shows preference for Canada when loyalties conflict. Would it be contrary to one's declaration of loyalty to send money to one's family overseas? To vote in a foreign election for a government whose goals conflict with the goals of the current Canadian government? Because of these difficulties, it is not too surprising that the proposed legislation makes no recommendations for altering Canadian dual nationality law.

Naturalisation rates

The level of naturalisation in Canada is high. According to Government estimates,[33] since 1977, the average rate of naturalisation has been 84 per cent. Of the 2 525 321 individuals who became permanent residents between 1977 and 1993, 2 052 738 became citizens. The yearly rates of naturalisation have varied significantly over this period. For example, in 1992, only 61 per cent of those who had been granted permanent residence three years previously, became citizens, while in 1986, 116 per cent of those who had been granted permanent residence three years previously did so.[34] Any opinion on the cause of these variations would be purely speculative.

Residential rights

Freedom of entry

The Immigration Act reserves two unqualified rights for citizens:[35] they have the unqualified right to come into Canada and the unqualified right to remain in Canada. The Charter guarantees these rights to citizens, and also guarantees to citizens the right to leave Canada. Non-citizens do not have these unqualified rights, although, as noted below, permanent residents have a qualified right to enter and remain in Canada. The qualifications are however, quite significant.

Residential status of non-citizens

Today, Canadian law recognises a number of categories of status for non-citizens. First and foremost, there is the permanent resident, also known as the landed immigrant. The person seeking this status will normally be required to apply from outside Canada and will be selected according to immigration criteria.

Also, there is provision for people to stay in Canada under a Minister's Permit, which allows for the temporary long term residency of a person who is unable to meet the standards required for entry and residence as a permanent resident. Generally, a permit is granted only if there are humanitarian or compassionate reasons for doing so, or if it is in the national interest to do so. A permit may be granted for up to three years but this may also be extended. A permit holder may apply for an employment authorisation from within Canada.

A Convention refugee is a person who meets the definition of 'refugee' found in the United Nations Convention Relating to the Status of Refugee. A person may apply for the status at a port of entry. Until a determination has been made one way or the other, the person who makes the claim will be allowed to stay in the country, at least for the duration of the process. There is no official description of this person's status, although the term 'refugee claimant' is widely used.

Except in specified circumstances, a person found to be a refugee is permitted to make an application for permanent residence from within Canada, and may also apply on behalf of dependants who are overseas.[36]

The Immigration Act provides that a 'visitor' is a person who is lawfully in Canada, or who seeks to come into Canada for a temporary purpose, other than a person who is (a) a Canadian citizen, (b) a permanent resident, (c) a person in possession of a permit or (d) an immigrant authorised to come into Canada. The essential characteristic of a visitor is the temporary nature of his or her (planned) stay in Canada. The status covers students and temporary workers, as well as tourists. People from countries with whom Canada has entered into trading agreements may have special rights to enter and remain in Canada. The North American Free Trade Agreement (NAFTA) recognises different categories of person engaged in trade activity: business visitors, professionals intra-company transferees and traders and investors. The General Agreement on Trade in Services (GATS) has similar provisions, as does Canada's trade agreement with Chile.

Requirements for permanent residence

The permanent resident will have applied either as an Independent Immigrant, that is under programmes that allow for the admission of skilled workers, entrepreneurs, investors and the self-employed, as a member of the family class who has been sponsored by a Canadian citizen or permanent resident, or under a humanitarian programme. In some cases, (for example, with some entrepreneurs), the status will be granted subject to terms and conditions, and will be lost if these terms and conditions are not met within a specified period.

There are two main grounds for determining inadmissibility. The first is medical grounds: if a person suffers from an illness and is likely to be a danger to the public health or safety or if their admission might reasonably be expected to cause excessive demands on health services, he or she may be excluded. Second is the grounds of criminality and state security. The provisions relating to criminality are detailed and complex and include sections dealing with the commission of offences inside and outside Canada, sections dealing with cases where there is a reasonable belief that an offence has been committed and with cases where there is anticipated criminal behaviour.

It should also be noted that a permanent resident, unlike a citizen, is subject to deportation or exclusion from Canada if he or she has committed a criminal offence. And like a citizen, a permanent resident may lose status if fraud or misrepresentation in the application process is discovered.

Alien registration and restrictions on re-entry

There is no alien registration process in Canada. A permanent resident may lose status if he or she leaves with the intent of abandoning Canada. Those who have remained more than six months outside the country in a twelve-month period are deemed to have abandoned Canada unless they can persuade an immigration officer that there was no intent to abandon. A returning resident permit is available for those who wish to show that there was no such intent.

Discrimination by country of origin

With few exceptions, Canadian law does not allow for discrimination by country of origin. De facto, it may in practice be easier for individuals from some countries to obtain status than it is for those from others. However, these differences may be attributed to a variety of factors such as the number of individuals who apply from that country, or whether an immigration post is located in that country. The principal exception is that an individual from some countries is exempted from applying for a visa before coming to Canada as a visitor. In general, a country appears on the list of those exempted if it is thought that there is little chance that individuals who arrive from there will remain illegally. Similarly, some applicants are exempted from applying for employment authorisation from outside Canada.

Social rights

Social rights and permanent residents

Permanent residents enjoy the same social benefits as enjoyed by citizens. This equality of status is recognised by a decision of the Supreme Court of Canada[37] which has held that a law which discriminates against individuals on the basis of their status as permanent residents violates the equality rights guaranteed in the Canadian Charter of Rights and Freedoms. One Supreme Court Justice cites as a reason for using section 15 to protect permanent residents, the fact that they hold an underprivileged position in society, on account of their lack of representation within democratic institutions.

Laws that are held to violate section 15 must be justified under section 1 of the Charter. While it has been held to be justifiable to draw distinctions in relation to rights to promotion within government employment,[38] it is unlikely that any attempt to allocate social benefits differentially would survive constitutional challenge, unless perhaps this is regarded as a necessary means to promote the meaning and value of citizenship.

The Canadian Pension Plan[39] makes available pension benefits to anyone who has contributed to the plan without referring to the legal status of the contributor. Also, The Old Age Security Act[40] makes available benefits to citizens or legal residents with more than ten years of residence in Canada. Reciprocal international agreements allow for international migration and deem residence in other countries to count as residence in Canada.

Benefits relating to health care, hospitalisation, emergency treatment and social assistance are governed by provincial law. In British Columbia, for example, under the Medicare Protection Act[41] and Hospital Insurance Act,[42] residents, and those deemed to be residents, are entitled to medical services and hospital benefits. These Acts identify as a resident a person who:

- is a citizen of Canada or lawfully admitted to Canada for permanent residence;
- makes his or her home in British Columbia; and
- is physically present in British Columbia at least six months in a calendar year. It does not include a tourist or visitor to British Columbia.

Under the B.C. Benefits (Income Assistance) Regulations,[43] income assistance is available to a person only if the applicant is a Canadian citizen, or is authorised under an enactment of Canada to take up permanent residence in Canada, or is determined to be a Convention refugee

Social rights and temporary visitors and illegal aliens

Temporary visitors will not normally be entitled to social benefits. However, there are exceptions. For example, in British Columbia, among those deemed to be residents by the Medical and Health Care Services Regulations[44] and the Hospital Insurance Regulations[45] are Convention Refugees, visitors holding student visas and visitors with work authorisations. Under the B.C. Benefits (Income Assistance) Regulations, an applicant, who must be a citizen, permanent resident or Convention refugee, may seek benefits on behalf of dependants who are defined more broadly to include holders of a Minister's Permit, and those making refugee claims. Under the same regulations, if an applicant is ineligible for income assistance, the minister may provide hardship assistance, but only if the minister considers that undue hardship will otherwise occur. Among those eligible are holders of a Minister's Permit or are in the process of having their claims for refugee status determined.

Illegal aliens have no legal entitlement to social benefits. However, *de facto*, a person without legal status will be provided with emergency medical treatment when required. The costs will be borne by the system where the person requiring treatment is unable to pay.

Multicultural education

In general, education is governed by provincial statute and is provided only in one of the official languages of Canada – English and French. However, in exceptional circumstances education may be offered in other languages. For example, the School Act in British Columbia permits a local school board, with the approval of the Minister of Education, to provide an educational program in a third language,[46] which has allowed for the provision of programmes in the languages of immigrant communities, such as Mandarin. As noted above, the

Constitution provides citizens whose first language is the minority language of the province with the right to have their children educated in that language but only if numbers warrant.

Economic rights

Property rights and aliens

Provincial legislatures may exclude non-residents from ownership of land within the province. However, a provincial attempt to exclude aliens from ownership might be regarded by the courts as an incursion into the subject matter of 'Naturalisation and Aliens' reserved in the Constitution for the Federal Parliament. The Federal Government has made only marginal attempts to restrict the property rights of aliens. The Foreign Ownership of Land Regulations[47] prohibit those who are neither citizen nor permanent resident from holding a property interest in controlled recreational land in Alberta.

The Bank Act[48] and the Canada Business Corporation Act[49] are more significant. They require that three-quarters of the directors of a Canadian bank and a majority of directors of a Canadian company be 'resident Canadians' and define this latter phrase in such a way as to exclude permanent residents who are eligible to have taken out citizenship but who have chosen not to do so. These provision provide a clear incentive for permanent residents to become citizens. To this point, these provisions have not been subject to constitutional challenge on the ground that they violate section 15 of the Charter.

Self-employment

Self-employment is regarded as a form of employment within the meaning of the Immigration Act. Visitors and others would not generally be entitled to engage in self-employment without previously gaining an employment authorisation.

The self-employed are one category of independent immigrant that the Canadian government attempts to attract. However, to obtain an immigrant visa as a self-employed person, a person must show that he or she has the ability to establish or purchase a business in Canada that will create an employment opportunity for himself and will make a significant contribution to the economy or the cultural or artistic life of Canada.[50]

Immigrants who have been professionals in their country of origin may have difficulty getting their credentials recognised within their province of residence. A person who has been permitted to come into

Canada under the skilled worker programme, will have to meet professional requirements imposed by professional organisations within each province. In the past, there has sometimes been an absence of co-ordination between federal immigration authorities and provincial professional organisations in relation to professional credentials, with the result that those who have been admitted into Canada to pursue professional careers have not been found not to possess professional qualifications.

National government jobs and aliens

The Public Service Employment Act[51] does not prevent non-citizens from holding government jobs. In fact an Order made under the Act, the Certain Non-Canadian Citizens Exclusion Approval Order,[52] goes out of its way to accommodate non-citizens. Section 23 of the Act requires those who are hired from outside the Public Service to take an Oath of Office and an Oath of Allegiance. The Order excludes from this requirement non-Canadian citizens who would forfeit their citizenship by subscribing to an oath of allegiance to the Queen.

The Public Service Employment Act does, however, discriminate against non-Citizens in relation to promotion within the service. Section 16 of the Act allows the Public Service Commission to restrict the competition for a job to citizens. The constitutionality of this section was challenged in the Federal Court, where it was held to be valid.[53] The court determined that the section discriminated against permanent residents contrary to section 15 of the Canadian Charter of Rights and Freedoms, but held that it was justifiable under section 1. The judge held that the provision had two basic purposes – to enhance the meaning, value and importance of citizenship and to provide an incentive to naturalise. In dealing with the former of these he suggested that 'if the differences between citizenship and permanent resident status disappear or are rendered virtually meaningless, then citizenship could suffer the same result.'[54] He also suggested that 'the greater the difference between citizenship and non-citizenship, the greater the value of citizenship.' As Joseph Carens, who was called as an expert witness in the case, has noted this need not follow.[55] A person may take more pride in his or her citizenship of a country which has a stronger commitment to equality and may have a stronger bond with his or her government if it treats its residents as it does its citizens.

Local government jobs

The general rule of non-discrimination between citizens and permanent residents apply provincially. By way of example, the Public Service Act of British Columbia[56] specifies merit as the sole criterion for determining employability. No statistics were available relating to the numbers of non-citizens in governmental employment.

Distinctions between some non-citizens

Anomalously, section 23 of the Constitution Act 1867 provides that British subjects may be appointed to the Senate. This allows permanent residents who possess this status from their country of origin to hold a Senate seat, while other permanent residents may not.

Political rights

National and provincial electoral rights

Section 3 of the Charter guarantees to citizens the right to vote and to be a candidate in federal and provincial elections. The guarantee appears inclusionary, rather than exclusionary, in the sense that others are not expressly barred from voting. Nevertheless, the Canada Elections Act, and most provincial acts governing elections, restrict the grant of voting rights to citizens. The difference between the inclusionary and exclusionary readings is important for understanding the meaning of citizenship and democracy in Canada. On the one hand, if the right to vote is reserved only for citizens, then the status of citizenship is regarded as a prerequisite for engaging in political decision-making. The tie to Canada by birth, by parentage or naturalisation with its requirement of an oath of allegiance, is regarded as vital as a qualification to participate in democratic decision-making. Moreover, the section may be interpreted as an incentive to encourage permanent citizens to take out citizenship. For most individuals taking out Canadian citizenship is not a difficult task. Nor does it require any sacrifice. Yet a sense of communal cohesion may be gained when people express their adoption of Canada as their country of citizenship. The restriction of voting rights to citizens may be one means by which this end is achieved.

An inclusionary reading of section 3 of the Charter would permit the various legislatures to grant voting rights to others while guaranteeing that citizens must have the right to vote. Such a reading could be justified by a broader conception of democracy – a conception which could allow that those who are affected by political decisions should have the right to participate in the electoral process. Furthermore, while most citizens lose nothing by taking out Canadian citizenship, some individuals do. They may be required to renounce their previous citizenship and as a result may lose guaranteed access to their country of origin, where they may have close kinship ties. Such individuals may have good reason for not taking out citizenship, while nevertheless wishing to be a part of the Canadian polity.

One anomalous electoral provision is section 28 of the Nova Scotia Elections Act,[57] which grants the right to vote to Canadian citizens and to 'other' British subjects. This provision rejects the exclusionary reading of section 3 of the Charter while also rejecting the idea that all permanent residents should have the right to vote. The provision should best be regarded as a legal anachronism which recalls an earlier era in which British subjecthood was the shared political status in Canada. The constitutionality of this provision has not been tested.

Another similar anomaly is found in the Saskatchewan Election Act.[58] This statute contains a 'grandfather' clause that grants the right to vote in provincial elections to British subjects who were qualified to vote in 1971. Oddly, section 35 of the Act also makes citizens and 'other British subjects' eligible for candidacy in provincial elections, without qualifying the latter group.

Local elections and political freedoms

Generally, the right to vote and the right to stand as a candidate in local elections is reserved for citizens. The data on non-citizens' turn-out and representation are not applicable in local, provincial and national elections.

Aliens, whether they be permanent residents, visitors or illegal aliens enjoy the same civil liberties as citizens. Section 2 of the Charter guarantees that *everyone* has freedom of conscience and religion, freedom of thought, belief, opinion, and expression, freedom of peaceful assembly and freedom of association.

Conclusion

In Canadian constitutional politics, there is an apparent tension between two political principles: the principle that equal treatment should be accorded to all individuals subject to the law; and the principle that different political statuses should be recognised that reflect the variety of bonds that may exist between an individual and the collectivity. The tension is particularly visible when one considers the status of permanent residents who are, for the most part, accorded the same rights and benefits as citizens while nevertheless, they are also, in general, denied democratic rights. As noted above, one Supreme Court Justice has identified the absence of access to democratic processes as a reason for requiring a strong justification for a measure which aims to distinguish between citizens and permanent residents.

The Constitution does allow for the commitment to egalitarianism to be trumped by other concerns, with the result that legislators and judges have the power to implement their own conception of the proper balance. On the one hand, they have revealed the desire to promote citizenship as a valued status, and to offer incentives to those who are eligible to become citizens to make the public commitment to do so. On the other hand, they have been disinclined to widen the gap between citizens and permanent resident to the extent that could rejection of egalitarian principles.

The result is a somewhat precarious status quo in which permanent residents who choose not to become citizens enjoy many benefits but also, perhaps, little security.

Notes

1 (UK), 30 & 31 Vict., c.3.
2 It was renamed in 1982 by the enactment of the Canada Act 1982, UK, 1982, c.11.
3 (UK), 28 & 29 Vict., c.63.
4 (UK), 33 & 34 Vict. c.14.
5 SC 1910 c.27.
6 SC 1921, c.4.
7 RSC, 1970, c.C-19.
8 RSC, 1985, c.C-29 (henceforth, 'CA').
9 Part 1 of the Constitution Act 1982, being Schedule B of the Canada Act 1982 (UK),1982, c.11 (henceforth 'CORAF').
10 CORAF, s.3.
11 CORAF, s.6(1). Section 6(2) of the Charter recognises the right of every citizen and permanent resident to move and to take up residence in any province and to pursue the gaining of a livelihood in any province.
12 CORAF, s.23(1).
13 Peter Hogg, *Constitutional Law of Canada* (4th student edn), (Toronto: Carswell, 1996), at pp. 643–4.
14 See Patricia E. Roy, *A White Man's Province: British Columbia Politicians and Chinese and Japanese Immigrants, 1858–1914*, (Vancouver: UBC Press, 1989).
15 See John P.S. McLaren, 'The Burdens of Empire and the Legalization of White Supremacy in Canada 1860–1910', in *Legal History in the Making*, (eds W.M. Gordon and T.D. Fergus) (London: Hambledon Press, 1991) c.13.
16 RSC 1985, c.I-2 (henceforth 'IA').
17 CORAF, s.15(1).

18 CORAF s.1.
19 See *R.* v. *Oakes* [1986] 1 SCR 103.
20 The Act also allows for some exceptional ways of becoming a citizen. For example, the Governor in Council (i.e. the Federal Cabinet) has unrestricted discretion to direct the Minister to grant citizenship in cases of hardship or to reward exceptional services to Canada. See CA, s.5(4).
21 CA, s.3(1)(a).
22 CA, s.3(2).
23 CA, s.3(1)(b).
24 CA, s.8. The detailed requirements of the process are outlined in s.6 of the Citizenship Regulations 1993, SOR/93-246. (as amended) (henceforth, 'CR').
25 The law relating to adopted children is to be found in the Immigration Act 1976 and the Immigration Regulations SOR/78-172 (as amended) (henceforth 'IR').
26 IA, s.24.
27 CR, s.15.
28 CA, s.9.
29 See, for example, *Switzman v. Elbling* [1957] SCR 285 and *Winner v. S.M.T.* [1951] SCR 887.
30 See *Nisga'a Final Agreement* (initialled, 4 August 1998) (Canada: Queen's Printer, 1998).
31 *Canadian Citizenship: A Sense of Belonging* (Canada: Queen's Printer, 1994), at p. 16.
32 *ibid.*, at p. 15.
33 Statistics were provided by Citizenship and Immigration Canada.
34 The fact that the number is over 100 % indicates that in that year people who had arrived in Canada as permanent residents more than three years previously took out citizenship.
35 IA, s.4. The Immigration Act grants these rights also to persons registered under the Indian Act. In exceptional circumstances, such persons might not be citizens of Canada.
36 See IA, s.46.04.
37 *Andrews v. Law Society of B.C.* [1989] 1 SCR 143.
38 *Lavoie v. Canada*, [1995] 2 FC 623 (TD) See below for a brief discussion of this case.
39 See Canada Pension Plan Act, RSC, 1985, c.C-8
40 RSC, 1985, c.O-9.
41 RSBC, 1996, c.286.
42 RSBC, 1996, c.204.
43 BC Reg. 75/97.
44 BC Reg. 426/97.
45 BC Reg. 25/61.
46 School Act, RSBC, 1996, c.412, s.5(3).
47 SOR/79–416.
48 SC 1991, c.46
49 RSC 1985 c.C-44.
50 Immigration Regulations, s.2(1).
51 RSC, 1985, c.P-33.
52 CRC c.1339.

53 *Lavoie* v. *Canada*, above, at note 38.
54 *ibid.*, at 658.
55 *ibid.*, at 660.
56 RSBC 1996, c.385
57 RSNS, 1989, c.140.
58 1996 SS E-6.

10

Change and Convergence: is American Immigration still Exceptional?

Thomas C. Heller

The lines between alienage and citizenship have generated intense debate in the United States from its foundation to the present. Political economists and political philosophers, lawyers and novelists, have made membership in the nation the focal point of both an asserted American exceptionality and its vehement denial.[1] Whatever the outcome of internal American contests over our self-representations of belonging, recent widespread transformations of classical lands of net emigration into the objects of immigration and asylum have led to claims of global convergence of problems and solutions that might replace American law and culture in a common framework of modernity.

This chapter comments on these debates and developments by posing four questions. First, what is the theory of members and outsiders in the United States? Second, what is the legal practice that may or may not institutionalise this theory? Third, how does this practice in the United States compare with that of other advanced industrial societies? Fourth, is this traditional practice or theory in the United States changing? To approach these questions, we can consider first the dimensions along which we might compare societies in the areas of entry and citizenship and then whether the United States is moving away from the patterns of practice that have defined its history along these dimensions. Thereafter, we may return to interpreting the meaning of American differentiation against the context of change that frames the current controversies over exceptionality and convergence.

To decide what we are comparing between national systems of alienage and citizenship, we might begin with the pool of potential members of the class of citizens. In each nation, there is a population of non-permanent residents who may or may not work and may be legally or illegally present. The size of this population will vary with the possibility of finding work, receiving social benefits, and the likelihood and cost of expulsion if they are illegal entrants or non-immigrant overstays. Members of this pool of non-residents may become legal or effective permanent residents, with or without the legal right to work or collect social benefits, depending in part on the ease of adjusting their status or being granted amnesty. In addition, the class of permanent residents may be more or less increased by the direct admission of immigrants as legal permanent residents, again with or without the rights to work or receive transfers.

From these several pools (resident and non-resident, legal and illegal) citizens may be drawn in several modes. The native born children of their members may or may not become eligible for citizenship in the receiving nation by birthright in the first, second or subsequent generations.[2] Moreover, the naturalisation of legal residents may be facilitated, required, prohibited or impeded by legal conditions of duration and qualification. The attractions of naturalisation, where application is in the discretion of permanent residents, may be affected by salient social, economic and political rights associated with citizenship alone. Finally, citizens may more or less easily lose their status through renunciation, acceptance of another nation's citizenship or the performance of acts seen as inconsistent with citizenship.

Comparisons between comprehensive national systems of alienage and citizenship could well focus on: the size of the several legally distinguishable population pools of aliens and citizens; the ease of entry to and expulsion from these classes; the ease of passage between them; the ability to sustain one's self through work or social transfers within each of the pools; the relative benefits and losses that attend acquiring different statuses of alienage; and the ease and importance of becoming a citizen for one's self and one's children. With so many variables relevant to the characterisation of a national system, multiple patterns of access and incorporation are possible. We will argue below that the US historical pattern is one of very large entry pools supported through good labour access, ease of adjustments of status between pools, ease of transition to citizenship through first generation birthright access, differential (long discriminatory) possibilities of naturalisation, poor border and internal administrative controls on residence, low expulsion, weak social benefits and low salience of citizenship. Put most simply, the dominant US system of immigration has been to create many jobs and keep them relatively open to international labour. It pays little attention to the thin fabric of social and political rights that US citizenship entails.

Broad characterisations of traditional patterns of alienage and citizenship in other industrial nations might diverge or converge along only some dimensions of this topography. Much of western Europe might be said to have a history of restricted general regimes for entry supported by strong frontier and local administrative controls, difficult passage between categories of alienage, a low naturalisation rate, low or long deferred birthright access, low work possibilities in highly regulated labour markets, strong social transfers, and a high salience of citizenship. The substantial import of social benefits and political enfranchisement in these systems implies that entry restrictions will be needed to preserve the value of these membership assets. These same patterns of low legal and illegal entry and restricted labour markets, reinforced by the limited availability of social benefits, have prevailed historically in Japan.

At the same time, especially in the latter half of the twentieth century, a number of supposedly exceptional circumstances have mitigated the formally closed boundaries of these systems. In Germany, entry to noncitizen status has been eased by a liberal understanding of constitutional provisions on asylum, by humanitarian concerns for family reunification after the termination of guest worker programmes in 1973, and by the grant of citizenship to the scattered populations of German ethnics after the collapse of the Soviet Union. In ex-colonial powers like France, the United Kingdom and the Netherlands, imploding empires built up political pressures and social networks that facilitated population adjustments and broad scale movement out of the resulting unstable political economies in Asia, the Caribbean and Africa. In such circumstances where migration once initiated is always hard to manage, what should be imagined as the exceptional and the normal is always contestable. But, again, in broad terms the immigration system in these polities has focused less on job creation and access than on integrating the limited numbers of the enduring streams of exceptional entrants – whether guest workers, former colonials or refugees – to the meaningful panoply of social and political rights that constitute their thicker sense of membership.

Contentions about change in the established patterns of alienage and citizenship may also be evaluated against alternative dimensions of national systems. For example, the 1996 law reforms in United States foreclosing certain state and federal social programmes to future resident aliens may have relatively little impact on an overall system where the magnitude of such benefits has always been low in comparison to the pull of access to jobs. Alternatively, new European policies that ease asylum, naturalisation or birthright citizenship for later-generation descendents may be significant where exceptional entry creates even a relatively small pool of aliens eligible for extensive social rights in economies pressured by global competition. My thesis is that the meaning of the law of alienage and citizenship should be read both as a whole and in a wider context of political economy and political philosophy. The significance of particular laws and legal reforms may be overshadowed by other provisions that mitigate or countervail the effect of those rules on the comprehensive operations of the system. And, more generous laws of entry and integration may mean less against a background of weak incentives to find sustainable work and professional identity for migrants and their families.

The need to compare rules of membership in the wider context of national systems appears also in the terminology in which these questions are debated. Terms such as residential rights or economic rights have little resonance in American legal discourse. Their common use reflects a background in which nations have normally largely closed their borders and labour markets, defining conditions of entry that made movement exceptional, work problematic and social integration essential. In this sense the template of this study has to be applied to America with some flexibility in order not to miss what may constitute the fundamental contrast among the case studies.

Nationality and citizenship (permanent residents)

Aliens in the United States may be divided into permanent residents, asylees and refugees, non-permanent residents and illegal entrants. Each category is subject to varied conditions of entry, period of stay and liability to deportation or other removal. Although substantially unrestricted entry to the United States was ended in 1921, a pool of around one million aliens each year is admitted to permanent residence or otherwise enters the United States with intention to reside indefinitely. In 1997, this pool was composed of 798 378 new legal permanent residents and there is an estimated net annual growth of approximately 275 000 illegal entrants.[3] Of the almost 800 000 new permanent residents, more than one-half were already living in United States and were adjusting their status as former non-immigrants, refugees and asylees, and illegal entrants. In addition, in a typical year of the current period admits of legal non-immigrants coming to reside and work for fixed terms in the United States as managers and investors, temporary workers and trainees, exchange visitors and intracompany transferees number between 600 000 and 700 000.[4] These figures do not include as additions to the domestic population children born in the US to any member of these alien groups because such children are US citizens at birth. The total legal and illegal immigrant flow is similar in scale to the average entry pool of the peak years of immigration between 1905 and 1917.[5] Although the total of the most recent years is somewhat reduced relative to the modern peak year of legal immigration in 1991, when approximately 1.8 million were admitted due to the regularisation of status of former illegal aliens under the Immigration and Control Act of 1986, entry levels that far exceed the average annual post-war flows from 1945–85 now seem stable.

Most of the pool of aliens entering the United States is eligible for citizenship. All admits to permanent residence may apply for naturalisation. General naturalisation provisions specify that a applicant must be at least 18 years old, lawfully admitted to permanent residence and resident in the country continuously for five years, have an ability to speak, read and write English, have a knowledge of US government and history, and be of good moral character.[6] Although the naturalisation process is neither complex nor difficult, the rate of naturalisation among eligible groups varies widely by age at the time of immigration, country of origin, profession and marriage status.[7] By 1995 45.9 per cent of the 1977 immigration cohort and 41.5 per cent of the 1982 cohort had naturalised. Illegal and non-immigrant alien populations are important to the composition of membership in the US in three ways. First, their US born children are automatically citizens.[8] The larger the size of the non-permanent resident groups, the larger their influence on the American citizen population.[9] Second, due to the relative ease of adjusting status after legal or illegal entry to the United States, illegal alien and non-immigrant groups may be better able to qualify for family or work based legal immigration once here.[10] This is especially true for those who become parents of American citizen children. Their subsequent admission as permanent residents will not usually change the total number of aliens granted this status, but does affect the selection of who comprises those so favoured.[11] Finally, a substantial and stable non-immigrant and illegal alien population may simply reflect the fact that there are not weighty net benefits to be acquired by changing status to permanent residents or citizens. To the extent that the differences in civil, political, and economic capacity that attend greater legal incorporation do not seriously affect the advantages that simple presence, legal or illegal, in a nation may afford, the distinction between classes of aliens and between aliens and citizens may not be salient for the analysis of membership.

Permanent resident aliens are admissible under an annual cap of 675 000 immigrants. The cap allows 480 000 family sponsored immigrants, 140 000 employment-based immigrants, and 55 000 diversity immigrants from nations subjected to what is now seen as excessive discrimination against entry by former US immigration rules. Immediate relatives of US citizens (parents, spouses, minor children) count as family sponsored immigrants, but their entry is uncapped. The total cap can then be exceeded if the number of immediate relatives and the minimum annual number of other relatives (226 000) exceeds 480 000. In addition to preferences for family reunification, work skills and historic inequities, immigration visas are allocated under a per-country limit of 7 per cent of the annual total and 2 per cent of this total for dependent areas. Spouses and minor children of legal permanent residents from high demand countries like Mexico are exempted from the per-country limits.[12]

A second pool of legal aliens are qualified refugees and asylees, who are admissible to the United States without subject to a numerical cap. Under the Refugee Act of 1980, annual limits are determined by the President, in consultation with the Congress, on the number of refugees in need of resettlement who are of special humanitarian concern to the United States. There has been a downward trend since 1992 (142 000) through 1995 (112 000) and the total quota is composed of regional sub-charges. Refugees, after one year of residence in the United States are eligible for adjustment to permanent residence status, and are exempt from worldwide annual limitations. Asylees, persons present in the United States who otherwise qualify as refugees under the definitions of 1980 Act, may be admitted to the United States with no limits set by law on their total number. More than 154 000 asylum applications, of which 104 000 were made by Central Americans, were filed or reopened in 1995. About 20 per cent of these applications were approved, a record high number. Asylee adjustments of status to permanent residence may take place after one year following approval of asylum, do not count against worldwide limitations on immigrants, and are limited to 10 000 per year.[13]

Residential rights (non-permanent immigrants)

A third major pool of legal residents with residential, and often work, rights in the United States is non-immigrants. Non-immigrants are defined by 8 USC 1101 (a)(15) as persons in any of eighteen categories who are temporarily admitted for restricted periods. A record 22.6 million non-immigrants in all categories entered the United States in 1995, of which 20.9 million were temporary visitors for business or pleasure trips. However, several categories of non-immigrants and their dependents are admissible to the United States for more extended periods of work for such time and under such conditions as the Attorney General may by regulations prescribe.[14] These included in 1995 131 777 treaty traders and investors (category E); 197 760 temporary workers and trainees (categories H and O); 201 095 exchange visitors (teachers, researchers or and other specialists or leaders in a field of specialised knowledge or skill) (category J); 112 124 intracompany transferees (category L) and 31 106 North American Free Trade Agreement Workers.[15] Added to the 364 220 non-immigrants admitted in that same year as students (category F), these populations are often able to spend significant parts of their working lives in the United States, make notable contributions to scientific and economic development in professional and technically advanced sectors where domestic populations may not supply comparably qualified employees, and, if desired, adjust their status to permanent residence through connections to children, spouses, and firms.

It has recently been estimated that about 5 million illegal or undocumented immigrants were residing in the United States in 1996 and that this population was growing by about 275 000 each year on a net basis. Mexico was the leading country of origin with 2.7 million (54%), with annual growth of near 150 000 since 1988. Other near-by Western Hemisphere nations contributed 725 000 of the total group. However, the INS believes that 2.1 million (41%) of the pool of illegal aliens are non-immigrant overstays, although the percentage of these entrants varies substantially by country of origin.[16] The stability with which illegal entrants and non-immigrant overstays can remain in the United States is dependent on several reinforcing factors. First, these populations are heavily concentrated in seven states (California, Texas, New York, Florida, Illinois, New Jersey and Arizona) and five metropolitan areas (New York, Los Angeles, Miami, Chicago and Washington, DC). Enforcement of deportation in dense alien communities is difficult. Second, although the INS began the publicised Operation Gatekeeper in 1994 along the heavily travelled San Diego–Tijuana border area and has had increased apprehensions in this region, non-border area deportations do not seem to have raised the risks of illegal residence and work in the United States.

Most undocumented captured aliens are not deported formally, but accept procedures called 'voluntary return under safeguard' or 'voluntary departure under docket control'. Although deported aliens may not generally be admitted to the United States for a period of five years after deportation, those who accept voluntary return or departure and pay the expenses of return to their countries of origin can be legally admitted in the future without penalty. Alternatively, given the large percentage of undocumented aliens from Mexico and Central America, voluntary departure can become no more than an occasional inconvenience. Recent statistics indicate that while deportations of aliens for convictions for or related to criminal or narcotics violations have grown from 1,702 in 1985 to 29 313 in 1995, deportations for simple entry without inspection and violation of non-immigrant status have fallen from about 19 000 to about 11 600 in those same years.[17] A portion of this decline may be due to the broad 1986 amnesty that had by 1995 regularised the status of 2.69 million undocumented aliens who had resided in the United States since 1982. However, the amnesty itself, combined with the low level of enforcement against the non-criminal, low-skill work force, underscores the fact that this stable pool of illegal aliens should not be distinguished qualitatively in a comprehensive study of the dynamics of membership in the United States.

The value to persons of being present in the United States will vary with the advantages and disabilities that characterise the different statuses of alienage and citizenship that they might occupy. In an expanding and relatively well-paying labour market, the attraction of the opportunity to work for extended periods with the assurance of protected civil rights may outweigh the immediate or long-term lack of political or social privilege. Or, rates of naturalisation to citizenship may be low in the United States because the losses attached to reduced capacity to own property in a nation of origin that forbids dual citizenship are more burdensome than the benefits acquired in the nation of destination.[18] In the US case, it makes sense to examine the pattern of incentives and sanctions that attach to legally distinct populations with respect to political and civil, economic and social rights; between citizens, legal and illegal aliens; and between state and federal (national) jurisdictions.[19] This categorisation will only describe formal legal differentiation. We will come back in interpreting the meaning of membership in America to the reasoning that underlies this variable treatment and the gaps between what is constitutionally allowed and what is politically practicable.

Political (and civil) rights

In general, equal civil rights are accorded by states and by the federal government to all 'persons', a term constitutionally broader than 'citizens'.[20] Immigrants, non-immigrants and illegal aliens in the United States are guaranteed trial by jury, due process in criminal and civil proceedings, freedom or speech and religion,[21] the services of a lawyer at criminal trials, freedom from self-incrimination and unreasonable searches and seizures,[22] the right to sue in state and federal courts,[23] and the coverage of federal anti-discrimination and labour statutes.[24] The principal civil distinctions in the treatment of citizens and aliens, as well as between classes of aliens, are in the area of immigration law itself.

Courts have pronounced the constitutional scope of the federal immigration and foreign affairs powers to be 'plenary'. Congress is unchallenged in its ability to set quantitative limits on the number of aliens who may be admitted to the United States as permanent residents or non-immigrants. Legal and illegal aliens may be removed from the United States on various and differentiated grounds of deportability. Citizens may not be removed unless they have lost their citizenship through renunciation or denaturalisation.[25] Only citizens can travel under US passports or receive consular protection outside the United States. Permanent residents are given fewer privileges in sponsoring family members' immigration to the US than are citizens.[26] Congress has been permitted to define for aliens subject to deportation processes fewer procedural rights than are normally accorded in other adjudicative forums and aliens at the border seeking initial entry are said to have no constitutional rights that go beyond the procedures statutorily granted to them.[27] Finally, realism requires notice that the willingness of illegal aliens to assert many of the civil rights to which they are legally entitled is constrained by the fear they may be deported, vindicated or not, as a consequence of announcing of their presence in the United States.

Aliens of any class, unlike citizens, are not entitled to vote in state or federal elections. Immigrants did vote in the United States throughout much of its history, with the last state eliminating the franchise for legal non-citizens in 1928.[28] Although there is no constitutional mandate that any state or local government empower any class of aliens to vote, several US localities have recently made permanent residents eligible to vote in local elections.[29] Because aliens are protected by the First Amendment, they would be protected against state or federal legislative initiatives to limit their participation in political demonstrations or related non-voting activities. However, all classes of aliens are statutorily prohibited from holding any job in the federal civil service on the theory that such work would conflict with the political function that is reserved for citizens.

A similar, though far more restricted, rationale has been the object of litigation at the state level. As discussed below, since 1972, state discrimination against permanent resident aliens has been considered constitutionally suspect and justifiable only when tested against a standard of strict scrutiny. An uncertainly wide political exception has allowed state laws to withstand a lesser standard of scrutiny when their distinction in the treatment of legal aliens and citizens touches on 'participation in . . . democratic political institutions.'[30] On the grounds that 'some functions are so bound up with the operation of the State . . . as to permit the exclusion from those functions of all persons who have not become part of the process of state government', immigrant aliens have been disqualified in some states from serving as teachers, probation officers or police.[31] It goes without saying that the denial of employment opportunities under the political function doctrine to permanent resident aliens extends to non-immigrants and undocumented aliens as well.

Economic rights

Subject to the reach of the political function doctrine, permanent resident aliens have the same state and federal rights as citizens to work in American labour markets.[32] Moreover, the direction of reform in the allocation of preferences for admission as a permanent resident has shifted in 1990 toward increased numbers of persons with valued economic skills undersupplied in domestic labour markets.[33] The access of non-immigrant aliens to work opportunities in the professional or managerial or technical sector of the US market is also ample. High-end workers are admissible as non-immigrants 'for such time and under such conditions as the Attorney-General may by regulation prescribe' as temporary workers, exchange visitors, intracompany transferees, or as importers 'of extraordinary ability in the sciences, arts, education, business or athletics'.[34] For all of these categories except exchange visitors, the Attorney General must consult with other appropriate agencies of the Government upon petition of the importing employer. Although continual political controversy attaches to the openness of the skilled end of the US labour market, the recent combination of economic growth and technological innovation have effectively expanded these opportunities and the populations that occupy them.

At the lower end of labour market, especially in the case of agricultural workers, labour certification usually requires the approval of the Departments of Labor and Agriculture and is subject to annual numerical limitations.[35] Beyond these limited cases, non-immigrant legal entry is more restricted and employment is available principally for undocumented aliens. Federal regulation of these informal markets was addressed in the Immigration Control and Reform Act of 1986 that imposed employer sanctions for the first time on firms hiring illegal aliens.[36] In addition, substantial investment has been made throughout the 1990s in improved border enforcement, especially in the Mexico–California corridor that leads to the largest supply of jobs. Finally, the economic return available through US low-end markets has been lowered by increased penalties for, and reduced procedural barriers to, deportation, as well as by various initiatives to cut off the effective access to social support and transfers systems by the undocumented and their children.[37] However, neither government statistics nor other analyses indicate that the net impact of these measures has seriously raised the wage or restricted the quantity of labour supplied in these transnational markets.[38]

Especially given the expansion of the American economy and the relatively effective regulation of wages and working conditions throughout in the US labour market, wage differentials for unskilled labour between the US and geographically proximate suppliers remain wide. In these circumstances, the marginal impact of the US proto-taxes on undocumented labour levied through higher costs for border crossing, wage interruption during voluntary deportation proceedings, and employer fines whose effective incidence lies on the work force have not reduced the undocumented pool.[39] Finally, American weak administration of residence or work controls at the local level lowers the probability of enforcement of alienage laws once the border has been breached. With no established tradition of bureaucratic penetration of daily life and continued resistance to the implementation of a national identity card system, there is little reason to believe the actual closure of the formally restricted low end of the American labour market is at hand.

Social rights

While economic and labour market policy is the predominant determinant of income for non-citizen populations, social transfers can substitute for or complement wage returns on sustained basis or during periods of transition. Among classes of aliens, the United States offers special social support only to refugees and that on a very limited scale. Presently a state agency where a refugee is relocated would receive about

$500 in Federal funds to cover basic needs for 30 days. Thereafter, the refugee would have recourse to the general welfare programmes. For all other aliens, the principal issues concern their eligibility under these general programmes and the interaction between the need for public support and qualification for legal entry.

Aliens who are likely become public charges are ineligible for visas or admission. For family sponsored applicants, the sponsor must execute an affidavit of support agreeing to maintain the alien at a level no less than 125 per cent of the Federal poverty line. This pledge is legally enforceable against him or her by the alien or by any level of government or other entity that provides the entrant with a means-tested benefit.[40] The main social thrust of the immigration laws is prophylactic, aiming to exclude from entry those who might burden transfer programmes aimed at citizenship. Moreover, the courts have ruled that the federal government may under its plenary immigration powers discriminate between citizens and permanent residents with respect to their eligibility for social support. *Matthews v. Diaz* denied a challenge to a federal Social Security Act provision that excluded aliens from coverage under Medicare unless they had resided in the United States as lawful permanent residents for at least five years.[41]

In 1996, in broad ranging reforms of the welfare system under the Personal Responsibility and Work Opportunity Reconciliation Act, further legal distinctions between the social rights of citizens and permanent resident aliens were elaborated. The original reforms denied both new and existing legal immigrants access to Supplemental Security Income (means tested cash assistance for the elderly) and Food Stamps until citizenship. In addition, most non-refugee immigrants entering after 1996 were barred from receiving Temporary Assistance to Needy Families (TANF), Medicaid, Title XX block grants, and other federal means-tested programmes. Since non-immigrants and undocumented persons are clearly less constitutionally enabled than permanent residents against differential treatment by the federal government, the operative boundary that governs federal social rights is distinctly between citizens and non-citizens. Correlatively, in years prior to the possibility of naturalisation, only family-based support or discretionary social assistance by states (where federal law allows this option) can supplement employment income for aliens.

The rights of legal permanent residents against the states have not been defined by a similar distinction between the constitutional treatment of citizens and aliens. Although the Supreme Court has struck down since 1886 state discrimination against aliens that it attributed to racial discrimination, many laws differentiating aliens and citizens were upheld throughout much of this century.[42] In 1971, *Graham v. Richardson* imposed a strict standard of scrutiny on welfare eligibility classifications in Arizona and Pennsylvania that limited benefits to citizens, intending citizens or long standing permanent residents.[43] Holding that aliens as a class were 'a discrete and insular minority' meriting 'heightened judicial solicitude' and that the shaping of incentive structures to affect immigration flows was the exclusive province of the federal government, the Court could find no compelling reason to justify lessened social rights for legal aliens at the state level. While the *Graham* suspicion of state discrimination against permanent residents still stands, the 1996 welfare reforms have complicated the legal picture by attempting to authorise a state's option to bar both current residents and new immigrants from non-emergency Medicaid, TANF and Title XX block grants, and all entirely funded state programmes. Since such unauthorised state action would have been unconstitutional under prior law, it is an open constitutional question whether the plenary federal power over immigration can in effect be delegated to the states.

The issue of state social transfers or provision of public services to illegal aliens is also unsettled.[44] In 1982 the Supreme Court struck down a Texas statute denying undocumented children access to the public schools.[45] Although the majority holding did not treat undocumented aliens as a suspect class, the law was struck down because the state had failed to show it had advanced a 'substantial state interest' in refusing an education. While the Court conceded that 'a state might well have a permissible interest in mitigating the potentially harsh economic effects of sudden shifts in population', the record in the case did not prove illegal immigrants imposed a significant burden on the State's economy. This door left ajar in *Plyler* has provided the doctrinal basis for the introduction by popular initiative in California in 1994 of Proposition 187. Building on a controversial documentation of the cost to the State of servicing its large undocumented population, 187 requires all state agencies providing public services, including public education and medical care, to verify recipients' immigration status, and when unsatisfied of its legality, to deny benefits and report the applicant to the Immigration Service.

Although the legal effect of most of Proposition 187 has been enjoined since its enactment,[46] the constitutional basis for disallowing states to discriminate between the social benefits afforded legal and illegal aliens is uncertain. The argument may turn less on the obligation of the state to recognise social rights for the undocumented than on a series of indirect harms caused by the effort to discriminate. Courts have suggested that the supposed economic benefits to a state from denying programmes to illegal aliens would be countervailed by the damage to public health or the costs of hosting a permanent uneducated underclass. Similarly, strict enforcement could interfere with the protected civil rights of the undocumented, permanent residents and citizens of Latino or Asian descent. Perhaps the only thing that is clear is that new restrictions on eligibility for social rights of all classes of aliens shift the United States even further toward a position where resources and services derived from the market overwhelmingly determine the calculus of immigration.

Recent reforms: continuity or change in American immigration?

The last fifteen years of the twentieth century, framed by the Immigration Control and Reform Act of 1986, the Personal Responsibility and Work Opportunity Reconciliation Act of 1996 (PRWORA) and the ongoing campaigns to clone widely Proposition 187, are frequently cited as a rising tide of a new American restrictionism. Yet, levels of legal immigration and participation of non-American labour in the US economy are near historic highs and the populations of undocumented workers are undiminished. In part, the sense that the politics of immigration have turned toward closure reflects an unremitting theme of American life that the social fabric has been stretched to its limits by the dilution of genetic and cultural homogeneity. The shift of the demography of incoming groups toward Latin America and Asia since 1965 is the latest occasion for such claims.[47] In part, the immigration debate has intensified because of it resonates with other political controversies including the economic effects of the continuing opening of global markets, the reduction in regulatory capacity of nation states, the asserted depreciation of social capital in American communities, and the widening distributional gap between advanced industrial and developing states. Scholarly arguments that America ought reverse the direction of immigration policy in confronting these problems have been reinforced at the popular level by lobbyists and popular books that have fuelled legislative calls for the reduction of legal immigration and the better enforcement of existing regimes against illegal aliens.[48] But examination of that legislative record offers less support for the thesis that the established patterns of American immigration law and politics are generally unstable.

Many initiatives touching on immigration have been introduced in the Congress since 1986. They might be categorised as attempts to reform: (1) the number and character of legal immigrants and non-immigrants; (2) the social transfer systems that are available to support legal immigrants on entry; (3) the legal procedures afforded to aliens seeking to enter or remain in the country; (4) the discouragement, detection, apprehension and expulsion of undocumented aliens. Although proposals to limit world-wide legal immigration of both permanent residents and temporary workers has been considered in almost every legislature since 1993, the only laws to pass have merely redistributed the quotas assigned to difference family preference groups and between family and work sponsored immigrants.[49] The restriction of access for aliens to social benefit programmes has enjoyed greater legislative success. As noted above, family sponsored permanent residents are now deemed to have more access to the resources of their relatives, and both established and future legal immigrants lost their eligibility for a wide range of federal benefits in the welfare reforms of 1996. These changes have been partially mitigated since that time for resident aliens already in the United States at the time of the reforms. The budget amendment of 1997 restored to that group disability payments under SSI and in 1998 food stamps were reinstated for some.[50] In addition, all but a few states used the option given them by the PRWORA to continue Medicaid and TANF benefits for legal aliens who arrived by the date of the Act. And, although states were given a mandate by PRWORA not to expend federal money for future immigrants during their first five years in the US, more than a third of the States chose to substitute state dollars to maintain benefits from the date of arrival of permanent residents.[51] Finally, it should be remembered that the limitation of access for aliens to social transfers occurred as a minor element in a comprehensive reduction of welfare benefits for American citizens. This implies that while future permanent residents will have more incentives to naturalise as soon as possible, thereby becoming eligible for remaining transfer programmes, the lowered value of social rights in general will reduce the importance of this distinction between citizens and aliens in the American community.

The Illegal Immigration Reform and Immigrant Responsibility Act of 1996 (IIRIRA) and the Anti-Terrorism and Effective Death Penalty Act of 1996 strengthened border enforcement, established a pilot phone-verification system to enable employers and social service agencies to verify the immigration status of applicants, made more difficult the appeal process by asylees denied entry by immigration officers at the border, and eased the exclusion criteria for such exclusions. The IIRIRA also made it harder for unauthorised aliens to avoid removal from the United States on hardship grounds and barred federal judges from reviewing deportation orders.[52] However, the effects of these changes must be understood in the context of the practice of deportation. The great majority of illegal aliens who have not been engaged in narcotics trafficking or have not otherwise committed crimes are offered and accept voluntary deportation as a tolerable risk of working in the United States. These changes in legal procedures, like the institution of employer sanctions in 1986 and subsequent attempts to deter undocumented entry to the United States, have not altered the reality of labour or political migration. In weighing the symbolic value of the legislative victories gained by restrictionist interests against the economic impact, it would be hard to suggest the former has prevailed. The larger picture is that in the 1990s access to the American labour market remains relatively unchanged and effective reform has focused on reducing of social transfers to legal and illegal aliens. Whether this change constitutes a convergence of American immigration practice with that of other advanced industrial nations depends on how we interpret the meaning of this pattern of shift and stability.

Concluding remarks: interpreting American immigration

The debate over American immigration is in part a struggle over self-representation. The predominant view of immigration has been a strand of a broader narrative of American exceptionalism.[53] In this narrative, the United States constructed its orthodox self-image by differentiating itself from the Old World nations its population left behind in search of refuge from repressive politics and the social immobility of ascribed identities. The transoceanic voyage became the defining act of individual autonomy, risk-taking and self-realisation that created and epitomised American identity. Maintaining, against increasing xenophobic pressures, open national boundaries symbolised the universality of liberal aspirations to equality by which subjective choice and political commitment rather than the accidents of birth determined membership in the community. Legal limitation of uncontrolled flows after 1921 has still allowed levels of immigration that approach historic highs at the century's close and reports of the immanent transformation of this abnormal pattern of receptivity are suspect.

In immigration, as in other areas of American historiography, revisionist accounts have assaulted this simple story.[54] They argue that citizenship was never universal and its denial to African-American was legally inscribed in the *Dred Scott* case. Naturalisation was permitted only for whites from 1790 and case law reiterated the litany of this proscription well into this century. Much immigration was always rotational rather than a one-way flight and racism controlled its demography with exclusion acts, barred zones, and national quotas from 1882 to 1965. But, in turn, the heaviness of this unremitting critique stimulates the instinct of reaction, especially in comparative terms. What was the short-term import of naturalisation restrictions in the context of first generation birthright citizenship? What is the meaning of the years of maximum numerical limitations and discrimination by nationality from the 1920s through the 1950s? Was this era the culmination and confession of a pervasive American illiberalism that belies a mythic universality? Or was it better seen as an epoch in which progressive impulses to manage emergent American power through the scientific organisation of society, bureaucratic administration, and corporatist regulation of the economy brought new experimentation with imported European ideals of state structure and national identity.[55] Should the years since 1965 of increased immigration and regional flows that reverse the effects of prior quotas be seen as political miscalculations or as corrections back toward a traditional course mistakenly abandoned?[56]

To recognise or understand change, there must be a baseline against which it is measured. Particular American immigration laws, regulations and politics can be characterised as a baseline of closure that converges with the policies of other industrial states or as no more than a compendium of exceptions to a baseline of openness that represents an American modernity that is itself exceptional. Worse, the pliability of interpretation can confound the other side of the comparisons we attempt. Does the protection of national cultures in European states demand segregation punctuated by populous exceptions of guest workers, asylees, refugees, ex-colonials, returning co-ethnics, denizens and European citizens? Or at some point does the pretence of non-immigration give way even as symbol? One response to this ambiguity is to embrace the logic of post-modernity. Rogers Smith asserts 'a multiple traditions' approach to nationality that embraces at once civic liberalism and ascribed community as intertwined strains of American (European?) identity.[57] We can, and do, always render asserted structures into alternative rhetorics, ready to hand, whose ebb and flow turns on the pragmatics of political competition.

Though I fully admit the complexity, even the malleability, of constructions like national discourses of immigration, I also suggest that there are material constraints on the evolution of the political and cultural institutions where discourse is played out. Differences in these constraints can induce idiosyncratic national tendencies in the formation of answers to the demands that modernity poses. The discrete laws and policies that emerge in specific sectors or times result from the ongoing interplay of differentiation and rapprochement between the opposing symbols and institutions that organise social life.[58] The structures from which this variation takes off, and to which its fluctuation often falls back, though neither fixed nor determined, may be more stable. If American exceptionality exists, it exists as a default case.

However, if America and other nations differ primarily through their periodic returns to distinct institutional patterns established during their particular adaptations to modernity, the interpretation of immigration must be both complex and derivative. It is complex because the vagaries and contradictions of immigration law and policy have an internal or local history that reflects the professional practice of immigration as an institutionalised system. It is derivative because the fixed points around which immigration practice is oriented reflect wider structures of political economy and philosophy. These fixed points and wider structures define the baselines against which national systems, or their convergence, should be measured.

In prior work I have argued that one fixed point, or default solution, in American political economy is a concept of 'thin citizenship'.[59] This concept is derived from the intersection between Marshall's typology of citizenship as composed on civil, political and social rights, and Hirschman's distinction between exit and voice.[60] My contention is that the United States in its constitutional period until 1850 relied on exit or mobility far more than on voice or political authority in creating institutions to allocate resources and settle disputes. Due in part to the relative abundance of land and in part to a colonial history that instilled distrust for a centralised administrative state, America developed a system relying on markets and decentralised institutions like courts and local governments that allowed those dissatisfied with outcomes to move on to other products or other jurisdictions. Because the relative roles and powers of political authorities were weak, organisations and cultural expectations adapted to self-governance through mobility and emphasised the primacy of civil rights that ensured the capacity of individuals to exercise that autonomy freely.

At the same time, neither political nor social rights took on the import they would assume in a system of governance that relied more heavily on voice than on exit. The ability to vote or otherwise influence political outcomes is devalued in a society where the scope of politics is reduced and escape is easy from the jurisdictions in which its results are enforced. Since social rights depend on inclusive political regulation to administer labour markets and decide how market income distributions be altered, Marshall's citizenship becomes thin in societies where exit is dominant and the salience of collective choice in the organisation of daily life is attenuated.[61] Moreover, in the United States the legal distinction between citizens and aliens is less meaningful because the prime attributes of citizenship are political and social rights of limited value. As long as aliens are given civil rights and economic access to participate in markets, their status is not much inferior to those whose citizenship carries few additional privileges. In a system where the default solution is exit-heavy, (im)migration becomes a central private strategy for problem solving and there is less reason to close (national) boundaries in order to protect the restricted package of rights that thin citizenship offers.[62]

In Europe, where the institutional balance has historically tilted more strongly to politics than to markets, membership matters more. Modern European nations were constituted in the nineteenth century with a higher population-to-land ratio than America and effective state bureaucracies carried over from displaced mercantile and absolutist regimes. External threats required both a standing military and a central state to support it, and generated a need for nascent national states to differentiate themselves from other polities contesting the loyalties of populations whose identities had been either fluid or local for centuries. In these conditions, the default case evolved as national voice with an accompanying ideal of thick citizenship. Given the installed base of the state apparatus, appropriated by the bourgeois class to liberal ends and scientific expertise, regular governmental intervention in European financial and industrial policy, trade, empire, diplomacy and social administration assumed a centrality that made the acquisition of political rights the predominant axis on which modern citizenship was defined until 1880. Thereafter, the management of the economy shaded into the establishment and regulation of national labour markets and ancillary social benefit programmes.[63]

National labour market interventions have generally resulted in a higher social wage that arguably limits job expansion and encourages capital intensive development, especially at the unskilled end of the market. The induced decline in demand for labour reduces the pull of wage-regulated economies for foreign workers. In addition, as Esping-Andersen has shown, continental European states have enacted complex and various social regimes with differentiated national styles that mirror diverse institutional histories and define the particular form of the relationship between state, church, guild, and other civil organisations.[64] These social regimes further pressured against immigration through their impact on social security (labour) taxes where the burden of transfers lies and by promoting a shared community of obligation demarcated by the boundaries of the nation. This imagined connection between alternative systems of social rights, national political institutions, and the local histories of ethnic populations gave material confirmation to the concept that modern nation-states were at once the embodiments, guardians and propagators of distinct cultural communities.[65] While each state configured a portfolio of political, social, cultural rights and implementing mechanisms that testified to the uniqueness of the society they governed, in all cases the modern European balance between voice and exit fell far closer to the pole of politics than it did in America.[66]

Thick citizenship expresses a commitment to national culture that carries with it the social rights and obligations of a shared communal product and the political rights to be heard in the collective process of community direction. The depletion of either of these rights through the entry of aliens whose fate is not linked by history or culture to that of members is not to be taken lightly. It is only in systems of governance where citizenship carries meaningful duty and privilege in social, political, and cultural processes that the presence of semi-members or denizens becomes problematic. To dilute the weight of voice or the bonds manifested in social transfers is to give up the main elements by which national culture is reproduced and abandon the particularity of history for the generality of principle. In a political economy that supports an ideal of thin citizenship, to reduce the social rights accorded to legal aliens is to tamper with a dimension of identity that carries little significance compared to expansive job creation. In a political economy that supports an ideal of thick citizenship, to mitigate the distinction between alien and citizen is to expose the labour market to competition that drives down the social wage on which equality within the community primarily depends and to risk the stability of transfer programmes. With thin citizenship, to close the door to the outside reverses the constitutional order in which mobility antecedes politics and redefines membership as more than individual commitment. With thick citizenship, to declare oneself unexceptionally open to immigration is to challenge the nationalist legitimation of political administration and to enter a universe of fluid subjectivity that depreciates social and cultural capital dearly accumulated.[67]

The default solution of a market oriented political economy overlaps imperfectly in America with a disposition toward liberal political philosophy. The debate on citizenship and immigration has tended to contest the latter more than the former. Republican and communitarian critiques of classical liberalism have been both positive and normative. On the positive side, Sandel suggests that it is not possible to avoid a sense of being thrown into by birth and socialisation into the objective circumstances of community. Kymlicka argues that all liberalism is necessarily national wherein the political reproduction of a dominant culture is a given.[68] Along this vein of thought, it is not the reality of classical liberalism as much as its illusory pursuit that entails psychological frustration. On the normative side, Putnam suggests that the social capital associated with political and civic community is not a constant.[69] He explicitly charges the polity with building up the stock of this capital at the risk of anomie and disorder. In either of these critiques, the price of excessive autonomy and mobility, imagined or actual, is the weakening of the communal fabric that organises social life and of the civic responsibility to ensure that political governance takes priority over the pursuit of private good. This elevation of the public domain places the issue of membership centre stage and, at the least, revives the question whether immigration and naturalisation are consistent with the maintenance or restoration of the American communal good.

Abstract political philosophy is often hard pressed to find empirical ground on which to test its propositions. It is not easy to imagine, for example, how to evaluate whether the social capital created by dense networks of community norms that structure common expectations and trust in the behaviour of compatriots is worth the cost, often in blood, that is paid for a strong sense of insiders and outsiders. Florence and Lucca were, after all, at each other's throats for centuries. If crime is lower in Japan or Sweden than America, other indicators of anomie like suicide are higher. In this regard, the law of immigration in the United States offers no very clear evidence of our commitments to particular notions of republicanism or liberalism. The constitutional support of the civil rights of all persons seems consistent with a non-national liberalism. However, the recognition of the plenary power of the Congress to limit political and social rights to citizens or special classes of aliens, or even, in theory, to end immigration entirely would easily support a communitarian ideal of nationality. But, here, going beyond the complexity of any local history, it may be important to note the profound absence of cultural rights in American law. In contrast to

European constitutions that normally allow, and even demand, the state to support major national cultural and religious traditions through financing and delegation of education, in America the use of state authority to establish such community building institutions is strictly policed. In this case, perhaps, it is the absence of the legal empowerment of cultural communities, when added to the political practice of continuing high immigration, which speaks to the prevailing political philosophy.

Liberal political philosophy is a fixed point of American history and, by derivation of the American interpretation of immigration, neither its content nor its context are unchanging. It is by now somewhat disingenuous to attack liberalism as a privileging of individualism to the negation of the collective foundation of social life. At the end of the twentieth century, there can be no coherent standpoint that ignores the constraining and enabling force of language, moral judgement, or identity as concepts that are always under inter-personal negotiation. The issue that distinguishes neo-liberalism from other political philosophies is not the inevitability of community, but the relationship between community and state power.[70] Men and women make themselves in relation to others; the question is what degree of flexibility they are allowed in moving between communities where they enact their construction of virtue and desire. Where the boundaries of jurisdiction are permeable, the effective capacity of political entities to reproduce themselves declines. Where the state cannot facilitate the establishment of culture, there is little incentive for cultural organisations to adopt strategies that aim at the capture of its agencies to that end. Mobility and immigration are not the denial of community, politics or social obligation, but they contribute to their localisation. And if globalisation means that the relative costs of exit are falling in relation to voice, then the stability of American patterns of immigration may be as much a harbinger of the future as a comment on the past.

Notes

1 For historical analysis of the debate see John Higham, *Strangers in the Land* (NY: Atheneum, 1963) and Thomas C. Heller, 'Immigration and Regulation: Historical Context and Legal Reform' in Jorge A. Bustamante, Clark W. Reynolds and Raul Hinojosa Ojeda: *U.S.–Mexico Relations: Labor Market Interdependence* (Stanford: Stanford University Press, 1992); for representative argument on current policy see T. Alexander Aleinikoff, *Between Principles and Politics: The*

Direction of U.S. Citizenship Policy (Washington: Carnegie Endowment for International Peace, 1998); Arnold H. Leibowitz, *A Time for Decision: Citizenship at the Millennium* (Office of Refugee Resettlement, US Dept. of Health and Human Services, 1998); Linda. S. Bosniak, 'Membership, Equality and the Difference Alienage Makes' 69 *N.Y.U.L. Rev.* 1047 (1994); and generally, the essays edited by Noah M.J. Pickus, *Immigration and Citizenship in the Twenty-First Century* (Lanham, Md: Rowman & Littlefield, 1998).

2 Parents or other relatives of these native born citizens may then more or less easily become eligible for permanent residency or citizenship themselves. See 8 United States Code Annotated (USCA) 1151(b)(2)(a).

3 See US Department of Justice, *Legal Immigration, Fiscal Year 1997* (Number 1, January 1999). p. 8 (hereinafter *Legal Immigration*); see also US Immigration and Naturalization Service, *Illegal Alien Resident Population*, at *http://www.-ins.usdoj./gov//stats/illegalalien/index.html* at 1.

4 In 1995 these categories of non-immigrant legal entrants, not including accompanying spouses and dependents, were approximately 642 000. Students admitted to full time study added another 364 000 non-immigrant residents. US Department of Justice, Immigration and Naturalization Service, *1995 Statistical yearbook of the Immigration and Naturalization Service* (March 1997), pp. 114–15, (hereinafter 1995 SYB).

5 See Legal Immigration, *op. cit.*, p. 1. Note that all entering immigrants in the earlier period were classified as legal immigrants since there were no quantitative restrictions on entry until 1921. Qualitative restrictions were enacted during this period and restrictions against the legal entry of Chinese and other Asians also existed, but statistics are not available on illegal entries by either qualitatively or nationally barred immigrants.

6 92 % of all naturalisations follow the general provisions. Spouses and children of US citizens and military classes constitute special naturalisation categories. Most individuals naturalising as spouses may do so in three years. 1995 SYB, *op. cit.*, p. 130.

7 1995 SYB, *op. cit.*, pp. 134–9

8 In the United States the practice of *jus soli*, citizenship by birth, was determined by the Supreme Court to be codified in the 14th Amendment to the Constitution: *U.S. v. Wong Kim Ark*, 169 US 669 (1889). In addition, *jus sanguinis*, citizenship by descent, has always applied to a child born to two citizen parents outside the United States. Where only one parent (mother or father) of a foreign born child is a US citizen, certain residency requirements may also apply to the grant of US citizenship. See Leibowitz, *op. cit.*, pp. 42–3.

9 In this sense, recent legislative proposals and debate has focused directly on a core pillar of US immigration policy in the controversial argument that birthright citizenship is neither mandated by the American legal tradition nor politically consistent with the communitarian nationality they advocate. See H.R.J. Res. 117, 103d Cong. (1993) and Gerald L. Neuman, *Strangers to the Constitution: Immigrants, Borders and Fundamental Law* (Princeton: Princeton University Press, 1996) pp. 165–87.

10 Immigration and Nationality Act (INA), Sect 245, 8 USCA 1255; for much of this decade until 14 January 1998 adjustment of status was especially facilitated by special procedures see INA 245(i), 8 USCA 1255 (i). About 68 % of

those adjusting status under 245(i) in 1996 were spouses and children of US citizens or permanent residents. 11% were professionals or foreign students who worked for US employers while in school and were to be retained after graduation. See Gary. P. Freeman, 'Clientelism or Populism? The Politics of Immigration Reform in the United States', conference paper, 11–12 June 1998, European University Institute, Florence, Italy.

11 The number of persons adjusting status from non-immigrant status to permanent residents is usually subtracted from the world-wide number of available immigrant visas in the appropriate preference categories. However, in some cases the total number of legal immigrants may increase through a large pool of changes in illegal or non-immigrant status. For example, the 1990 Immigration Act, still in effect, set a maximum of 480 000 for family-sponsored preferences: 8 USCA 1151(c). Immigrant status granted to immediate relatives of US citizens in any year reduces this total in the subsequent year's quota. However, the Act also specifies a minimum of 226 000 family-sponsored admits annually. Therefore, if a large number of immediate relatives of US citizens (including illegal or non-resident aliens who are parents of US born children) is granted adjustment, this limit may be reached and total admissions will increase. In addition, when illegal aliens are given amnesty and not counted against annual caps on immigrants, as was the case the Immigration Control and Reform Act of 1986 for persons illegally resident in the United States since 1982, or are made legal through special procedures like suspension of deportation, then the size of these populations is relevant to the size as well as the composition of legal alien populations.

12 The 1990 Act both expanded the aggregate number of legal immigrants by approximately one-third over previous levels and altered the preferences according to which they are selected. Congress reduced the number of visas available for adult children of legal permanent residents and expanded visas available for their spouses and minor children. In addition, the number of visas available for highly-skilled immigrants and their families and for certain other skilled and unskilled workers and their dependents was raised from 54 000 (27 000; 27 000) to 120 000 (110 000; 10 000). There are currently four preferences for family-sponsored immigrants and five employment based preferences. For summary see 1995 SYB, *op. cit.*, pp. 15–17; 8 USCA 1153 (a) and (b).

13 More complete discussion of refugee and asylee entry and adjustments may be found at 1995 SYB, *op. cit.*, pp. 72–8.

14 8 USCA 1184(a)(1) and (2); see this code section generally for specific definitions of who may qualify under these various employment categories as non-immigrants, the conditions for entry and exit of such employment, and details of the labour certification process that applies to those admitted under 101(a)(15)(H).

15 1995 SYB, *op. cit.*, pp. 114–15

16 These figures are generally based on the INS report on *Illegal Alien Resident Population, op. cit.*

17 1995 SYB, *op. cit.*, p. 170.

18 These balances may shift over time and may be dynamically interrelated. For example, although the United States does not officially recognise dual citizenship, dual citizenship is now widespread. It no longer presents a serious

legal issue as courts have restricted the cases in which an American can be threatened with the involuntary loss of his or her citizenship. Nor does the United States distinguish between nationality and citizenship. However, as the United States made the benefits of citizenship more valuable by disallowing certain forms of social transfer to immigrants acquiring permanent resident status after 1997, Mexico responded by redefining its rules on dual citizenship. By creating a new status of nationality, distinguished from full citizenship, Mexico allowed Mexicans who naturalised in the North to apply to reacquire 'Mexican nationality'. They thereby retain the right to travel on a Mexican passport, to own coastal and border land forbidden to aliens, and to take advantage of a wide range of economic and commercial privileges normally denied in Mexico to aliens; see Aleinikoff, *op. cit.*, pp. 25–40 and Leibowitz, *op. cit.*, pp. 59–63.

19 In the final part of this essay I will extend Marshall's trilogy of rights to cultural rights. However, I will not discuss cultural rights in this section because there is little direct American recognition of such rights to linguistic, religious or other cultural establishment for either citizens or aliens. Rather, the protection of cultural identity is limited to the liberal prohibition of governmental authorisation or empowerment of any particular cultural practice. I will reserve the question of cultural rights because of its relevance to the liberal–communitarian debate that dominates the political philosophical consideration of immigration.

20 *Wong Wing v. United States*, 163 US 228 (1896); *Plyler v. Doe*, 457 US 202, 215 (1982) extended this inclusive reading of the term person to the Fourteenth Amendment.

21 *Bridges v. Wixon* 326 US 135 (1945)

22 *Almeida-Sanchez v. U.S.* 413 US 266 (1973); the Supreme Court in dicta has more recently questioned whether undocumented aliens would receive full Fourth Amendment protections since that amendment uses the term 'the people' rather than the perhaps more inclusive term persons used in the Fifth and Sixth Amendments, see *United States v. Verdugo-Urquidez*, 494 U.S. 259, 272 (1990).

23 *Bolanos v. Kelley*, 509 F.2d 1023 (2d Cir. 1975).

24 See discussion and accompanying citations in Bosniak (1994a), *op. cit.*, pp. 1100–1101 and 1115–17.

25 Permanent residents who leave the United States temporarily may be subject to re-entry restrictions, a process usually triggered by assertions of criminal activity or material misrepresentations of qualifications for permanent residence. Both re-entry restrictions and loss of citizenship processes have been increasingly constrained by recent jurisprudence, see Aleinikoff, *op. cit.*, pp. 21–4.

26 8 USCA 1153 (a).

27 See Sup Ct reversal of 9th circ. on rights in deportation proceedings; see *also American Arab Anti-Discrimination Committee v. Meese (ADC)*, 714 F. Supp. 1060 (C.D. Cal. 1989) holding that, in spite of the extraordinary power of Congress in the immigration area, First Amendment protections for political speech would apply even in the context of deportation; on exclusion see *United States ex. rel. Knauff v. Shaughnessy*, 338 US 537 (1950); *Shaughnessy v. United States ex. rel. Mezei*, 345 US 206 (1953).

28 See Gerald M. Rosburg, 'Aliens and Equal Protection: Why not the Right to Vote?', 79 *Mich. L. Rev.* 1136 (1977).

29 See Jamin B. Raskin, 'Legal Aliens, Local Citizens: The Historical, Constitutional, and Theoretical Meanings of Alien Suffrage', 141 *U. Penn. L. Rev.* 1391 (1993).

30 See *Sugarman v. Dougall*, 413 US 634 at 648 (1973).

31 See *Ambach v. Norwich*, 441 US 68, quote above at 73 (1979); *Foley v. Connelie*, 435 US 291 (1978); *Cabell v. Chavez-Salido*, 454 US 432 (1982).

32 As a practical matter, the need for security clearances in advanced technology or other defence-related industries may be more of a problem for persons with foreign histories, but the grant of such clearances is decided on an individual rather than a categorical basis related to alienage.

33 8 USCA 1153 (b). There have also been numerous proposals since 1990 to move further toward skills related admission the balance between family sponsored and economically justified immigration. Even the restrictionist Smith House omnibus bill rejected in great part in the 1996 reforms would have increased work-related admissions. See Freeman, *op. cit.*, p. 6.

34 8 USCA 1101(a)(15)(H), (J), (L), or (O).

35 8 USCA 1184 (c) and (g); USCA 1182(a)(5) and (n).

36 See 8 USCA 1324 and 1324a. States, whose jurisdiction is preempted by federal power in most matters affecting alienage law, were recognised to have the authority to penalise the employment of illegal aliens. *De Canas v. Bica*, 424 US 351 (1976). The exceptional holding of *De Canas* might be differently resolved today because of the passage of IRCA in 1986 since at the time of the opinion the federal government did not itself regulate the employment of undocumented persons. This proposition is untested because states have not been active in this field of labour market regulation. For more general discussion of the question of federal preemption of state authority in the immigration area, see Peter J. Spiro, 'The States and Immigration in an Era of Demi-Sovereignties', 35 *Va. J. Int'l L.* 121 (1994); Linda S. Bosniak, 'Immigrants, Preemption and Equality', 35 *Va. J. Int'l L.* 179 (1994), Hiroshi Motomura, 'Federalism and Immigration Law', 35 *Va. J. Int'l L.* 201 (1994).

37 See Freeman, *op. cit.*, pp. 10, 13.

38 See *Illegal Alien Resident Population, op. cit.* The ongoing effort since IRCA by legislators and interest groups who seek to fortify border controls, punish more harshly both illegal aliens and their American employers, and develop more sophisticated registration and identity systems for citizens and legal aliens in order to lower the population of undocumented aliens testifies to the failure of existing rules and programmes to achieve this end. See Freeman, *op. cit.*, p. 6.

39 Note that increased penalties for deportees do not apply to voluntary deportation procedures and that employer penalties are limited for firms that comply with all other wage standards and regulations of working conditions applicable to legal and illegal workers.

40 8 USCA 1182(a)(4) and 1183a. These so-called deeming provisions were considerably strengthened in the 1996 reforms. Public Law 104–208; Section 551(a). The effectiveness of the deeming affidavits ends once the alien has worked for the equivalent of 40 qualifying social security quarters in the United States.

41 426 US 67 (1976); see discussion in Bosniak (1994a), *op. cit.*, pp. 1065–7 and 1103–5.
42 On improper discrimination see, e.g. *Yick Wo v. Hopkins*, 118 US 356 (1886); *Takahashi v. Fish & Game Commission*; for allowable alien based classifications, see, e.g. *People v. Crane*, 108 NE 427 (NY), aff'd 239 US 195 (1915).
43 403 US 365 (1971).
44 I know of no instance where states have been required to provide social assistance to non-immigrants, nor of any case where states have attempted to deny provision of public services to non-immigrants legally working in their economies.
45 *Plyler v. Doe*, 457 US 202 (1982). Where aliens, legal or illegal, do attend the public schools, they are presumably entitled to the same rights to a bilingual or multicultural education that are extended to citizen children. Educational programmes are generally a matter of state law, but the Supreme Court has held on statutory rather than constitutional grounds that school districts that accept federal aid may be required to consider how to rectify the educational disadvantages suffered by non-English speaking children: *Lau v. Nichols*, 414 US 563 (1973). Since that ruling a wide variety of state and local programmes have proliferated, amidst political and academic controversy on where on the continuum between cultural maintenance and English immersion students will be best served. In California, where some school districts have children from as many as 80 language groups, extended teaching in major languages like Spanish or Chinese continues in spite of recent legislation that emphasises the necessity for rapid acquisition of proficiency in English.
46 Federal courts blocked the implementation of all 187 provisions except those imposing criminal penalties for the use of fraudulent documents. A final settlement of the 187 controversies was reached on 29 July 1999 when California and all opposing parties agreed to drop appeals of court decisions that voided all the referendum's core provisions including those that prevented illegal immigrants from attending public schools and receiving social services and health care. The agreement also left standing the judicial overturning of the requirement that law enforcement authorities, school administrators and social workers turn in suspected illegal immigrants: *New York Times*, 30 July 1999 at A1 and A15.
47 See Gabriel J. Chin, 'The Civil Rights Revolution Comes to Immigration Law: A New Look at the Immigration and Nationality Act of 1965', 75 *N. Car. L. Rev.* 273 (1996).
48 Michael Lind, *The Next American Nation: The New Nationalism and the Fourth American Revolution* (NY: Free Press, 1995).
49 See Freeman, *op. cit.*, pp. 5–11 on legal workers; 20–2 on proposals concerning temporary workers.
50 *ibid.*, p. 15.
51 *ibid.*, p. 16.
52 Many of these procedural provisions have been the subjects of litigation with variant outcomes since their enactment. See *ibid.*, p. 15.
53 See Louis Hartz, *The Liberal Tradition in America: An Interpretation of American Political Thought since the Revolution* (NY: Harcourt, Brace, 1955); see also Thomas C. Heller, 'Modernity, Membership and Multiculturalism', 5 *Stanford Humanities Review* 2, 39–45 (1997).

54 See for summary of critical revision arguments and cases Peter J. Spiro, 'The Citizenship Dilemma', 51 *Stan. L. Rev.* 597, 598–606 (1999).

55 See Heller (1997), *op. cit.*, pp. 39–52 suggesting caution in seeing events in any of the industrial powers during the inter-war period as typical expressions of a nation's preferred system of governance. The extremism produced by the disruptions of WWI, the economic turbulence that followed it, and widespread moral and political backlash against liberalism and industrial capitalism led everywhere to departures from established institutional practices. These experiments often were themselves left behind after WWII.

56 See Chin, *op. cit.*, pp. 303–21, 336–45.

57 Rogers M. Smith, *Civic Ideals: Conflicting Visions of Citizenship in U.S. History* (New Haven: Yale University Press, 1997).

58 For a fuller attempt to elaborate this theme see Heller (1997), *op. cit.*

59 *ibid.*, pp. 15–30; also Robert H. Wiebe, *Self-Rule: A Cultural History of American Democracy* (Chicago: University of Chicago Press, 1995) pp. 17–111

60 Albert O. Hirschman, *Exit, Voice and Loyalty* (Cambridge, Mass: Harvard University Press 1970). I will not explore the loyalty term separately here since in modern societies loyalty generally reflects commitments built up through the prior operations of exit and voice, rather than through traditional or charismatic attachments.

61 See Theda Skocpol, *Social Policy in the United States: Future Possibilities in Historical Perspective* (Princeton: Princeton University Press, 1995).

62 As noted above, this description of American institutions is a default case. At various times, for various reasons, there have been turns toward the increased reliance on public administrative management and denser political regulation more characteristic of European modernity. In this century the First World War and the New Deal best exemplified this turn. This was also the period in which immigration controls were strengthened. Indeed, immigration management was earlier instituted than most other elements of the regulatory state because there was less legal resistance to the centralisation of what was constitutionally accepted by the courts to be an exclusive federal competence. See Heller (1997), *op. cit.*, pp. 42–5.

63 *ibid.*, pp. 46–52.

64 Gosta Esping-Andersen, *The Three Worlds of Welfare Capitalism* (Princeton: Princeton University Press, 1990), pp. 9–35.

65 Following Anderson, I use the term 'imagined' to admonish the point of view that the historical traditions that undergird national cultures are artifacts of that history itself. See Benedict Anderson, *Imagined Communities* (London: Verso, 1983).

66 For analysis of national styles in European politics see Frans van Waarden 'Persistence of national policy styles: A study of their institutional foundations' in Brigitte Unger and Frans van Waarden, *Convergence or Diversity: Internationalization and Economic Policy Response* (Aldershot: Avebury, 1995), pp. 333–72.

67 Although I refer to American and Europe to develop the opposition between thick and thin citizenship, I do not think the concepts are useful only in these regions. Many developing nations modelled themselves on the European states with which they had become familiar and interested during colonialism. The difficulty of applying this model of the state and its narratives of

cultural homogeneity and political competence to ex-colonial polities is obvious. Other nations of immigration like Argentina or even Canada have more hybrid notions that lie between thick and thin citizenship. These may reflect the longer or better established colonial status of these nations and the greater appropriation of the institutions of the colonial administration by creole elites. Still other nations like Japan, which openly borrowed European models of state and law during Meiji, have created thick ideals of citizenship that centre more on the reproduction of common cultural capital than on social and political rights.

68 Michael Sandel, *Democracy's Discontent* (Cambridge, Mass.: Belknap Press, 1996); Will Kymlicka, *Multicultural Citizenship: A Liberal Theory of Minority Rights* (Oxford: Clarendon Press, 1995). I have extensively argued that Kymlicka's characterisation confuses European modernity, where liberalism is national, with American liberalism that is not. See Heller, *op. cit.*

69 Robert D. Putnam, *Making Democracy Work* (Princeton: Princeton University Press, 1993).

70 See John Rawls, *Political Liberalism* (NY: Columbia University Press, 1993), pp. 89–129.

11
Comparative Citizenship and Aliens' Rights

Atsushi Kondo

Introduction

Every country has its own unique history of migration policy and a specific context within which migration has taken place. For example, some countries have had colonies (Japan, France, UK and the Netherlands) and some countries have themselves been colonies (Australia, New Zealand and the USA). In the past some countries have been emigration states (Japan, Germany, Sweden and the UK). In recent times, we can classify states into classical immigration states (Australia, New Zealand, Canada and the USA),[1] European immigration states (France, the UK, Sweden, the Netherlands and Germany) and states with only modest levels of immigration (Japan). Table 11.1 shows the size of the foreign populations and foreign-born populations in the countries analysed in this book. Generally, foreign populations and foreign-born populations grew in the 1990s except in the Netherlands, where the foreign population fell due to high rates of acquisition of citizenship after the amendment of the administration of naturalisation practice.

Immigrants in the traditional immigration states have been granted many rights in contrast to non-immigrants. In the 1970s and 1980s, immigration policy changed and aliens' rights were improved in many European states which stopped labour immigration because of the first oil crisis in 1973. On the one hand, the International Covenant on Economic, Social and Cultural Rights (ICESCR) obliged ratifying states to guarantee residential, social and economic rights to resident aliens. However, the USA has not ratified this treaty, perhaps reflecting the difference of social rights between citizens and permanent resident aliens in the USA. On the other hand, the International Covenant on

Table 11.1 Size of foreign population and foreign-born population in selected countries (thousands and percentages)

Country	*Foreign population*		*Foreign-born population*	
	1990	*1996*	*1990*	*1996*
Australia			3 753.3*	3 908.3
% of total population			22.3*	21.1
Canada			4 342.9*	4 971.1
% of total population			16.1*	17.4
New Zealand			527.3*	605.1
% of total population			15.8*	17.5
Germany	5 342.5	7 314.0		
% of total population	8.4	8.9		
France	3 596.6			
% of total population	6.3			
Sweden	483.7	679.9	834.5**	943.8
% of total population	5.6	6.0	9.6**	11.0
USA	11 770.3		19 767.3	24 600
% of total population	4.7		7.9	9.3
Netherlands	692.4	679.9	1 217.1	1 407.1***
% of total population	4.6	4.4	8.1	9.1***
UK	1 723	1 972		
% of total population	3.2	3.4		
Japan	1 075.3	1 415.1		
% of total population	0.9	1.1		

* 1991 data ** 1992 data *** 1995 data

Source: SOPEMI, *Trends in International Migration – Annual Report* (Paris: OECD) 1992 edn, p. 131; 1995 edn, p. 194; 1998 edn, pp. 223–4; 1996 Census of Population and Dwellings. National Summary (Statistics New Zealand: Wellington, 1997), p. 24.

Civil and Political Rights (ICCPR) have been ratified by all the states in our comparative study. Most civil rights are granted to resident aliens and political rights also extend to resident aliens to a certain degree. In the 1990s, the European Union established special privileged status for EU citizens. But at the same time economic depression has hindered the acceptance of refugees and has had the effect of strengthening control of irregular resident aliens.

Some recent constitutional laws stipulate aliens' rights, for example in Sweden, the Netherlands and Canada. Other constitutional laws are inclined to make light of the distinction between citizens and aliens even if they do not stipulate aliens' rights. Some constitutional laws guarantee equality before the law for aliens. Courts have contributed to reduce discrimination on the basis of alienage.[2]

Citizenship and nationality

Acquisition and loss of nationality (1.1)

Generally, citizenship can be acquired in any one of four ways: by descent (*jus sanguinis*), by birthplace (*jus soli*), by naturalisation or by registration.[3]

Citizenship attribution at birth is divided into two principles: *jus sanguinis* (right of the blood) and *jus soli* (right of the soil). Roughly, we can describe Japan, Germany, Sweden, France, and the Netherlands as *jus sanguinis* countries and the UK, Australia, New Zealand, Canada and the USA as *jus soli* countries. However, there are significant exceptions from each pure model and many countries adopt both elements and give greater weight to one or the other. In order to compare the character of birthright citizenships, namely 'nationality of origin', it is best to classify them into four types: (i) strict *jus sanguinis*; (ii) flexible *jus sanguinis*; (iii) limited *jus soli*; (iv) unconditional *jus soli*.

Even in strict *jus sanguinis* countries (Japan and Sweden), the principle of *jus soli* has exceptionally been extended to a child (in order to avoid statelessness) when both parents are unknown in a case where the child is born within a country's territory. On the one hand, non-strict *jus sanguinis* countries (Germany, France and the Netherlands[4]) add the element of *jus soli* or double *jus soli* by way of the 'optional model'. Therefore, the second or third generations of immigrants can acquire the citizenship of the settlement country. On the other hand, limited *jus soli* countries (the UK and Australia) add the condition that one parent must be a citizen or a permanent resident. As a result, most second generation immigrants can acquire citizenship in a settlement country of *jus soli* type. In non-limited *jus soli* countries (New Zealand, Canada and the USA), even children of irregular residents, short-term residents and travellers have the automatic birthright of citizenship. There is a minority opinion that birthright citizenship for the children of irregular and temporary-visitor aliens should be limited,[5] but majority opinion in the USA[6] is against such limitation.

There is no 'second generation problem'[7] in the non-limited *jus soli* countries such as the USA, and it is a tiny problem in the limited *jus soli* countries such as the UK. There is no third generation problem in non-strict *jus sanguinis* such as France. However, even a fourth generation problem still remains in strict *jus sanguinis* countries such as Japan. Table 11.2 illustrates the main criteria for determining attribution of citizenship at birth.[8]

Table 11.2 Main and secondary criteria for determining the attribution of citizenship at birth

Country	*Born in the country (jus soli)*		*Descent (jus sanguinis)*	
	Citizenship automatically granted	*One parent must be a national or a permanent resident*	*One parent must have been born in the country (double jus soli) etc.*	*One parent must be a national*
Non-limited *jus soli*				
USA	O			X
Canada	O			X
New Zealand	O			X
Limited *jus soli*				
Australia		O		X
UK		O		X
Jus soli combined with *jus sanguinis*				
Germany		X		O
France			X	O
Netherlands			X	O
Strict *jus sanguinis*				
Sweden				O
Japan				O

O = main criteria X = secondary criteria

Citizenship acquisition after birth is generally explained in two ways: naturalisation and other means such as registration, declaration and restoration. Regarding the adult citizenship acquisition, *jus domicili* (right of the domicile) is referred to as the principle by which citizenship may be granted to persons with real or effective residence in the state.[9] This is a principle by which citizenship entitlement is on the basis of long-term residence rather than origin.[10] Even in some *jus sanguinis* countries (France, the Netherlands, Sweden and Germany), *jus domicili* is applied on the condition of a certain period of domicile or education in the settlement country.

Distinctions between nationality and citizenship (1.2)

As discussed in the introduction, the terms nationality and citizenship vary from country to country and among various academic disciplines. Nationality has two main meanings: (i) membership of a state; and (ii) membership of a nation.[11] Citizenship also has two main meanings: (i) membership of a state; and (ii) a set of rights and duties in a polity.

The former is called 'formal citizenship' and the latter 'substantial citizenship'.

The concept of citizenship (1.3)

There are two types of contemporary conceptions of the substantial citizenship; (i) regional and reciprocal citizenship; and (ii) residential and universal citizenship. Firstly, European Union citizenship is the new concept of regional and reciprocal citizenship in EU Member States such as the UK France, Germany, the Netherlands and Sweden. Recently, the notion of 'Nordic citizenship' has been introduced to describe a similar concept.[12] Secondly, there are new concepts of universal citizenship for permanent or long-term resident aliens in France, the UK, the USA, Germany, the Netherlands, Japan and Sweden even if they do not have a legal counterpart. They are called *la nouvelle citoyeneté*,[13] new citizenship,[14] post-national citizenship,[15] *Niederlassungsrecht*,[16] *eijû shiminken*,[17] and denizenship respectively.[18] This regional and reciprocal citizenship is connected with the formal citizenship of its member states and this is practical, whereas residential and universal citizenship is only theoretical. Denizenship is the most influential concept of these transnational citizenships but it is not a legal term and its definition is different from person to person. For example one Austrian researcher has translated it into '*Wohnbürgershaft*' which means 'residential citizenship'[19] and I translated denizenship into the Japanese phrase '*eijû shiminken*' which means 'permanent-resident citizenship'.[20] Even if there is no such new concept, non-citizen residents have developed rights of quasi-citizenship in Australia, New Zealand and Canada. In the context of indigenous rights, however, 'cultural citizenship' is discussed in these countries rather than denizenship.

Stateless persons (1.4)

Generally, there are few cases of stateless persons because every country has tried to eliminate them. Minor exceptions are the cases of asylum seekers who may lose their former citizenship before gaining a new one, and children of undocumented mothers who also may not acquire any citizenship at the time of their birth.

Dual nationality (1.5)

In contrast, dual nationality is relatively common in some states (Australia, New Zealand, the USA, Canada, the UK and France).[21] Indeed, to counter this, the Council of Europe introduced the 1963 Convention on Reduction of Cases of Multiple Nationality. However in 1993, following the growing trend in certain states to give wider acceptance to multiple nationality due to the increase of international marriage and migration, the Second Protocol amending the 1963 Convention was adapted. This has been drafted in such a way as to allow, or even to encourage, dual national status in two specific contexts: that of unity of nationality within the same family, and that of the integration of second-generation migrants.[22] Furthermore, the 1997 European Convention on Nationality is neutral on the issue of the desirability of multiple nationality, so Member States are free to allow multiple nationality in addition to the cases of international marriage.[23] Since 1992, plural nationality has been officially accepted and is no longer seen as problematic and a cause for refusing naturalisation in the Netherlands.[24] In Germany, the Nationality Law was amended in 1999. The 'option model' allows the children born of foreign parents to have dual nationality if one of the parents is a permanent resident. In the future however, they must chose to become exclusively German between the ages of 18 and 23 or lose their German nationality.[25] The Swedish government is also planning to amend the Citizenship Act in order to allow wider dual nationality.[26] The exact number of dual nationality persons is not clear, but the advantages of it are considered to outweigh the disadvantages. Japan and Korea limit the increase of dual nationality by way of the option system for the children of mixed marriage and the requirement for renouncing the former nationality. Sweden has the same rule but there are many exceptions in practice.

Changes in the naturalisation rate (1.6)

Changing citizenship law or practice has had the effect of increasing the naturalisation rate in Australia and the Netherlands. In Germany, the rate increased because of a climate favouring naturalisation among 'Germans'. Table 11.3 is the number of acquisitions of citizenship after birth and the naturalisation rate in a broad sense. Australia, Canada, New Zealand and the USA are countries where a native-born/foreign-born distinction is prevalent, so it is not so easy to identify the naturalisation rate. Currently, about 18 000 people gain New Zealand citizenship annually (see Chapter 8).

Some countries, such as Sweden, regard citizenship as a step towards integration, while others, such as Germany, consider it a reward for the successful completion of integration. In multicultural communities, for example the USA, political allegiance and basic language abilities are part of the naturalisation process. In communities where membership

Table 11.3 Acquisition of citizenship after birth and the naturalisation rate (thousands and percentages)

Country	*1988*	*1989*	*1990*	*1991*	*1992*	*1993*	*1994*	*1995*	*1996*	*1997*
Japan	5.8	6.1	6.8	7.8	9.4	10.5	11.1	14.1	14.5	15.1
	0.7	0.6	0.7	0.7	0.8	0.8	0.8	1.0	1.1	1.1
Germany	40.8	68.5	101.4	141.6	179.9	199.4	259.2	313.6	302.8	271.8
	1.0	1.5	2.1	2.7	3.1	3.1	3.8	4.5	4.2	3.7
France	74.0	82.0	88.5	95.5	95.3	95.5	126.3	92.4	109.8	116.2
				2.7						
UK	64.6	117.1	57.3	58.6	42.2	45.8	44.0	40.5	43.1	37.0
	3.5	6.4	3.2	3.4	2.4	2.3	2.2	2.1	2.1	1.9
Netherlands	9.1	28.7	12.8	29.1	36.2	43.1	49.5	71.4	82.7	59.8
	1.5	4.6	2.0	4.2	4.9	5.7	6.3	9.4	11.4	8.8
Sweden	18.0	17.6	16.8	27.7	29.3	42.7	35.1	32.0	25.6	28.9
	4.5	4.2	3.7	5.7	5.9	8.5	6.9	6.0	4.8	5.5
Australia	81.2	119.1	127.9	118.5	125.2	122.1	112.2	114.8	111.6	108.3
	5.7							7.4		
Canada	58.5	87.5	104.3	118.6	116.2	150.6	217.3	227.7		
				9.1						
USA	242.1	233.8	270.1	308.1	240.3	314.7	407.4	445.9	1044.7	600.0
			2.3							

Source: SOPEMI, *Trends in International Migration – Annual Report* (Paris: OECD, 1999), p. 265, table A.1.7; Dilek Çinar, 'From Aliens to Citizens: Rules of Transition' in Rainer Bauböck (ed.), *From Aliens to Citizens: Redefining the Status of Immigrants in Europe* (Aldershot: Avebury, 1994), pp. 63–4; Stephen Castles and Mark J. Millar, *The Age of Migration* 2nd edn (New York: Guilford, 1998), p. 239.

was defined by descent, such as Germany, naturalisation has been much more difficult[27] although as mentioned earlier, the German Nationality Act was amended in 1999.

Residential rights

Restriction on freedom of entry (2.1)

Following the international legal principle of territorial sovereignty, states possess extensive authority to control the ingress of foreigners into the their territory. The International Declaration of Human Rights states that everyone has the rights to freedom of movement within the borders of each state, and everyone has the right to leave any country (article 13). The right of everyone to enter any country is not provided for. The International Covenant on Civil and Political Rights stipulates that no one shall be arbitrarily deprived of the right to enter his own country (article 12-4). Generally, aliens do not have the freedom of entry to other countries. However, Nordic co-operation, EU citizenship, EEA treaties and the Trans-Tasman Travel Arrangement regulate the exceptions on the basis of special treaties.

Residential status of foreigners (2.2)

Usually, residential status is categorised into two types: (i) temporary stay; and (ii) permanent residence. In the traditional immigrant states where there is a migration programme (family, skill and investment), it is necessary to apply for permission before entering such states and temporary immigrants need to return to their country of origin to apply for such permission. Sweden will give a permanent residence permit before a person has entered the state in some cases and temporary residents can be granted permanent residence after a few years. In other countries temporary residents apply for a permanent resident permit after residence for a certain number of years.

Tomas Hammar suggests a model of three entrance gates for immigrants – temporary residence, permanent residence and naturalisation – into European countries.[28] However, in the classical or traditional immigration countries, immigrants go directly to the second entrance. Usually, residential periods for acquiring a permanent residence permit are shorter than for naturalisation except in the case of Japan (see Table 11.4). The reason why the second hurdle is higher than the third hurdle in Japan is that the government is especially reluctant to grant permanent residence permits and is fond of an assimilation policy of citizenship.

Table 11.4 Permanent residence and naturalisation requirement[29]

	*Requirement for permanent resident permit**	*Requirement for citizenship**
Australia	0 year	2 years
New Zealand	0 year	3 years
Canada	0 year	3 years
USA	0 year	5 years
Sweden	0–3 years	2–5 years
France	3 years	5 years
UK	4 years	5 years
The Netherlands	5 years	5 years
Germany	8 years	8 years
Japan	10 years	5 years

* It should be noted that spouse/child of citizen/permanent resident can apply for the permanent residence status and citizenship after two to five years in many countries.

Requirements for permanent residence status (2.3)

Generally, permanent residence status is granted only after the alien immigrant has been lawfully resident for some years, has sufficient income or stable employment, and has not recently committed serious offences. Sufficient knowledge of the language is a requirement for this status only in Germany and Japan.[30] It is estimated that the majority of resident aliens in all our comparative European states currently hold a secure residence status (permanent residence status and privileged status such as EU citizens): over 50 per cent in Germany, over 66 per cent in the Netherlands and Sweden and more than 90 per cent in France.[31]

Restrictions on freedom of re-entry (2.4)

It is necessary to receive permission to re-enter before departing the domiciled state and if permanent residents do not want to lose their permission they must return for 6 months (Germany), 9 months (the Netherlands), 2 years (the UK) and 3 years (France). In Japan, special permanent residents can reside abroad for a maximum of 5 years (others 2 years) without losing their status. In Australia and New Zealand, permanent residents need to return while the original entry visa is still valid In Canada, permanent residents need to persuade an immigration officer that there was no intent to emigrate if they remained more than 6 months outside the country in a year.

Discrimination according to country of origin (2.5)

Citizens from the EU/EEA/Association Treaty with EU have a better residence position in EU States. Furthermore, citizens of Belgium and Luxembourg have the automatic right to a permanent residence permit in the Netherlands. Citizens of Iceland and Norway also have permanent residence status in Sweden. Likewise, in Australia and New Zealand, mutual citizens are permitted permanent residence.

In France, citizens of the former colonies Tunisia, Morocco and Algeria will gain permanent residence more easily. There are some relevant issues in Japan, such as former colonial Koreans and Taiwanese who had lived in Japan before the end of the Second World War, and their descendants, who are given the status of special permanent residents. People of Japanese origin of the second and third generations, who came mainly from Brazil and Peru, are given the status of quasi-permanent residents. In Germany, ethnic Germans who came from mainly Eastern Europe are granted immediate citizenship.

Problems in the alien registration procedure (2.6)

There are special alien registration processes in many countries such as police registration (UK), and civil registration (Japan, France, Germany and the Netherlands). In Sweden, popular registration and personal ID cards are available for resident aliens as well as for citizens.

In the USA, Canada, Australia and New Zealand, there is no alien registration system because population registration and identity cards have been rejected on grounds of civil liberty.

In EU Member States, fingerprinting for non-EU citizens such as irregulars or persons subject to deportation is required. Japan will abolish fingerprinting for all resident aliens in 1999 but aliens are still obliged to carry the registration certificate with them at all times.

Social rights

Restrictions for permanent residents (3.1)

Legally, resident aliens have access to a set of social services almost identical to those available to citizens.[32] The main line of division in both cases is not between citizens and aliens, but between permanent residents (and, in Europe, resident foreigners from common market states) and others.[33] Among the factors bearing on immigrants' eligibility for social benefits, citizenship is a relatively insignificant matter. More important factors include: (a) physical presence in the territory;

(b) legality of residence and/or work; (c) specific immigrant status (for example, permanent, short-term, tourist); (d) nature of the welfare programme (for example, contributory, non-contributory, emergency); (e) country of origin (for example, EU Member States); (f) length of residence; (g) zeal with which eligibility rules are administratively enforced; and (h) the state or province of residence in federal states.[34]

Generally, there is no restriction in the social service system for permanent or long-term residents. For example, minimum living standard welfare is permitted only to permanent or long-term residents in many countries. Exceptionally, it is also available to all persons who have a domicile in Sweden, while many social rights are limited even to permanent resident aliens in the USA.

Insurance-based (contributory) benefit depends on prior payments by individuals. Thus, they are open to all categories of legal aliens, except those who are supposed to be insured in their home countries (for example contract workers). In contrast, assistance-based (non-contributory) benefits are financed by general taxes.[35] As a result, limited-term resident aliens tend to be excluded from non-contributory benefits for fear of the rejection to renew a residence permit, while permanent residents tend to have more access to social services financed by taxes.

Limitations for temporary residents (3.2)

In many countries, temporary residents or visitors do not have access to medical and social benefits except where there are reciprocal agreements with their own country.

Limitations for irregular residents (3.3)

In some countries such as Sweden, irregular residents (overstayers and illegal entrants) are excluded from medical and social benefits except for emergency medical care. In other countries such as the Netherlands, irregular residents are entitled to health insurance. The transformation of the Nightwatch State into a Welfare State follows that social rights are increasingly seen as 'universal human rights' in the same manner as civil rights. It is however important to note that in all welfare states irregular residents have been excluded from the social rights.[36] There are rare exceptions such as personal injury under New Zealand's comprehensive accident compensation and medical treatment of atomic bomb victims in Japan.

War-related compensation (3.4)

Discrimination on grounds of citizenship regarding war-related compensation for former soldiers remains a serious problem only in Japan.

Multicultural education (3.5)

Education has been a crucial dimension of social integration for migrants. There is an increase in immigrant minority pupils who speak a language at home other than the national standard language. Generally, support and orientation services are available for foreign pupils, particularly for new arrivals who are not immediately able to enter mainstream education. Additionally, proposals to teach immigrants' mother tongues are based on the premise that this would not only generate self-respect, but also facilitate host country language training.[37]

From a historical point of view, some countries introduced mother-tongue instruction to children of immigrants to ensure family remigration to their countries of origin. However, this justification was virtually abandoned because of the lack of substantial family remigration and mother-tongue instruction came to be seen more negatively as a considerable source of problems and deficiencies. In order to defend mother-tongue education a new justification was developed and some countries emphasised the importance of knowledge of immigrant languages and cultures from a cultural, legal and economic perspective.[38]

Mother-tongue instruction is sometimes given to children of immigrants in private ethnic schools with the financial support of governments. Even in general public schools, it is often afforded to them in such countries as Sweden, the Netherlands and Canada. Its implementation is different from municipality to municipality and schools in areas of immigrant settlement are usually active in support of their ethnic cultural activities.

Economic rights

Property rights (4.1)

Generally, property rights are granted to resident aliens as well as to citizens.[39] Exceptionally in Japan, the existence of a reciprocity treaty is required for ownership of land, ship and patent rights and there are some restrictions to holding stocks for broadcasting and telephone companies. There is a nationality requirement regarding industrial property and commercial property in France. In Canada, three-quarters of the directors of a bank and a majority of the directors of a company need to be resident Canadians.

Self-employment (4.2)

Generally, permanent residents have full rights to self-employment and to establishing businesses.[40] Regarding the freedom of business and free choice of occupation, resident aliens who have resident permits with restriction in activity cannot engage in other than permitted jobs, while those who have resident permits without restriction in activity can engage in almost all jobs in the same manner as citizens. Irregular residents have no legal working rights.

However, there seems to be a difference between the strict vocational qualification countries such as Germany and the non-strict vocational qualification countries such as the United States. Immigrants in Germany have to wait eight years until they are eligible to establish business. They are also required to fulfil requirements set by the Chamber of Crafts and so on. In the United State, by contrast, these vocational qualifications are not strict and it seems to be easier for even irregular residents to live and work.[41]

Restriction on employment in central government (4.3)

The right to be employed as civil servants is not included in the content of EU citizenship since in Europe, freedom of movement for employment has an exception for 'employment in the civil service' (Article 48 EC Treaty). However, the Court of Justice of the European Community interpreted its meaning in a narrow sense – that it is those posts involving the exercise of powers conferred by public law and whose purpose is the safeguarding of the general interests of the state or the public authority. Generally, the Continental European countries have drawn a distinction between civil servants with public status and employees with private-contract conditions of employment. The positions as employees had been made totally open to resident aliens and positions as civil servants without public authority tend to be open to EU citizens.[42] In contrast, Anglo-Saxon countries and Japan do not have such a distinction in respect of posts in public administration.

Across continental Europe, positions as civil servants in Sweden and the Netherlands are widely opened to resident aliens if their functions are not directly subordinated to government and relate to national security. In Germany and France, non-EU citizens cannot be civil servants but EU citizens can be, and non-EU citizens can be employees and workers. France is more exclusive and even EU citizens cannot be employed as civil servants whose exercise involves sovereignty or public authority.

New Zealand is the least restrictive country in the field of civil service. Except for the positions of Member of Parliament or employee of the New Zealand Security Intelligence Service (because of issues of national interest, loyalty and national security), almost all public employment is widely open to permanent residents. In the UK, government posts such as national political office, senior posts in the civil service and armed forces are closed to non-citizens except for Commonwealth citizens, Irish citizens and British Protected Persons, on grounds of loyalty. In Australia the permanent government positions are closed to aliens except on a probationary basis, provided they undertake to apply for Australian citizenship. In Japan, positions as university professors, doctors and nurses are open but high and low national civil servants are closed to aliens because of the constitutional popular sovereignty clause.

Restriction on employment in local government (4.4)

Generally, employment as local civil servants is more open to resident aliens than employment as national ones. In Australia, New Zealand, Sweden and the Netherlands, there is no citizenship requirement for the employment as local civil servants. In Germany and France, employment as civil servants is closed to non-EU citizens in the same manner as national governmental jobs. In Japan, some local governments have closed the door to all posts for public office work, while others have rules barring only promotion to managerial status because of the popular sovereignty clause in the Constitution and its nationalistic interpretation.

Data on aliens' governmental posts (4.5)

It is difficult to compare the data on the number of aliens working in governmental posts because no statistical data are available in many countries.

Distinction between categories of nationals in public employment (4.6)

EU citizenship has some relevance for public employment. For example, public employment is open to EU citizens as distinct from other resident aliens in Germany. In France, EU citizens can access employment which is independent from the exercise of sovereignty or does not involve direct or indirect participation in the exercise of national or local public authority. In the Netherlands, EU citizens are in the same position as citizens except for the function of security. Other aliens may be employed if no qualified EU citizen can be found for the job.

Political rights

National electoral rights (5.1)

Generally, resident aliens are not permitted electoral rights (suffrage and eligibility for election) in the national Parliament. Exceptionally, the UK grants the citizens of Ireland and British Commonwealth citizens the suffrage and the eligibility for election to the national Parliament. Canada is gradually weakening the relationship with the British Commonwealth and since 1975 British subjects cannot vote federally.[43] In Australia, a British subject enrolled to vote before 26 January 1984 is permitted national electoral rights.[44] New Zealand grants not only British Commonwealth citizens but also permanent residents the suffrage of the national Parliament.

In New Zealand there are a number of unusual factors. First there is the British Commonwealth tradition of granting electoral rights for British subjects and British Commonwealth citizens. However, the difference between New Zealand and other British Commonwealth states cannot be explained by this alone. A second factor is that it is an immigration state where the extension of voting rights may help integrate new members into the community.[45] However, this can not explain the difference from other immigration states, either.[46] A third factor may be that the improvement of indigenous Maori people was closely connected with the equal treatment of foreign residents as a minority group. Yet this does not clarify the reasons for the difference from other multicultural countries (Canada, the USA, Australia and Sweden). A fourth factor is a lack of a popular sovereignty clause in the constitution, which is considered to be an obstacle to aliens voting in Japan,[47] France[48] and Germany.[49] However, the difference from other countries (the USA, the Netherlands, Canada and Australia) whose constitutions also lack in a popular sovereignty clause cannot be explained by this. A fifth determining factor may be that nationalist feeling is not strong in New Zealand.

Local electoral rights (5.2)

In local elections, there is a general tendency to grant local electoral rights to certain resident aliens in Europe. They are roughly classified into two types: (i) 'universal', and (ii) 'limited'. The universal type grants local electoral rights to all adult resident aliens who have been living for some time in the country. The limited type grants local electoral rights to selected aliens who came from specified countries.

Strictly speaking, since the establishment of the European Union, some universal types are transformed into the mixture of 'universal and reciprocity model'. For example, all resident aliens who reside more than three years in Sweden have been granted local electoral rights, and nowadays EU citizens and Nordic citizens are granted local electoral rights on the same condition as Swedish citizens. Also, in the Netherlands, resident aliens who reside for five years or more and EU citizens who reside more than six weeks have municipal electoral rights.

As a limited type, the UK is the 'traditional model' which derives from the tradition that Irish citizens and British Commonwealth citizens who reside in the UK can vote in every election. Recently, EU citizens who reside in the UK have been given local electoral rights. The UK can be called the 'traditional and reciprocity model'. The 'reciprocity model' grants local electoral rights to selected aliens who come from countries connected by bilateral or multilateral treaties among supranational organisations such as the EU. Germany and France are reciprocity models.

New Zealand is a universal type regarding suffrage but a limited type concerning eligibility because only New Zealand citizens and British citizens enrolled before 22 August 1975 can stand for election.[50] Generally, many states regard suffrage and eligibility as one and the same. According to the democratic principle that identifies the ruling and the ruled, there is a need for an interchange of personnel between the electorate and the representatives.[51] However, eligibility to be a mayor is not open to EU citizens in two states of Germany (Bayern and Sachsen) and in France.[52] Furthermore, the Queen appoints mayors in the Netherlands and the posts are not open to EU citizens because their function is considered to be relevant to the secrets of the state.

Turnout (5.3)

Generally, the turnout of foreign and immigrant voters is lower than that of voters as a whole, as we see in Tables 11.5 and 11.6.[53] The turnout of foreign voters is in long-term decline, and the difference compared with turnout as a whole is increasing. Although a high turnout of foreign voters might be expected in Australia where voting is compulsory, no actual data is available.

Ratio of representatives of aliens (5.4)

Generally, the ratio between the numbers of foreigners or immigrants and their representatives is not as good as for citizens. Table 11.7 shows

Table 11.5 Foreign citizens' turnout in local elections in Sweden (%)

Election year	*All voters (a)*	*Foreigners (b)*	*(a)–(b)*
1976	90	60	30
1979	89	53	36
1982	90	52	38
1985	88	48	40
1988	84	43	41
1991	84	41	43
1994	87	40	47
1998	81	34	47

Table 11.6 Ethnic groups' turnout in municipal elections of four Netherlands cities (%)

	Amsterdam		*Rotterdam*		*The Hague*		*Utrecht*	
	1994	*1998*	*1994*	*1998*	*1994*	*1998*	*1994*	*1998*
Turks	67	39	28	42	–	36	55	39
Moroccans	49	23	23	33	–	23	44	26
Surinamese/ Antilleans	30	21	24	25	–	27	–	22
Total	56.8	45.7	56.9	48.4	57.6	57.6	59.8	56.5

the ratio of representatives of foreign-born persons and foreign citizens in Sweden.[54] By comparing this data with the ratio of voters of foreign-born persons (about 8 % in 1979) and foreign citizens (3.8% in 1979), we can estimate how far they are under-represented compared with residents. In Sweden, the percentage of foreign-born persons and of foreign citizens was 5.1 per cent in 1979; 4.9 per cent in 1982; 4.6 per cent in 1985; 5 per cent in 1988; 5.7 per cent in 1991; and 6.1 per cent in 1994. In the Netherlands, there is a tendency to research the data not on foreign residents but on *allochtonen* (non-indigenous people). In the 1990 elections some 50 ethnic council members (out of a total of slightly more than 11 000) were elected.[55] Table 11.8 shows the elected non-indigenous (defined as all people of non-Netherlands citizenship and/or born outside the Netherlands, plus all those who have at least one parent born outside the Netherlands) candidates and the total number of seats in four Netherlands cities in 1994 and 1998. We can estimate their underrepresented situation from the ratio of their residents in big four cities.

Table 11.7 Ratio of representatives of foreign-born persons and foreign citizens in Sweden (numbers and percentages)

	Foreign-born						*Foreign citizens*					
	1979	*1982*	*1985*	*1988*	*1991*	*1994*	*1979*	*1982*	*1985*	*1988*	*1991*	*1994*
Elected to Parliament	?	6	6 1.7%	9 2.6%	7 2.0%	7 2.0%	–	–	–	–	–	–
Regional Council	43 2.5%	54	61 3.5%	69 4.0%	64 3.7%	78 4.4%	4 0.2%	3 0.2%	7 0.4%	11 0.6%	? 0.5%	8 0.5%
Municipal Council	490 3.7%	528 4.0%	569 4.2%	589 4.3%	? 4.2%	625 4.6%	84 0.7%	89 0.7%	101 0.8%	106 0.8%	? 0.7%	119 0.9%

Table 11.8 Elected non-indigenous people in four Netherlands cities, 1998

City	*Number of total seats*	*Number of elected non-indigenous people*	*Percentage of non-indigenous municipal councillors*	*Percentage of non-indigenous population*
Amsterdam	45	11	25%	44%
Rotterdam	45	9	20%	42%
The Hague	45	6	13%	39%
Utrecht	45	6	13%	30%

In such countries as Australia, although there is a growing number of immigrants who have become local and state level politicians of immigrants, they remain under-represented in relation to their share in the population.

Eligibility to stand for office (5.5)

In New Zealand, permanent residents have only the right to vote, without the eligibility to stand for office, if they were not registered as electors of British subjects on 22 August 1975. In many countries, the electorate should be eligible because democratic theory identifies the governor and the governed. Exceptionally, the position of chief of local government is specially limited to citizens in the Netherlands, France and two states of Germany.

Political freedom (5.6)

Traditionally, rights of expression for political matters are not guaranteed for alien residents. Currently, however, alien residents can establish a political party and enjoy the freedom of electoral campaigning. Theoretically, there are no limitations on the rights of aliens to express their views and engage in political activities. But in some countries they are under pressure to limit their political activities in case protesting against their home government could result in deportation because of the concern for public safety.

Conclusion

In discussing foreigners' rights, it is necessary to distinguish between foreigners in various categories of resident aliens according to the nature of the rights. First, on residential rights, we classified them as: (1) permanent residents and privileged citizens; (2) short-term residents; or

(3) irregular residents. Second, on social rights, they are categorised as: (1) permanent residents and privileged citizens; (2) long-term residents; or (3) short-term residents and irregular residents. Third, on economic rights: (1) permanent residents and privileged citizens; (2) short-term residents; or (3) irregular residents. Fourth, on political rights: (1) permanent and long-term residents and privilege citizens; or (2) short-term residents and irregular residents.

Residential rights are divided into many categories. Social rights and economic rights are not fully guaranteed to temporary alien residents but settled aliens have equality with nationals regarding social rights. There are some restrictions on economic rights for aliens, but there is a tendency to guarantee settled aliens the right to employment as local civil servants. Moreover, there is a huge support for the granting of local voting rights to settled aliens. Their residential, social, economic and political rights are considered as citizenship-like rights, as distinct from formal citizenship, that is, nationality.

Finally, it might be necessary to consider cultural rights as the fifth element of a foreigner's citizenship. In this book, we have dealt with only multicultural education from the viewpoint of social rights. Cultural citizenship is not well established in some states, for example Japan. In general, the main stream of immigration to European states thirty years ago comprised migrant workers. The re-uniting of families has increased in the last twenty years, and the numbers of asylum seekers and refugees has increased in the last decade. Owing to the growing economic cost and high unemployment rates, there has developed an atmosphere of racism and cultural friction, and a demand for the reduction of the cultural rights of immigrant residents. However, multicultural legal and political policy is a significant issue not only in Canada and Australia but also in every modern country. At present, every government needs to regulate harmony between the majority culture and various minority cultures. To improve the basic standard of these regulations, the concept of cultural citizenship must be developed more clearly in the near future. The future direction of this study will encompass refugees and asylum seekers; more careful examination of irregular residents is also required.

Three 'gates' and sets of admission rules are needed for immigrants (immigration control and regularisation; permanent residence permits and denizisation; and citizenship and naturalisation) corresponding to the three categories of status (temporary residents; denizens; and citizens).[56] There is a need discuss the differences between these three sets of admission rules; and for long resident undocumented children especially, regularisation should be considered in response to 'the best interest of the child' as proposed in article 3 of the UN Convention on the Rights of the Child.

Notes

1 See United Nations, *International Migration Policies* (New York: United Nations, 1998), pp. 67–80.
2 *ibid.*, p. 54; Virginie Guiraudon, 'Citizenship Rights for Non-Citizens,' in Christian Joppke (ed.), *Challenge to the Nation-State* (Oxford: Oxford University Press, 1998), pp. 297–301.
3 See Sarah A. Adams, 'The basic right of citizenship: a comparative study,' *Backgrounder*, Nos. 7–93 (Washington, DC: Center for Immigration Studies, 1993), p. 2.
4 Strictly speaking, the Dutch system is double *jus domicili* rather than French double *jus soli*, but both characters are relatively similar. See Chapter 2 on the Netherlands.
5 Peter H. Shuck and Rogers M. Smith, *Citizenship without Consent* (New Haven: Yale University Press, 1985), pp. 2–3.
6 See T. Alexander Aleinikoff, *Between Principles and Politics: The Direction of U.S. Citizenship Policy* (Washington, DC: Carnegie Endowment for International Peace, 1998), p. 10.
7 David A. Martin, 'Membership Without Consent: Abstract or Organic?' in *The Yale journal of international law* 11 (1985), pp. 283–4.
8 See SOPEMI, *Trends in International Migration – Annual Report 1994* (Paris: OECD, 1995), p. 160, table III. 2; United Nations, *op. cit.*, note 1, p. 31, Box 1.
9 Tomas Hammar, *Democracy and the Nation State: Aliens, Denizens and Citizens in a World of International Migration* (Aldershot: Avebury, 1990), p. 76.
10 See Rainer Bauböck, *Transnational Citizenship: Membership and Rights in International Migration* (Aldershot: Edward Elgar, 1994), p. 32; Stephen Castles and Mark J. Miller, *The Age of Migration: International Population Movements in the Modern World* 2nd edn (New York: Guilford, 1998), p. 241; Chikako Kashiwazaki, 'Jus sanguinis in Japan: The Origin of Citizenship in a Comparative Perspective', *International Journal of Comparative Sociology* vol. 39, no. 3 (1998), p. 279.
11 Paul Weis, *Nationality and Statelessness*, 1956 (Westport: Hyperion, 1979), p. 3.
12 See Allan Rosas and Markku Suksi, 'Finland' in Bruno Nascimbene (ed.), *Nationality Laws in the European Union: Le droit de la nationalité dans l'union européenne* (Milano: Butterworths, 1996), pp. 267–8; Allan Rosas, 'Citizenship as a Process: The Concept of Nordic Citizenship' in Siofra O'Leary and Teija Tiilikainen (eds), *Citizenship and Nationality Status in the New Europe* (London: Sweet & Maxwell, 1998), pp. 53–62.
13 Saïd Bouamama, 'Réinventer la société', in Saïd Bouamama *et al.* (eds), *La citoyenneté dans tous ses etats* (Paris: L'Harmattan, 1992), pp. 325–6; C.W. de Wenden, *Citoyenneté nationalité et immigration* (Paris: Acantère, 1987), pp. 72–3.

14 J.P. Gardner, 'What Lawyers mean by Citizenship' in Commission on Citizenship (ed.), *Encouraging Citizenship* (London: HMSO, 1990), p. 71.
15 See Yasemin Nuhoglu Soysal, *Limits of Citizenship* (Chicago: University of Chicago, 1994), p. 139; Peter H. Schuck, *Citizens, Strangers, and In-Betweens* (Oxford: Westview, 1998), p. 202.
16 Fritz Franz, 'Renaissance des Niederlassungsrechts' *ZAR* (1985), p. 14; Fritz Franz, 'Der Gesetzentwurf der Bundesregierung zur Neuregelung des Ausländerrechts', *ZAR* 1/1990, pp. 5–6.
17 Atsushi Kondo, *Gaikokujin sanseiken to kokuseki* [The Aliens' Voting Rights and Citizenship] (Tokyo: Akashi Shoten, 1996), p. 18; Atsushi Kondo, *'Gaikokujin' no Sanseiken: Denizenship no hikaku kenkyu* [A Comparative Study about Denizenship] (Tokyo: Akashi Shoten, 1996), pp. 12–13.
18 Tomas Hammar, 'Legal Time of Residence and the Status of Immigrants', in Rainer Bauböck (ed.), *From Aliens to Citizens* (Aldershot: Avebury, 1994), p. 189.
19 Rainer Bauböck, *Immigration and the Boundaries of Citizenship* (Centre for Research in Ethnic Relations University of Warwick, 1992), p. 8; Rainer Bauböck, 'Changing the Boundaries of Citizenship', in Rainer Bauböck (ed.), *From Aliens to Citizens* (Aldershot: Avebury, 1994), p. 226.
20 Atsushi Kondo, *Gaikokujin sanseiken to kokuseki supra*, note 17, p. 18; Atsushi Kondo, *'Gaikokujin' no Sanseiken: Denizenship no hikaku kenkyu supra*, note 17, pp. 12–13.
21 See Kay Hailbronner, *Einbürgerung von Wanderarbeitnehmern und doppelte Staatsangehörigkeit* (Baden-Baden: Nomos, 1992), pp. 100–101.
22 Ruth Donner, *The Regulation of Nationality in International Law*, 2nd edn (Irvington-On-Hudson: Transnational, 1994), p. 214; Europarat, 'Zweites Protokoll zur Änderung des Übereinkommenes über die Veringerung von Mehrstaatigket und die Wehrpflicht von Mehrstaatern' in Klaus Barwig *et al.* (eds), *Vom Auslander zum Burger* (Baden-Baden: Nomos, 1994), pp. 411–12.
23 Appendix: European Convention on Nationality and Explanatory Report, in Síofra O'Leary and Teija Tiilikainen (eds), *Citizenship and Nationality Status in the New Europe* (London: Sweet & Maxwell, 1998), pp. 211, 243.
24 Hans van Amersfoort, 'Migration Control and Minority Policy: The Case of the Netherlands' in Grete Brochman and Tomas Hammar (eds), *Mechanism of Immigration Control* (Oxford: Berg, 1999), pp. 138–9.
25 Rupert Scholz and Arnd Uhle, 'Staatsangehörigkeit und Grundgesetz' *NJW* no. 21 (1999), p. 1515.
26 SOU 1999:34, p. 13.
27 United Nations, *op. cit.*, note 1, p. 57.
28 Hammar, *op. cit.*, note 9, p. 21.
29 See Jonas Widgren, *The Key to Europe* (Stockholm: Fritzes, 1994): SOU 1994: 135, p. 70.
30 There is another case in Hungary. Kees Groenendijk *et al.*, *Security of Residence of Long-Term Migrants: A Comparative Study of Law and Practice in European Countries* (Strasbourg: Council of Europe Publishing, 1998), p. 99.
31 *ibid.*, p. 101. At the beginning of 1997 in Japan, permanent residents (42.2%), spouse/children of Japanese citizen (18.5%), spouse/children of permanent residents (0.4%) and quasi-permanent residents (13.7%).
32 Soysal, *op. cit.*, note 15, p. 124.

33 William Rogers Brubaker, 'Membership without Citizenship: The Economic and Social Rights of Noncitizens', in William Rogers Brubaker (ed.), *Immigration and the Politics in Europe and North America* (Lamham: University Press of America, 1989), p. 156.
34 See Jens Magleby Sorensen, *The Exclusive European Citizenship: The Case for Refugees and Immigrants in the European Union* (Aldershot: Avebury, 1996), p. 60.
35 Thomas Faist, 'Immigration, Integration, and the Welfare State', in Rainer Bauböck *et al.* (eds), *The Challenge of Diversity* (Aldershot: Avebury, 1996), p. 257.
36 Hans van Amersfoort. 'International Migration and Civil Rights: the Dilemmas of Migration Control in an Age of Globalisation' in Elspeth Guild (ed.), *The Legal Framework and Social Consequences of Free Movement of Persons in the European Union* (The Hague: Kluwer Law International, 1999), p. 76.
37 United Nations, *supra* note 1, p. 55.
38 Peter Broeder and Guus Extra, 'Language' in Hans Vermeulen (ed.), *Immigrant Policy for a Multicultural Society. A Comparative Study of Integration, Language and Religious Policy in Five Western European Countries* (Brussels: Migrant Policy Group, 1997), pp. 93–4.
39 It was remarked that 'for example, in Sweden citizenship is required in order to start a company with shareholders' (Soysal, *op. cit.*, note 15, p. 126). However, the important requirement is that the founder shall be domiciled in one of EEA countries even if he or she does not have a Swedish citizenship. See Aktilebolagslagen (SFS 1975:1385) Ch. 2§1.
40 There are a few exceptions. Foe example in Japan, there is prohibition for aliens to have mining rights.
41 Thomas Faist, *Social Citizenship for Whom?* (Aldershot: Avebury, 1995), pp. 41–2.
42 Astrid Auer, *Civil Services in the Europe of Fifteen* (Maastricht: EIPA, 1996), pp. 40–41; Matthias Niedobitek, 'Recht des öffentlichen Dienstes in den Mitgliedstaaten der EG', in Siegfried Magiera and Heinrich Siedentopf (eds), *Das Recht des öffentlichen Dienstes in der Mitgliedstaaten der Europäischen Gemeinschaft* (Berlin: Duncker & Humblot, 1994), pp. 59–62.
43 Ronald G. Landes, *The Canadian Polity* 4th ed. (Ontario: Prentice-Hall Canada, 1995), p. 352. However, pursuant to section 23 of the Constitution Act 1867, British subjects may be appointed to the Senate.
44 Peter J. Hanks, *Constitutional Law in Australia* (Sydney: Butterworths, 1991), pp. 43–53.
45 Report of the Royal Commission on the Electoral System, *Towards a Better Democracy* (1986), p. 232.
46 In the 19th century and the beginning of the 20th century, although electoral rights had been granted to resident aliens in many states in the USA, such alien's vote were abolished by the rise of nationalism. See Gerald L. Neuman, '"We are the People": Alien Suffrage in German and American Perspective', *Michigan Journal of Law* vol. 13 (1992), p. 303; Jamin B. Raskin, 'Legal Aliens, Local Citizens: The Historical, Constitutional and Theoretical Meanings of Alien Suffrage', *University of Pennsylvania Law Review* vol. 141 (1993), pp. 1462–3.
47 *Hanreijihô* [Selected Court Reports] no. 1452 (1993), p. 38.

48 92-308 DC (9.4.1992) and 92-312 DC (2.9.1992) in Louis Favoreu, *Recueil de jurisprudence constitutionnelle 1959–1993* (Paris: Litec, 1994), pp. 500, 508.

49 BverfGE 83, 37 (31. Oct. 1990), pp. 51–2; BverfGE 83, 60 (31. Oct. 1990), p. 72.

50 Electoral Act 194-F; Local Elections and Polls Act 112 (5) (b).

51 Jörg Sennewald, 'Kommunalwahlrecht für Ausländer?' *Verwaltungsrundschau* 1981, p. 83

52 It is forbidden in France for EU citizens to be a deputy mayor or participates in the Senate election. As to German states, see Katarina Barley, *Das Kommunalwahlrecht für Ausländer nach der Neuordnung des Art. 28 Abs. 1 S. 3 GG* (Berlin: Duncker & Humblot, 1999), pp. 121, 140.

53 See Jean Tillie, 'Migranten die stemmen', Utrecht: FORUM (forthcoming); M. Berger, M. Fennema, A. van Heelsum and J. Tillie, *Politieke participatie van etnische minderheden in Nederland* (Den Haag: Ministerie van Binnenlandse zaken) (forthcoming); Jean Tillie, 1994, Kleurrijk kiezen – Opkomst en stemgedrag van migranten tijdens de gemeenteraadsverkiezingen van 2 maart 1994, Utrecht, p. 8. Tables 11.4 and 11.6 are based on the information from Dr Jean Tillie at Amsterdam University. Furthermore, see at http://www.onstat.amsterdam.nl/ cijfers/grotesteden.php3

54 See Tomas Hammar, *Invandrarkandidater i 1979 års kommunara val* (Stockholm: EIFO, 1982), p. 37; Hammar, *op. cit.*, note 9, at 181; Statiska Centralbyrån, Tema Invandrare '(Stockholm: SCB, 1991), p. 114; Tomas Hammar, 'Participation politique et droits civils en Suede' in Andrea Rea (ed.) *Immigration et racisme en Europe* (Brussels: Interventions, 1998), p. 157; Henry Bäck and Maritta Soininen, 'Invandrarna, demokratin och samhället', *Föevaltingskolans (Göteborg) rapporter no.* 2 (1996), pp. 57, 63. Furthermore, Table 11.5 is based on the information from Tomas Hammar.

55 Rinus Penninx *et al.*, *The Impact of International Migration on Receiving Countries: the Case of the Netherlands* (The Hague: NIDI, 1994), p. 215. In the elections of 1986 approximately 25 aliens were elected in municipal councils. In the elections of 1998 more than 50 aliens were elected in the municipal councils. See Kees Groenendjk and Paul Minderhoud, 'The Netherlands' in Rainer Bauböck *et al. Rechtliche Instrumente der Integration von Einwanderern im Europäischen Vergleich* (Wien: European Centre, 2000) p. 337.

56 See Hammar, *op. cit.*, note 18, p. 189.

Select Bibliography

Japan

Hanami, Tadashi, 'Japanese Policies on the Rights and Benefits Granted to Foreign Workers, Residents, Refugees and Illegals' in Myron Weiner and Tadashi Hanami (eds), *Temporary Workers or Future Citizens?* (London: Macmillan, 1998).

Iwasawa, Yuji, *International Law, Human Rights, and Japanese Law* (Oxford: Clarendon Press, 1998).

Kashiwazaki, Chikako, 'Citizenship in Japan: Legal Practice and Contemporary Development' in T. Alexander Aleinikoff and Douglas Klusmeyer (eds), *From Migrants to Citizens* (Washington, D.C.: Carnegie Endowment for International Peace, 2000), pp. 434–71.

Kondo, Atsushi, *Gaikokujin sanseiken to kokuseki* [The Aliens' Electoral rights and Citizenship] (Tokyo: Akashi Shoten, 1996).

Kondo, Atsushi, 'From "Mono Ethnic State" to Cultural Pluralism in Japan' in Janina W. Dacyl and Charles Westin (eds), *Governance of Cultural Diversity* (Stockholm: CEIFO, 2000), pp. 112–52.

The Netherlands

de Groot, Gerard-René and Bollen, Carlos, 'Netherlands Nationality Law' in Bruno Nascimbene (ed.), *Nationality Laws in the European Union* (Milano: Butterworths, 1996), pp. 545–90.

Groenendijk, Kees and Minderhoud, Paul, 'The Netherlands' in Rainer Bauböck *et al.*, *Rechtliche Instrumente: Der Integration von Einwanderern in europäischen Vergleich* (Wien: Europäischen Zentrum, 2000).

Kuijer Aldo and Dteenbergen, Hanneke, J.D.M., *Nederlands vreemdelingenrecht*, 4th edn (Nederlandes Centrum voor Buitenlandes, 1999).

Penninx, Rinus *et al.*, *The Impact of International Migration on Receiving Countries: the Case of the Netherlands* (The Hague: NIDI, 1994).

Sweden

Hammar, Tomas, *Democracy and the Nation-State: Aliens Denizens and Citizens in a World of International Migration* (Aldershot: Avebury, 1990).

Inrikesdepartementet, *Medborgarskap och identitet* (SOU 1997:162, Stockholm).

Kulturdepartementet, *Svensk medborgarskap* (SOU 1999:34, Stockholm).

Westin, Charles and Dingu-Kyrklund, Elena, *Reducing Immigration, Reviewing Integration* (Stockholm: CEIFO, 1997).

France

Fassin, Didler *et al.*, *Les Lois de l'inhospitalité* (Paris: La Découverte, 1997).
Guiguet, Benoît, *Citoyenneté et nationalité: limites de la rupture d'un lien* (PhD, IUE, Florence, 1997).
Lagarde, Paul, *La Nationalité française*, 3e édition (Paris: Dalloz, 1997).
Weil, Patrick, *Mission d'étude des législations de la nationalité et de l'immigration* (Paris: La Documentation française, 1997).

Germany

Barwig, Klaus *et al.* (eds), *Neue Regierung – neue Ausländerpolitik?* (Baden-Baden: Nomos, 1999).
Hailbronner, Kay, 'Die Reform des deutschen Staatsangehöigkeitsrechts', *Neue Zeitschrift für Verwaltungsrecht* (1999), pp. 1273–80.
Hailbronner, Kay, 'Doppelte Staatsangehörigkeit', *Zeitschrift für Ausländerrecht und Ausläenderpolitik* (1999), pp. 51–8.
Renner, Günter, 'Von der Rettung des deutschen Asylrechts', *Zeitschrift für Ausländerrecht und Ausländerpolitik* (1999), pp. 206–17.

United Kingdom

Bulmer, Martin and Rees, Anthony M., *Citizenship Today: The Contemporary Relevance of T.H. Marshall* (London: UCL Press, 1996).
Dummett, Ann and Nicol, Andrew, *Subjects, Citizens, Aliens and Others: Nationality and Immigration Law* (London: Wiedenfeld and Nicolson, 1990).
Fransman, Laurie, *British Nationality Law*, 2nd edn (London: Butterworths, 1998).
Marshall, T.H., *Citizenship and Social Class and Other Essays* (Cambridge: Cambridge University Press, 1950).
Modood, Tariq *et al.*, *Ethnic Minorities in Britain: Diversity and Disadvantage* (London: Policy Studies Institute, 1997).

Australia

Castles, Stephen *et al.*, *Immigration and Australia: Myths and Realities* (Sydney: Allen & Unwin, 1998).
DIMA, *Australian Citizenship*, Fact Sheet 66 (Canberra: Department of Immigration and Multicultural Affairs, 1998).
Galligan, B. and Chesterman, J. 1997, 'Aborigines, citizenship and the Australian Constitution: did the Constitution exclude Aboriginal People from citizenship' *Public Law Review* vol. 8, no. 1, 1997, pp. 45–61.

New Zealand

Bedford, Richard *et al.*, 'Regulating International Migration: A New Zealand Perspective', *International Migration: Conference Proceedings and the Regulation of*

International Migration in New Zealand (Auckland: Asia–Pacific Migration Research Network, 1998).
Fleras, Augie and Spoonley, Paul, *Recalling Aotearoa, Indigenous and Ethnic Politics in New Zealand* (Auckland: Oxford University Press, 1999).
Haines, Rodger 'Citizenship and Nationality', in Robin Cook *et al.* (eds), *The Laws of New Zealand* (Auckland: Butterworths, 1994).
McKinnon, Malcolm, *Immigrants and Citizens. New Zealanders and Asian Immigration in Historical Context* (Wellington: Institute of Policy Studies, 1996).
Trlin, Andrew, D. and Spoonley, Paul (eds), *New Zealand and International Migration. A Digest and Bibliography, Number 1* (Palmerston North: Massey University, 1986).

Canada

Berezowski, Nan M. and Trister, Benjamin J., *Citizenship* (Scarborough, Ontario: Carswell, 1996).
Galloway, Donald, *Immigration Law* (Concord Ontario: Irwin Law, 1997).
Kaplan, William (ed.), *Belonging: The Meaning and Future of Canadian Citizenship* (Montreal: Queen's McGill Press, 1993).
Kymlicka, Will, *Multicultural Citizenship* (Oxford: OUP, 1995).

United States of America

Aleinikoff, T. Alexander, *Between Principles and Politics: The Direction of US Citizenship Policy* (Washington, D.C.: Carnegie Endowment for International Peace, 1998).
Heller, Thomas C., 'Modernity, Membership and Multiculturalism', 5 *Stanford Humanities Review* 2, (1997).
Neuman, Gerald L., *Strangers to the Constitution: Immigrants, Borders and Fundamental Law* (Princeton: Princeton University Press, 1996).
Pickus, Noah M.J., *Immigration and Citizenship in the Twenty-First Century* (Lanham, Md: Rowman & Littlefield, 1998).

Comparison

Bauböock, Rainer (ed.), *From Aliens to Citizens* (Aldershot, Avebury, 1994).
Brubaker, Rogers (ed.), *Immigration and the Politics of Citizenship in Europe and North America* (London and New York: University Press of America, 1989).
Joppke, Christian (ed.), *Challenge to the Nation-State: Immigration in Western Europe and the United States* (Oxford: Oxford University Press, 1998).
Kondo, Atsushi, *'Gaikokujin' no Sanseiken: Denizenship no hikaku kenkyu* [A Comparative Study on Denizenship] (Tokyo: Akashi Shoten, 1996).
Layton-Henry, Zig (ed.), *The Political Rights of Migrant Workers in Western Europe* (London. Sage, 1990).

Index